MARY JANE'S GHOST

The Legacy of a Murder in Small Town America

• • •

TED GREGORY

UNIVERSITY OF IOWA PRESS • IOWA CITY

University of Iowa Press, Iowa City 52242
Copyright © 2017 by Ted Gregory
www.uipress.uiowa.edu
Printed in the United States of America

Design by April Leidig

The University of Iowa Press is a member of Green Press Initiative
and is committed to preserving natural resources.

Printed on acid-free paper

Library of Congress Cataloging-in-Publication Data
is on file at the Library of Congress.

978-1-60938-523-1 (pbk)
978-1-60938-524-8 (ebk)

For Mom

CONTENTS

ACKNOWLEDGMENTS

I'M DEEPLY GRATEFUL to many people involved and uninvolved in the case for their time and consideration, especially Mike Arians, Greg Beitel, Doug Blodgett, Sarah Cooper, Matt Davis, Steven Di Naso, Scott Doody, Greg Farnham, Jack Fredrickson, Bonnie Hendrickson, Philip Kendall, Doug Oleson, Dr. Mark Peters, Warren Reed, Frank Schier, George Seibel, Michael Verde, Gary Wagle, Nathan Wallick, and Rich Wilkinson. I also must thank Jerry Glover for his sage, sharp-eyed advice and Bill Riddle for his friendship and support during all my writing projects.

Thank you, Catherine Campbell Cocks, for your kindness, open mind, and perceptive, steady guidance that took me through the dark forest into the bright meadow; Jim McCoy for taking a chance on a different book; Faith Marcovecchio for being a copy editor who allows writers to sleep much easier at night and who would have made Ring Lardner beam with pride; Susan Hill Newton for friendly guidance and good cheer; and all my other friends at University of Iowa Press. I'm so appreciative of your hard work on my behalf.

Thanks, Irene, Nick, and Leah—and now Michael—for making your distracted father so proud.

And, as always, thank you, Terri, for your patience, for understanding what it takes and for helping me get there, for showing me how to keep it flowing, and for your love.

AUTHOR'S NOTE

I CHANGED THREE NAMES to respect a family's privacy and in a couple of instances finessed the chronology of events to accommodate the narrative. Otherwise, I presented this story as accurately as I could, given the fallibility of humans and the mischief of ghosts.

—Ted Gregory, October 2016

MARY JANE'S GHOST

Death of a Butterfly,
Lost in the Weeds

• • •

THE LETTER I SHOOK from the packed envelope was typed on lavender stationery. Later, someone who knows about these things would tell me lavender's the color of romance, mourning, mistrust, and cruelty. Makes sense now.

In six paragraphs on that stationery, Mike Arians sought help. He was looking into the unsolved murders of two young lovers who died way back in 1948 in the small, scenic river town of Oregon, Illinois. It was a shocking crime that started with a man shot to death on a lovers' lane, followed by the kidnapping of his date, and ending with her murder.

Newspapers from Chicago to Iowa described the crime, Mike wrote, as "the most heinous of its time known to the Midwest." Coverage actually extended much farther, from the *Portland Press Herald* in Maine to the *Long Beach Press-Telegram* in California. But the killings faded from the headlines after a few days. In the nearly six decades since, they'd become lost.

Mike had been "extensively involved in researching" the case for roughly five years, he said, and he had a scandalous theory about what happened to Mary Jane Reed and Stanley Skridla late one summer night in 1948. He wanted to exhume one of the victims' bodies in hopes of finding DNA evidence and anything else that might be illuminating.

I read the letter in my cubicle at the *Chicago Tribune*, where I worked as a general assignment reporter marooned in the suburbs. It was 2003. The ground under the newspaper business was starting to get soft but hadn't yet turned into the quicksand that would swallow more than a hundred newspapers and put somewhere in the neighborhood of 25,000 journalists out of work. At this point, it was still pretty much the Good Ol' Days. At least newspapers largely pretended it was.

Mike described himself as the "recent" former mayor of Oregon and a retired insurance fraud investigator. He ran the Roadhouse, a rustic restaurant and tavern on the outskirts of town.

"There is little question in my mind who the perpetrator of this crime was," he wrote. "Probably the more interesting story is the cover-up that has gone on for over 50 years."

He had enclosed copies of old newspaper clips, fascinating anthropological relics available without having to scratch through the dirt using a toothbrush. They're raw history as it happens, unrefined by bloviators. I love old newspaper clips.

These were from 1948. Seven of them. Six from the *Tribune*, a model of midwestern understatement that called itself "The World's Greatest Newspaper." Five months after the dates on these clips, the World's Greatest Newspaper ran history's most infamously wrong headline, "DEWEY DEFEATS TRUMAN." Decades later, you could buy T-shirts and posters of a photograph of Harry Truman, freshly elected president over Thomas Dewey, holding up the newspaper headline and beaming.

On June 26, 1948, the paper ran a front-page story about Frances Dewey, Thomas's wife. She revealed that she weighed 120 pounds and liked "off the face hats and all kinds of colors." Next to that story was a grim dispatch from Oregon.

"SUITOR KILLED, HUNT FOR GIRL," the headline read. "Fear She Is Dead or a Suitor's Captive."

"The slaying of a handsome young man from Rockford, and the mysterious disappearance of an 18-year-old girl he had dated a few hours earlier" —she actually was seventeen—"sent authorities on a wide hunt for the young woman tonight in the belief that she, too, is dead or is the captive of a jealous suitor," the story reported.

"Sheriff's deputies were searching banks of the Rock River and ditches and culverts for some trace of the girl, Miss Mary Jane Reed, comely telephone operator here."

The story went on to say that "a love triangle theory was advanced" by Ogle County sheriff Joseph Maas when he'd learned that Mary Jane had not been seen since her date with twenty-eight-year-old Navy vet Stanley Skridla. His body had been found that morning along the lovers' lane south of town. Maas already had questioned six men who were acquaintances of Mary Jane's, but none "could throw any light on the case." The sheriff said he planned to question any other boyfriends she might have had.

The newspaper reported that Mary Jane weighed 120 pounds, same as Frances Dewey, I noted. Stanley worked as a telephone lineman. His hometown of Rockford, then a city of 90,000, was about twenty-five miles northeast of Oregon.

"He met Miss Reed recently after they became acquainted thru telephone conversations while he was testing and repairing wires," the paper reported. "Miss Reed worked until 10 p.m. Thursday and was seen leaving an Oregon tavern with Skridla about 11:30 p.m. The next to the youngest of six children of Mr. and Mrs. Clifford Reed of Oregon, she was to have been a bridesmaid today at the wedding of Donald Reed, a brother." The family postponed the wedding.

The couple had stopped at a number of nightspots, including the establishment that later would become the Roadhouse, before heading to lovers' lane. The shooting occurred between 1 and 2 a.m. on that gravel road, where police found shells and a "big pool of blood" the next morning, the newspaper reported. "The slayer had a .32 caliber and he pumped four bullets into Skridla's chest and abdomen," Sheriff Maas told the *Tribune*. "After the shooting, somebody dragged the body several feet into the ditch," a task that would have taken considerable strength, the sheriff added. Stanley weighed 175 pounds. Someone also had moved Stanley's Buick about a mile north, to a lot across the street from what would become the Roadhouse.

"The sheriff said he still believed Miss Reed was overpowered by the slayer and carried from the scene, either dead or as a prisoner," the *Tribune* reported. "Search for her body continued today with several hundred volunteers aiding deputy sheriffs in beating thru near-by woodland."

On Tuesday, June 29, 1948, the *Tribune*'s banner headline was "REDS

DEMAND TITO OUSTER," a reference to Communists' push to dump the Yugoslavian premier, who had "veered from the party line."

Tucked deeper in the newspaper was a peculiar four-paragraph story about Mary Jane's father meeting with a fortune-teller who assured Clifford that his daughter was safe.

"Reed, a blacksmith, said the fortune-teller told him Mary Jane is alive, unharmed, and held prisoner by a man of dark complexion," the story reported. "The sheriff said he still is without any clew to Mary Jane's whereabouts. He was told by a farmer yesterday that a gray haired man has made a habit in recent weeks of coming to the lane alone in an automobile and parking for hours at a time."

I turned to the next clipping. It included a photo of Mary Jane, in full profile, on the back page of the paper. She's seated in the grass, dressed in white shorts that had inched up high on her thighs and a white bikini top. Her hands, palms pressed to the ground, are behind her a few inches. Her elbows are locked. Her left leg is crooked at the knee, right leg bent at a higher angle. She has full, wavy dark hair—people described it as auburn— that stopped just above her shoulders.

She is lovely and she is smiling, and not the smile you might get from a Sunday school teacher after reciting this week's prayer. More like a smile from a woman who knows she has something you want, something you'd like very much.

I stared at the photo. What it must have been like to be Mary Jane Reed, blossoming into full womanhood, with all its anxiety and restlessness, in a small town so far from any real action when so much action was to be had in post–World War II America. She was the child of a machine repairman —newspapers were wrong when they called Clifford a blacksmith—and a homemaker. She lived in a hectic, needy household, and she'd found a job that connected her to the outside world in what was then a very modern way. It must have been fascinating and frustrating. She may have wanted out of Oregon, like so many young people in small towns, but had so much holding her there.

A date with a sailor, who'd likely seen the world, was adventurous, perhaps even exotic, at least for a seventeen-year-old girl from a town of 3,000 people. And that photo. Did she entertain a fantasy that it would lead to being discovered by a modeling agency or Hollywood? Maybe it was nothing more than a little fun on a boring summer afternoon.

A fourth clipping ran the same picture again—this time closely cropped around her face. It was on the front page of the June 30th *Tribune*.

"Missing Girl Found Slain," the headline read, "2d 'Lovers Lane' Victim."

"Two 'lovers' lane' slayings were linked definitely to the same mysterious killer tonight," the story said, "with the report that Mary Jane Reed, whose nearly nude body was found in a ditch this morning, was shot with the gun used to riddle her boyfriend.

"The attractive and popular girl, a telephone operator here, had been missing since Skridla's body was found Friday morning ¾ of a mile from Oregon. She was found dead in a weed-filled ditch beside a lonely road about two miles from here and the same distance from the scene of Skridla's death."

Mary Jane had been shot once in the base of the skull, the story reported, adding curiously that "the condition of the body" led to the coroner's earlier theory that she had been shot in the back. Examination of the bullet cartridges showed they were from the same gun. Her father had passed twice within four feet of the place where Mary Jane's body was found, under a box elder tree near a sandpit and along a road Clifford traveled to and from his job at the National Silica Company plant. Harold Sigler, twenty-eight, an Oregon trucker who was hauling sand from the pit, found her.

"Mary Jane was nude, except for panties and brassiere," the story read. "The rest of her clothes—brown slacks, embroidered blouse, shoes, and socks—had been tossed upon the body in the weeds."

I set down the papers. A double homicide unlike anything locals had seen; the swarm of state police, reporters, and photographers; national news coverage; intense pressure to make progress at the crucial early stages of an investigation. It must have been overwhelming for the Oregon Police Department and Ogle County Sheriff's Office. Even for big city and federal authorities, investigative tools were laughably primitive compared to what exists today.

The next clip Mike had included was from the *Chicago Herald-American*. Next to a story about a zoo bear chewing off the arm of a twelve-year-old boy—"zookeepers said the bears had been on a vegetarian diet ever since their capture and were considered very tame"—was this headline: "Seek Jealous Wife in Love Lane Killing."

Police were theorizing that the wife of one of Mary Jane's suitors may have killed the couple. "Close friends told police, 'Mary Jane didn't care whether a man was married or not,'" the article stated. "Authorities in both Oregon and near-by Rockford admitted the murders would be hard to unravel because 18-year-old [sic] Mary Jane Reed, the beautiful telephone operator, led such a complicated life."

Calling her—again—"the comely, blue-eyed girl with the reddish brown thatch of hair," the story said police were questioning her "male friends," but that "it is still anybody's guess who perpetrated the crime."

The *Herald-American* quoted her sobbing mother, Ruth Reed.

"Mary Jane was such a happy little girl, just like a butterfly," the grieving woman said. "She was so happy with life." Mrs. Reed talked of Mary Jane helping ease the mother's arthritis pain and of Mary Jane's thrill at wearing her mother's wedding ring, a gift from Ruth.

In the classic, subtle newspaper style of the time, those tender recollections were followed by this: "Ironically, the girl was wearing the ring when her nearly nude body was found in a ditch where it had been rolled after she had been shot in the head and criminally assaulted."

Police also were talking to four of Stanley's girlfriends from Rockford and looking for two railroad employees who had disappeared since the murder. They were questioning a nineteen-year-old Navy veteran from La Crosse, Wisconsin, a former suitor of Mary Jane's, and looking for a dark blue-and-gray Pontiac. They were checking into a report that Mary Jane had mentioned seeing a gun in a date's glove compartment two months earlier, and they were looking for "a mental incompetent from Mount Morris who had threatened Mary Jane unless she was true to him alone."

The *Tribune* said authorities had questioned "a parade of 50 persons" but were still "up against a stone wall." Police had arrested "a Negro" for speeding in a Pontiac similar to the one spotted near the crime scene at the time of Stanley's shooting. The newspapers suggested Mary Jane's diary might contain clues, but her father refused to pass it on to authorities.

In other words, they were lost in the weeds.

Five decades later, they hadn't emerged. A solution was well past the point of being hopeless. Yet here was this seemingly sane individual digging into the mystery. What in the world was he thinking? I took another spin through his letter. The tone was obvious: something sinister—"the cover-up that has gone on for over 50 years"—hovered over the entire case.

"I would like to bring you up to date on our story," Mike wrote. "If you find you have interest in this subject matter, in my opinion it would be a huge set back to contact local authorities."

I had interest. As hopeless as Mike's endeavor appeared, and in part because of that, all of what he packed in that envelope—Mary Jane, Stanley, and the other characters, the old newspaper clips, the history, the setting —started circulating in my head like a funnel cloud, but slower: like an assemblage of ghosts swirling in a gentle eddy.

I stood and started walking to my editor's office, lavender stationery in hand, a grin spreading on my face.

Field Trips Downstate

• • •

AN ICONIC BIG CITY newspaper, the *Chicago Tribune* was established in 1847 and is largely credited with propelling Abraham Lincoln to the White House and playing a vital role in the formation of the National Football League. It was a champion of emancipation and prided itself on exposing corruption, something it still executes with astonishing, aggressive regularity. The *Tribune* was anti-Roosevelt, anti–New Deal, pro-isolationist, and remains, on its editorial pages, predominantly and moderately Republican. Far less pretentious than the *New York Times* and *Wall Street Journal*, it's stocked with very smart, resourceful, eloquent journalists who put their egos aside and put their shoulders into the joy—mostly—of hard work every single dang day. Along the way, those journalists have collected twenty-seven Pulitzer prizes.

The *Tribune*'s landmark neo-Gothic thirty-four-story headquarters has stood since 1925 along what is arguably the most prominent and beautiful boulevard in the City of Broad Shoulders. At any given moment, a dozen or so tourists pause at the base of the building to marvel at 120 stones from structures all over the world embedded in the exterior walls of Indiana limestone. Walk around the Tribune Tower and you'll find chunks of the Parthenon, great pyramids of Egypt, Taj Mahal, Great Wall of China, Alamo, Fort Sumter, White House, and Kremlin. Many visitors also venture into the cathedral-like lobby, where a giant map of the United States made from shredded money dominates one wall and is surrounded by other walls of engraved quotes thematically connected to freedom of speech. It's a place that generates serious, inspirational mojo. Nearly everyone who works for the company simply refers to the building as "the Tower."

Where I worked, in the suburbs, was slightly less prestigious. We were in an office park. No pieces of the Parthenon in those walls. No hustle and buzz. No cabbies, street musicians, or sidewalks jammed with people in a hurry. And no scenic views of Lake Michigan or the Chicago River. Just a boxy gray building surrounded by expansive asphalt parking lots filled with minivans, SUVs, and lots of Honda sedans. A swanky shopping mall covered acres of ground about two miles down the six-lane. Once every few hours, a near-empty commuter bus hissed to a stop outside. We didn't even have a sidewalk until a couple of years earlier.

General assignment reporters sprinkled through the cubicle farm inside that building were low on the food chain at the World's Greatest Newspaper. The action is downtown, where ambitious Serious Journalists jockeyed so they could continue their rise to prime beats—city hall, federal court, science, the environment, national staff, investigative team. Working at the Tower also was often the launching pad to the Washington, D.C., bureau, a foreign correspondent gig, or a glass-enclosed corner office from which one could lead the troops.

I was married, living in the suburbs with three kids under five years old, a minivan, and an obese cat. My career path, for reasons of domestic tranquility, personal sanity, and a desire to have a little more control over my life, kept wending around suburbia, for the most part.

But city or suburb, a reporter occupies an important place in the democratic republic for which we stand. Reporters primarily are watchdogs keeping track of how our institutions and officials spend public money or how they lose sight, willfully or otherwise, of noble ideals. It's more than important, actually. It's vital, as vital as any branch of our government.

And when they're not covering the mayhem of crime, fires, and car crashes—and sometimes even if they are—peripatetic general assignment reporters, or GAs, often help ordinary, sometimes overlooked communities and people tell their stories. Those stories not only define a place but they help preserve its memory and soul—they keep its ghosts alive. From there, it's not too much of a stretch to see how producing those stories may even help draw us closer to each other. For decades, while I was scrambling from place to place, story to story, I never fully grasped that idea. But I like to think that it existed deep down in me somewhere and kept me interested in the nomadic life of a GA.

The variety is another reason I stayed with the job. Depending on what editor tapped me on the shoulder or what idea I concocted, I wrote about a cease-fire in Nicaragua and local murder trials. The national desk dispatched me to wildfires in Colorado and Arizona, and the political editor asked me to cover the Illinois governor's race. I wrote a travel story from Key West and a story about freight train–hopping "weekend hobos" from the Chicago suburbs. I tackled subjects as different as the statistical analysis of drunk driving arrests and the experience of a young woman receiving her second double-lung transplant.

It dawned on me that I was one part chameleon and one part savant, trying to pass for an expert. I was trying to persuade readers and sources that I knew what I was talking about when, many times, I'd stumbled across the topic a few hours before then called an expert and poached information from him or her. It's a slightly artificial way of building a career. But it also makes the job stimulating, intellectually challenging, a cognitive rodeo of fun.

A very tangible downside, however, is story scramble mode, a condition I can never cure, only manage.

You know all these compelling stories are out there, but finding the right one can take time. Meanwhile, editors are under pressure to feed the gargantuan, always-famished news beast. That makes them prone to come up with half-baked ideas that they pass along with more than a nudge to the anxious reporter, who then develops a headache trying to contort the idea into a rational story someone would want to read.

For me and many other reporters, a natural effect of that existence is that we grow, figuratively speaking, story-idea antennae. Refined from the overabundant curiosity reporters emerge from the womb with, these antennae are a little like those on Uncle Martin from the ancient sitcom and unfortunate 1999 comedy feature film *My Favorite Martian*. They are almost always on alert for potential ideas, and they accompany us everywhere

—in the shower, at parties, wedding receptions, the dinner table, while driving.

But story antennae aren't enough to get the job done, which leads to one of the sausage-making aspects of the work: how I find stories.

Like any job, many parts of mine aren't quite as thrilling as what you see on the big or small screen, or what I'd talk about at cocktail parties, if I ever attended a cocktail party. Since the emergence of the world wide webbed internets and staff cuts that have gutted all newsrooms, finding stories involves a fair amount of sitting on one's arse, more or less anxiously working the phone and scouring the aforementioned webbed internets.

The ideal scenario is to find a promising story idea floating around undetected, then coax it from the shadows, nourish it, and dress it in a lovely gown. After that, you release it and let it sweep across the ballroom like an elegant dancer. Throughout the process, you're on the lookout for the next conquest.

I undertake all sorts of tactics to try to make that happen. Sometimes, while dodging editors, I make phone calls to sources and institutions—museums, zoos, universities, national laboratories—asking if they've got anything newsworthy. Sometimes a colleague will email an idea to me. (Bless you, Brother Ray Long.) Sometimes PR people send intriguing ideas. Sometimes I'll fish out a keeper from the oceans of social media. Sometimes I'll poach, which is to say I'll read other papers. They might be smaller papers with ideas that haven't made it to the bigger stage or haven't been fully developed. They also could be larger papers with snippets that have a significant, under-pursued angle. Sometimes I look through academic journals. Sometimes I plead with family, friends, and strangers for story ideas. Sometimes an editor will come to me with an idea that won't give me a headache. Sometimes I'll look to update an earlier story. Sometimes a former colleague who left the business for medical school will bump into me at the Billy Goat Tavern and mention an African American physician raised in one of Chicago's most violent neighborhoods who now makes house calls in Chicago's most violent neighborhoods and mentors struggling minority medical students. That story will soar like an Apollo rocket to page one Sunday, and I will send thoughts of bountiful blessings to Dr. John Biemer, his family, friends, and whatever pets they love.

Now you see why it's called story scramble mode. Once a reporter finds a story idea that he or she thinks will ring the bells of readers and does the same—more or less—for the reporter, he or she must persuade an editor that the idea's worthy.

Sometimes you find an idea that rings your bell but is less intriguing to an editor. Sometimes the ringing bell is obvious to everyone. Sometimes it wouldn't be obvious to any unimpaired human being, but presenting that idea to the editor is a somewhat pitiful, desperate effort to show her or him that you really are out there giving it the old college try. The scramble can get complicated, and for me, it ends up being more peculiar performance art than calculated science, a controlled agitation with far less logic than I'd prefer. Much of it can be slightly pathetic to observe.

All of that makes the life of a general assignment reporter programmed for distraction. We move from one unrelated assignment to another. To hedge against that anxious existence, GAs over time tend to gravitate toward a subject area, sometimes called a sub-beat—might be teen drug abuse, gays, traffic, parenting, technology, legalized casino gambling—that ensures the reporter always will have a well of ideas into which they can dip. I hated sub-beats and avoided them, opting instead for the high-wire adventure of finding what ideas I could, taking what I had to from editors, and sometimes making chicken salad out of chicken shit.

My one conciliation to a sub-beat, mostly because I love field trips, was to harvest ideas from the outback of Illinois. Many people in the Chicago news business call it "downstate," never mind that the term geographically dismisses a giant swath of the state north and west of Chicago and is mildly pejorative of everyplace seventy-five miles outside the city.

All sorts of poignant, curious, and intriguing stories existed "downstate": the restoration of the tallest, most heinous Abe Lincoln statue; the invasion of massive flying Asian carp; a community reconciling the discovery of lost graves from a shameful massacre; the effort to change the name of Negro Creek. There was the small-town Jaycees president who became a serial bank robber turned in by his police officer son; the bagel capital of the world in Mattoon, Illinois, of all places; the battle for Lee Harvey Oswald's tombstone; farm implement demolition derbies.

Those stories emanated from mostly small, often disregarded places populated by open, friendly, helpful people who loved their communities. And I enjoyed hitting the road to explore them. I'm a simple man. Few things resonate with the contemplative joy and serenity I experience while driving on a two-lane though the emerald fields and small towns of my home state. I relish spotting little oddities like a car parked on a tiny island in the middle of a large pond, a sculpture garden of old outboard motors, a stump of a tree carved and painted to resemble an ear of corn, a tall-steepled, lovely redbrick church sprouting trees from its windows and shrubs from its belfry.

These places had their own distinctive, if subtle beauty. I'd come upon a scene that had the feel of an Edward Hopper painting, or the surprising elegance of courthouse squares, or the intriguing allure of restored buildings that were 150 years old, or the melancholy beauty of their slow descent into ruin. Then I'd roll through the clear shimmer of those emerald farm fields against a summer sunset. Each place and its story were a colorful tile in a mosaic, a found jewel. And, they got me out of the office.

Some politicians—former Illinois governor James Thompson comes to mind—have called Illinois the most American state in the United States. It's a persuasive view, one that acknowledges Illinois as the confluence of cultures and history.

Settled from the north by urban opponents of slavery from New York and New England and from the south by rural slave owners from Tennessee and Kentucky, Illinois's northern boundary aligns geographically with Boston. Its southern tip is south of Richmond, Virginia, capital of the Confederacy during the Civil War. The mores of southern culture—those that are appealing and those less so—are entrenched in counties south of Effingham.

Illinois includes the world's most fertile farmland and pockets of near-breathtaking beauty—the "world's most beautiful drive" is how Theodore Roosevelt described Grandview Drive in Peoria. That town, by the way, is considered so American that since the 1880s, stage producers, movie studios, politicians, and makers of everything from disposable diapers to McDonald's McRib sandwiches have used it as a test market before going national.

Illinois is where the fabled artery that separates east from west, the Mississippi River, flows from Minnesota or South Dakota to the Gulf of Mexico. It's where Abraham Lincoln became a man, where Ronald Reagan and Hillary Clinton were born and raised, and where Barack Obama won his first elected office after starting his career of public service there.

Within its borders is one of the greatest American cities, which is also the nation's transportation hub. Skyscrapers were invented in Chicago. It's where Muddy Waters and his buddies transformed Delta blues into the electric version that gave birth to rock 'n' roll.

I'll acknowledge up front that violence is a very serious problem in Chicago, although the number of murders declined generally between 1994 and 2015 and violent crime dropped between 2006 and 2015. I'll also point out that it's concentrated, sadly, in the south and west sides of the city. I could argue that the violence in those areas is a very American micro-cosm. It happens in places where locally owned businesses, decent jobs, and functioning schools have been absent for decades, allowing problems to simmer. Then hopelessness, fueled by the availability of guns, erupts like an improvised explosive device.

However you want to analyze or qualify it, the violence is unacceptable and underscores another American issue: race. Chicago is a very segregated city that needs to do better for its young black males, needs to train its police much better, and needs to stop the tidal wave of illegal guns flowing into the city.

Yes, corruption is also an issue in Illinois. Two recent governors, Republican George Ryan and Democrat Rod Blagojevich, served consecutive terms in office then served terms in federal penitentiaries. Those gentlemen did their level best to keep my home state among the top 10 in public officials' corruption in many surveys. But in a 2012 "data-driven assessment of transparency, accountability and anti-corruption mechanisms in all 50 states," the Center for Public Integrity gave Illinois a C grade, better than Maine, New York, Florida, and Minnesota, to name a few.

And, let's face it, public officials' corruption is a very American—even universal—reality. Someone less cynical than I might contend that the Center for Public Integrity's rating and the convictions of two consecutive governors from different political parties show a state that is serious about rooting out corruption.

Finally, in demographic marker after marker, Illinois shows up as a composite portrait of the entire country.

Take race, for example. In an Associated Press analysis of Census Bureau data from 2000–06, Illinois lined up almost exactly with the U.S. average of 68 percent white, non-Hispanic, 15 percent Hispanic, 13 percent black, and 5 percent Asian.[1]

In fact, the AP reported, "Illinois most closely matched the national average on a combination of demographic factors, including race, income, education, mix of industry, age, immigration and share of people living in rural and urban areas."[2]

In 2015, *Time* magazine came to a similar conclusion. An article headlined "Find Out If Your State Is America's Past or Future" outlined how researchers crunched data from 2013 to determine what year each state most closely reflected the demographic makeup of the entire country.[3]

None matched. Some, like Iowa, Montana, and North Dakota, were stuck in 1930 America. Others, like California and Texas, looked like America of 2060. Only one came closest to the racial and ethnic demographics of the U.S. in 2013. Yep. The Land of Lincoln, the Prairie State, Illinois.

In the outback of that most American place was where I found my subbeat. When Mike Arians's fat envelope plopped on my desk—it's still a mystery to me how it got there—and I read through the materials enclosed, all of it resonated somewhere deep inside me, like hearing a mysterious song float across a snowy, moonlit landscape.

Although I didn't know it at the time, the case would stay in that deep, resonant place for more than a decade, through all the distractions. At the outset, I knew part of the reason. This was a scandalous murder of two innocent young lovers that remained unsolved for more than a half century, and some guy was now trying to get to the bottom of it.

Over the years, the reasons grew into something broader and deeper, something about the damage inflicted by all unexplained murders and the desire to forget; about disposable victims and the mysterious beauty of a place; about the value of pursuing truth; and about an eccentric man's pursuit of his ghosts.

For now, though, I merely was glad my editor gave me the green light on another field trip.

In Memoriam

· · ·

"ROADHOUSE," the guy answered when I called the phone number on the lavender stationery. The voice was a little deep, likeable, folksy, intimate; it would have been perfect for a late-night talk radio host, and it belonged to Mike Arians.

We talked for a few minutes, mostly reviewing the information he'd sent, filling in a gap here or there. As excited as I was about the story, I wanted to determine if this case was all that it appeared to be, if it was worth a two-hour drive. More important, I wanted to determine if Mike was a nut.

He didn't sound like one. He was very open to all my questions, even a little passive. The more we talked, the saner he seemed. Pausing from time to time to draw on his cigarette, he told me about the Roadhouse. He said he had notebooks and files full of other material and photographs on the Reed-Skridla case that he was happy to share. He made a vague reference to a Mary Jane Reed memorial he'd set up and mentioned something about her presence visiting the restaurant from time to time. That set off a tiny alarm bell in my head, but overall, the conversation went smoothly. In the end, he registered somewhere around "eccentric" on my personal psycho-meter. That, combined with his willingness to talk for as long as I wanted about any element of the case, was ideal for a story like this. We arranged to meet at his restaurant in a couple days.

• • •

OREGON, ILLINOIS, is 101 miles from the Tower, past the office and condo high-rises of Chicago's Loop, past rehabbed factory lofts and the University of Illinois at Chicago, the bombed-out west side, gritty inner-ring suburbs, and the Waldheim and Concordia Cemeteries; past angular, gleaming office parks that stand in the far west suburbs, past the thirty-screen multiplex and billboards touting new subdivisions and the Hollywood Casino.

Chicago radio reception started to fade about the time vinyl-sided McMansions appeared on one side of Interstate 88 and fields of corn and soybeans sprouted on the other. The stench of torches burning off landfill methane hung in the air near DeKalb, and then the landscape turned very flat and listless, the kind of landscape that gets drivers talking to themselves surprisingly fast.

I turned north on Interstate 39—the E. J. "Zeke" Giorgi Highway, named for a state rep who was the Father of the Illinois Lottery—then west on Illinois Route 64. Three miles later, traffic came to a halt at a stop sign at a lonely intersection where an exhausted-looking restaurant stood. It would be blown to bits by a tornado a few years later. Then came a tiny graveyard and a dot of a town called Kings. There, about 200 feet and a bone-jarring set of railroad tracks separated an old church from a small bar called the Shakey Rooster. The route passed Skare Road and tourist attraction signs for Granny's Berries and Hidden Timber Gardens.

Thirteen miles west along Route 64, the land undulated and the road curved. Farm fields gave way to trees and the rolling, at times steep, rocky landscape of the Rock River valley. Views of wooded, hilly scenery extended farther and farther. Native American lore tells of this area being so beautiful that the river doubles back on itself just south of Oregon to show its reluctance to leave. Its beauty is not breathtaking and certainly is helped by its emergence from the tabletop farmland. But it is refreshingly Vermont-like, scenic in a subtle way.

Over a ridge, stopped at a traffic light, I got my first view of Oregon, just beyond a colorful sign adorned with the carving of a bald eagle. "Oregon, Illinois" the sign read, "a beautiful place in the country." That sentiment was more than local boosterism. The town is surrounded by nearly 5,000 acres of state parks.

The spire of the old courthouse protruded above treetops. On the left was a closed bait and tackle shop with a sign announcing "24 hours guns and ammo." Water rushed over the dam of the wider-than-expected Rock River. Upriver on a bluff promontory was a striking sight—a giant statue of a contemplative Native American that looked to be made of stone, gazing over the valley. On the main drag were a vintage drive-in restaurant, riverside bar, gently restored stone buildings, and deteriorating redbrick businesses that looked to be more than a century old.

Left on Illinois Route 2, I passed the courthouse and two mismatched cannons on its front lawn, a beauty salon, and a quick mart gas station, then a McDonald's. Old frame houses—some well-maintained or restored, others dilapidated—lined the road, which bent at a bronze statue of a young Abraham Lincoln playing with children. A few feet past a car dealership on the left was a low, brown, wooden structure that looked like an outpost: the Roadhouse.

It was the end of July, the time of year in Illinois when sunshine, no matter how bright, always seems veiled by humidity hanging in the air. It can be tough to breathe, especially if the air-conditioning on your six-year-old Kia sedan is dysfunctional. My shirt was stuck to my chest.

The Roadhouse was closed that day, and the parking lot was empty, except for a white van close to the back of the building. Waves of heat emanating from the asphalt wrinkled my vision. After a couple of knocks on the screen door at the rear of the place and a call inside, a compact man in a goatee and glasses appeared from the kitchen. He looked a little like Peter Sellers's Inspector Clouseau from the Pink Panther movies and a little like Humphrey Bogart. He was Mike Arians. We shook hands, and he invited me inside, where it was cool and dark. He asked how the ride went and gave me a tour.

Mike said the structure dated back to the mid- to late 1800s. It had the feel of a place that had been remodeled seven or eight times: layered, catacombed. The faint aroma of smoke and grease carried through the restaurant, but it was very clean. The motif was what might be called Wild West Country Kitchen, where Martha Stewart duels Billy the Kid and Billy wins. The walls bore antique guns and steel hunting traps, miniature horse-drawn wagons, steer horns, and silhouettes of bronco-riding cowboys.

Framed photos and news clippings of Ronald Reagan, whose boyhood home is in nearby Dixon, were mounted on a wall.

Mike walked through the bar, where coins on the bar top glinted through layers of polyurethane. A mannequin dressed as a prospector sat at the bar. Then we entered the main lounge and stopped. There she was, in silicone.

On the balcony, eerily illuminated with stage lighting, was another mannequin. Her brown wig looked a little askew. Her right arm was raised, bent at the elbow, her graceful hand lifting a finger as if she was calling for the waiter. She was wearing a lavender gown. She was Mary Jane, in memoriam.

A chill ran up the back of my neck and settled somewhere in my ear canals. Mike was gazing at the mannequin.

"She was a beautiful girl," he said, pausing for a long and awkward moment. Then he turned. "Have you seen this?"

Mike walked to a hall off the lounge. On one wall was a pencil rendering of Mary Jane from the side-view photograph of her as coquette, seated on the grass. Other photos of her were mounted around it. It was a shrine to Mary Jane and included about twenty-five framed photos and newspaper clippings from the case. We sat in a booth. Mike started telling me his backstory.

What I came to find out, from that conversation and from other sources, somewhat illuminated what he would have difficulty explaining for years: why Mike had devoted so much time, money, and energy on the decades-old murders of two people he'd never met and had no connection to.

Childhood trauma might be the obvious cliché in a case like this. Mike's childhood was a little more nuanced, an uneven mix of stability and neglect, idyllic farm boy life and anxiety rooted in the perception that he was unwanted.

Born in 1949 and raised largely by his grandparents on a 65-acre family farm forty miles northwest of Chicago, Mike was unsure who his father was. The man who married his mother shortly before Mike was born looked nothing like Mike, who'd been told he had at least some Native American lineage. Apparently, relations were cordial between residents of a nearby reservation and pale-faced women in Mike's ancestry.

He had wistful memories of the farm. It was his playground, and as a boy, Mike was outside all the time, year-round, playing along a creek in what he described as "almost a Huck Finn/Tom Sawyer existence." He also remembered getting in trouble often, for leaving his grandfather's tools by the creek, coming home muddy and wet, or committing some other, similar infraction.

"My grandma always clopped me beside the head and hooked me in the house," Mike recalled. "To this day, I have a problem with my one ear where she would clop me all the time, my right ear."

His mother was unpredictably petty and, like the man she married, promiscuous. She worked as a secretary at a large manufacturing company. Mike's stepfather was a salesman and easily agitated World War II vet who drank too much and would disappear for days. Mike missed kindergarten, he said, because no one in his family would drive him to school. His family would manage to get him to religious youth group activities only occasionally, then leave him stranded afterward. At a couple of Christmas celebrations for the extended family, he was the only kid who didn't receive a present. "I was kind of the redheaded stepchild . . . bastard child," Mike once told me. "Looking back—and I'm not crying or whining—but I don't think I was off on the same playing field with most kids my age."

Most troubling was an older stepbrother, C. C., and his friends, who would pick on Mike constantly. An incident in which they collapsed a hollowed-out snowbank on him nearly suffocated him. Another time, C. C. and a friend tied Mike to a tree, placed lit flares around it, and told him the flares were dynamite. "Fun crowd," Mike told me, chuckling.

He attended a four-room schoolhouse in the tiny town of Plato Center, near the farm, then rural Burlington Central High School, where he worked on the student newspaper and yearbook, was in the library club, Future Farmers of America, and AV club. President of the chess club, Mike played on the football and baseball teams and participated in theater. He enjoyed history and geography and liked to write, he said, but little else engaged him academically. He gravitated toward subjects in which he could work with his hands: auto shop, woodworking, and the like.

After graduating in 1967, Mike enrolled in a vocational school in deep southern Illinois, 300 miles from home. Poor and enduring the penurious unpredictability of his mother, Mike developed stomach ulcers. He fell short of a degree but became proficient in auto mechanics, returned home, married his college roommate's sister, and worked as a mechanic and auto body repairman in Elgin, about thirty-five miles northwest of Chicago. She gave him a daughter in 1974, and the three returned to the family farm near Plato Center as renters.

His career was on a busy upswing. Mike became a body shop manager, testified in insurance fraud cases, then began working as an insurance adjuster. At one point, he held that job while he ran a body shop and boarded nearly fifty horses at the farm. His mother would push him to make more money, Mike recalled, then raise the rent at the farm.

His mix of talents led to him cracking fraud cases for insurance companies, Mike said, and he became more intrigued by the law. He enrolled in paralegal classes, looking to become a lawyer.

He divorced his first wife and was hired as a claim investigator for a large insurance company. "They used to call them pecker checkers in those days," Mike told me. He married again.

About this time, he hit a rough patch. His new wife drank all the time, often while spending the day in her pajamas. When he was at paralegal classes, she had an affair and got pregnant, he claimed. Mike wrote up legal documents and obtained a divorce.

The insurance gig soured on him, too. After he uncovered a fraud scheme involving an insurance company attorney, Mike said, he eventually was forced out of the corporation in the late 1980s.

While all this was going on, Mike opened a playhouse in a barn on the family farm. The Oak Dell Farm Theatre staged a handful of performances. A revival of a 1960s comedy, *Luv*, and *Driving Miss Daisy* were a couple of crowd-pleasers. He'd even taken to the stage himself in several other community theater productions, playing Doc—and receiving rave reviews in the local press—in Tennessee Williams's play *Small Craft Warnings*. He also appeared in *Driving Miss Daisy*, *Move Over Mrs. Markham*, and *The Man with the Plastic Sandwich*.

He met a new woman, June, a schoolteacher who stabilized his life and helped raise Mike's daughter. They married, and that one stuck. Oak Dell, meanwhile, was hounded by zoning complications and closed in about 1991. But Mike's agitation with local government officials over the matter prompted him to run for county board as a Democrat. He lost by a 2–1 margin, switched to the Republican Party, ran for the same spot, and won. About the same time he lost reelection, in 1998, an attorney acquaintance told him of a vacant restaurant in Oregon. Mike was intrigued, visited, found a different vacant restaurant, and acquired it.

That was also the year he happened to read a series of stories in the local press on the fiftieth anniversary of the unsolved murders of a local girl and her Navy veteran date, Mike told me. The case read almost like a mystery novel to him.

"I was intrigued by it, and I just kind of made a mental note of it," Mike said while we sat in the booth at the Roadhouse.

But he'd decided to run for mayor, and the campaign consumed him. When, in April of 1999, he beat the twenty-year-incumbent mayor by 265 votes from a total of 1,131 ballots cast, Mike kept hearing whispers about the murders of Mary Jane and Stanley. He remembered a waitress telling him about overhearing local law enforcement officers and power brokers chatting furtively about it in her diner. She couldn't hear specifically what they said, but Mike recalled that she was upset by their demeanor.

Something else about the case gnawed at Mike's conscience. Mary Jane was from Sandtown, a section of Oregon on the east side of the river where residents were viewed as lower-class troublemakers and slouches. From Mike's perspective, many in Oregon viewed Sandtown people as disposable, and that annoyed him, given his own biography. When Sandtown residents encouraged him to look into the case, he didn't have to reach too deep for motivation. He started paying closer attention, dug up background on the murders, and talked with people—many of whom told him that a law enforcement officer was involved.

"They felt that there should be some justice done," Mike said of the people who approached him about the case, "and they felt that I was in a position to do something about it."

He got around to calling Warren Reed, Mary Jane's youngest brother and the only surviving immediate family member.

Then Mike was indicted.

The state's attorney in Kane County, where Mike had been residing and serving on the county board, charged him with perjury, official misconduct, and disregarding election law. Turns out Mike might have been residing in two counties at the same time and fudging about it.

As a Kane County commissioner, he was required to reside in Kane County. To run for mayor of Oregon, he was required to live in Oregon, which is about sixty miles past the Kane County line, in Ogle County. After he was indicted, Mike must have decided the best defense was a robust counterattack. He sued the state's attorney, claiming prosecutorial misconduct.

While his criminal case made its way through the legal system, Mike continued to chip away at the Reed-Skridla case.

Warren Reed, perhaps the most sympathetic and forlorn soul in the ordeal, agreed to meet Mike at the Roadhouse and walked in with Jerry Brooks, Ogle County sheriff from 1970 to 1990. Jerry reportedly had his own personal file on the case. Mike had mentioned to me that he thought Jerry, as a teenager living in Oregon at the time of the murders, had helped police push Stanley's car to a garage after his body was found.

The three men talked. Jerry shared his theory that two brothers from out of town killed Stanley over a gambling debt, or to rob him or even the score on some other perceived slight. Mike offered that it could have been one person. Warren said Mike might be right. At that point, Mike recalled, "Jerry got mad and stormed out of the restaurant."

This might have been the key moment for Mike, when a minor agitation grew a little more persistent, when he turned the corner from interest and headed down the dark alley toward obsession. Maybe the ghosts of his earlier life—his mother issues, stepfather issues, stepbrother issues—drove him in some way to pursue Mary Jane's and Stanley's.

When I stopped and thought about all this, a few things became evident: Mike wasn't a guy inclined to feel sorry for himself. In fact, he brushed aside observations that he tumbled through a life of constant instability, especially in childhood. And, he wasn't afraid of a fight; he wasn't above fudging here and there, and he probably liked the limelight. He'd been cast aside, willfully neglected, bullied, and cuckolded. He was someone who uncovered wrongdoing by the powerful and sought justice, and was fired for doing so. A man with a past he couldn't shake, tactical ethics, and a desire to set things straight.

So when he read a local newspaper account of the unsolved killing of a girl from the wrong side of the river—a crime her community's collective memory had dismissed, a crime that may have been perpetrated, or at least facilitated, by powerful interests—something must have reverberated inside him, something that even he didn't want to acknowledge or couldn't articulate.

The criminal case against Mike ended in a mistrial. In October of 2001, both sides settled. Mike agreed to pay $3,000—the approximate amount of his Kane County salary while he was living in two places—and drop his civil suit against the state's attorney. With that cleared up, Mike had more time to investigate the murders. He dug deeper. Then strange things started happening, he said.

At that point in the conversation, Mike got uncomfortable, squirming in his seat. He took a pull from his cigarette and blew a long stream of smoke toward the ceiling. He paused.

"We purchased the place . . ." Then he stopped again, sighed. "People who worked here said it was haunted. I don't like the word *haunted*, and that's not how I perceive the energy here."

He let a moment pass, took another pull off the cigarette then snuffed it in the ashtray, watching it as he jabbed, and kept jabbing. He exhaled smoke. "It's not a black-and-white situation."

Now, let me just say here that when people talk about spirits inhabiting a home, or a jail, or a dormitory, or a roadhouse on the outskirts of a small midwestern town, I have three fairly distinct responses: (1) This person is nuts; (2) This is bullshit and this person is trying to play me; (3) I am scared witless. When Mike told me the place was haunted, my reaction was somewhere between numbers two and three.

The story, as Mike grudgingly told it, is that when he came to Oregon in the late 1990s with an interest in buying the restaurant that would become the Roadhouse, it was called the Seven Seas, and "it was in a shambles." Still, he saw something in it. The restaurant drew him toward it.

"When I first walked into the place, it had a very powerful, almost warm, inviting, cordial type of feeling," he said. "I don't know how to explain it. It's like it came to life before my eyes. I walked in here, and I could see how things were and how things used to be and . . . the potential, and it just kind of grabbed me."

He acquired the building and started sleeping there overnight while he was remodeling it. He remembered drifting easily into a deep, sound sleep. But sometimes the place would creak a lot, even for an old wooden building. He started hearing "peculiar noises." Once or twice, a stack of plates or a collection of pots and pans would collapse in the middle of the night, sending an eruption of noise through the place. After the Roadhouse opened and the disturbances continued, he and the staff shrugged and chuckled that it was Esther Stenhouse, the no-nonsense woman who owned the establishment with her husband in the 1930s and '40s. Legend has it that she died of a heart attack in a bathtub upstairs and that, since then, her ghost walks around from time to time, making sure the place is cleared out.

But other occurrences were more unnerving. The jukebox would spontaneously play the same song, "After Sunrise" by Sergio Mendes & Brasil '77, a guitar melody dominated by the haunting voice of a woman. Mike admitted that he started seeing connections to Mary Jane in his everyday life, that maybe he was looking for them: An Illinois Environmental Protection Agency letter to him on storm water management was signed by a Mary Reed. A fax from an equipment manufacturer included the name of the woman who transmitted it—Mary Jane. While Mike was away from the Roadhouse, a deliveryman showed up with flowers on November 15, Mary Jane's birthday, and was turned away. Mike never did find out who sent them.

"It was getting to the point where myself, my wife June, and our help were experiencing these 'incidents,' and they were so abundant that we just kind of accepted it and in kind of a jovial way said it wasn't Esther, it was Mary Jane."

But a woman bartender quit, saying she was creeped out by the vibe in the place at night. Then, Mike said, one of his waitresses saw an apparition or something resembling one in a hallway near the restrooms after closing. Finally, encouraged by others—namely Warren Reed—Mike stepped into the ethereal.

"There was no way I could explain what they saw," he said of his employees. "I was starting to question my own sanity. I was lost, and I was looking for a way to think outside the box."

He contacted a psychic, who visited in the summer of 2002. The woman said one of the spirits in the Roadhouse was named Ruth—the first name of Mary Jane's mother—but the psychic was having difficulty going deeper.

"To be honest with you," Mike said, sitting across from me in the booth, "I do believe there are other dimensions out there that we don't understand."

He took a pull from a new cigarette, blew a stream of smoke upward again, looked a little distant. "There's a presence at the Roadhouse that is very determined. I almost feel like—as crazy as this sounds—that Mary Jane and I have a relationship—not a romantic relationship."

Nervous laughter bubbled into my voice.

"Well," I said, exhaling, "that's a relief." I stared up at the mannequin. My palms tingled.

Just as I was about to ask him a little more about the psychic sessions, Mike suggested he take me for a tour of important sites in the case. The psychics could wait, I thought. We hopped in his truck.

He drove to lovers' lane, a gravel road cut between two farm fields, got out, and walked to the spot where he thought Stanley and Mary Jane had parked. He pointed to where Stanley had been shot and where his body had been found. Then we got back in the truck and Mike drove to the weedy patch along a curvy, remote road a couple miles north, where Mary Jane's body had been found. He gave a quick tour of town, noting large restored Queen Annes and more modest clapboard Victorians and Colonials, and the contemporary, expansive ranches where the wealthy lived. He crossed the river, drove to Sandtown and to what had been Mary Jane's home, a small, gray frame house that had been expanded but still looked beaten down, bowed, leaning. Definitely the wrong side of the river.

Throughout the drive, he explained his theory of the case.

From Mike's point of view, Mary Jane may not have been as pure as the crystal waters of the Rock River. She'd had quite a few admirers, and Mike suggested she'd allowed some to do more than admire her. One of those boyfriends was Vince Varco, a chief deputy sheriff and something of a bully who puffed on a cigar jammed in a smoking pipe clenched in his teeth. They had a brief fling that Mary Jane ended before Vince wanted it to. The deputy showed up at the Reed house the afternoon before Mary Jane's disappearance, pulled her outside, and wanted to persuade her, in his less-than-subtle way, that they should continue seeing each other. Other accounts say Vince ran into Mary Jane in a bar a few hours before the shooting. It's possible both incidents occurred.

This was an awkward relationship for Mary Jane. Vince was married. Maybe it was a little forbidden fun for her—and for Vince—but she didn't see much reason to continue, Mike told me. Besides, she had been making progress with a much more exciting prospect: Stanley, the handsome Navy vet who was single, from the big city of Rockford, and liked to spend his money late into the evening. Her kind of man.

It sounded as if she was tossing Vince aside and moving on. He had different plans. That day, he grabbed her by the arm. She struggled to get away. Vince held on.

And then he hit her. Then he hit her again, and again, Mike said, before throwing her aside and taking off.

The next night, Mary Jane's date was shot four or five times. At least three bullets entered the abdominal area, which someone might interpret as Mr. Stanley Skridla having his balls shot off. Mary Jane was abducted, probably raped, murdered, and tossed in a ditch. The morning of the murders, according to Mike, Vince showed up for work without his service revolver, a .32 caliber, the same caliber weapon used in the killings. It was simple logic: Vince was the killer.

"They've covered this thing up for fifty-five years," Mike told me.

Vince had died in the mid-1980s. Precisely how Mike arrived at his theory was a little befuddling, but it sounded plausible, and he had done exhaustive research. He was hoping the exhumation of Mary Jane's body would help connect the dots.

If he was right, Ogle County officials had reason to be nervous. They might be on the hook for a conspiracy that could result in a huge court judgment. How much is a half-century cover-up of a double homicide worth? Millions? Many millions? And what about the criminal culpability if current local officials were aware of the cover-up? Neither Mike nor Warren nor Stanley's relatives had filed suit, but that was a logical extension of where they were heading.

Still, Mike had made a few leaps and twists to connect the dots, and as months passed, his theories started sounding fairly desperate, until one shocking detail in a later investigation revealed itself. But that was still years away.

At the time of our first visit, Mike had filled four three-ring binders with news clippings, reports, letters, and other information. He'd hired private investigators and bought the books *Practical Homicide Investigation* and *How to Solve a Murder*. He'd collected aerial photos of the area and dug up various police files on the murders. He'd interviewed people and contacted forensic pathologists. He'd even hired a local reporter to start a book on the case. And, a would-be producer from California had visited to gather research for a screenplay. Both projects fizzled in fairly short order.

Mike said he'd spent $20,000—a figure, excluding the hours of personal time he'd invested, that would grow more than fivefold by the end of his ordeal.

That investment looked like the proverbial "pouring money down a rat hole," so it was no surprise that Mike had been enduring a fair amount of grief for embarking on this odyssey. I started thinking about what that must be like on a daily basis. It's one thing to pursue an endeavor like this in the anonymity of a metropolitan region of nine million people, quite another in a small town where you run a business and are looking to be reelected as mayor.

News accounts of Mike's effort, mine included, would quote critics who questioned his integrity and sanity. People around town who'd been willing to talk about the case with him became uncooperative. When he'd see one of his restaurant customers at the grocery store, instead of stopping to say hi or chat, they'd turn their carts in the opposite direction, Mike told me.

He estimated that one-third of the community didn't care about the case, one-third was on his side, and one-third "wanted my ass." Those who would speak with him told Mike that the Reed family was taking advantage of him or that he was crazy. They'd criticize the mannequin memorial on his balcony or say he was trying to get rich through a movie deal or piece of a court settlement.

If Mike was trying to orchestrate a huge windfall off this, he had a curious way of going about it. Most everything he tried crumbled in his hands. To me, that didn't sound like a guy trying to make a bunch of money. It sounded like a guy who may be obsessed, a guy haunted by lives lost and never redeemed by justice, a guy who was in over his head emotionally, perhaps, maybe even a guy in love.

The cumulative effect was reflected in business at the Roadhouse, which ultimately fell to about half of what it was before Mike started researching the case, he told me, and in his reelection campaign, which he lost.

Not to mention the death threats.

One night, Mike recalled, he and a manager were eating dinner at a local restaurant when a younger man who may have had a few too many cocktails approached their table, formed one hand into a gun, pointed it at Mike, and kept flicking his thumb.

"He said he had people who would take care of me," Mike recalled. "That was pretty freaky."

He tried to shake it off as hot air from a gasbag, but the incident was unsettling. A couple years later, Mike said he got a phone call from a long-time customer, "Bob," an attorney who'd worked in Chicago, inherited a sizable amount of money, and built a beautiful home west of Oregon. Like the young man who'd approached Mike at the restaurant, Bob also might have been drinking, Mike told me.

"You gotta drop it," he recalled Bob saying about the case. "You just gotta drop it. I got a call from the boys in Chicago, and they've got a hit out on you."

"That scared the shit out of me," Mike said. He responded by placing black stage curtains on windows at his restaurant so no one outside the building could see exactly where he was. He also contacted the state police, who apparently spoke with Bob. Nothing materialized, except that Mike said he bought a couple of guns.

I wanted to believe all of what he was telling me. To healthy skeptics, conspiracy theories are as enticing as catnip to a feline. But Mike's retelling of events, especially the death threats, was nebulous enough to make me wonder. When I'd press him for details, he'd have difficulty recalling. When he'd hit on a particularly intriguing nugget, he'd quickly move to something else, and he could walk a long way down Tangent Avenue, which I'd let him do. I wanted to absorb as much as I could about him and the case.

But there was no doubting the amount of effort and money he was investing, and that gave him credibility. I'd start to shake my head in doubt at something he was saying, then an incident would occur to make me think Mike was, in his own circuitous way, tracking down suspicious, even criminal, conduct.

Like our encounter with a receptionist at the sheriff's office that muggy July afternoon.

Days before, I'd arranged to view the sheriff's file on the case. But when we parked and entered the sheriff's building, all that changed.

"I'm sorry," the receptionist said, "we can't let you look at that file."

She hunched and turned toward her paperwork, trying to dismiss the issue with one quick sentence. I wouldn't let her. We debated the point for a few minutes. I noted that this was precisely what I'd sought to avoid by getting approval from the deputy chief days earlier, before driving 100 miles to get here. She said the file was part of "an ongoing investigation" and that, as such, was unavailable for public review.

"Ongoing investigation," I said, in what might have been a disrespect-ful tone. I asked where the deputy chief was and whether I could speak with him. She said he was in a meeting. I chuckled in a way that, again, might have been disrespectful. *Of course he's in a meeting,* I thought, and I might have expressed that view aloud, again in what might have been construed as a disrespectful tone. I asked when the meeting would end. She said she was unsure. I nodded, perhaps with a snide grin.

"I'm sorry," she said for about the fifth time, blinking at me. She looked a little bored and a little agitated.

We held our positions for a few seconds, both of us silent, staring at each other.

A reporter has choices in moments like these. I could have waited, but she and I knew that would burn valuable time with little chance of a pay-off. I could start ratcheting up the volume and outrage and see where that led, or I could leave it be. I've done all three.

This time, waiting seemed like my least promising option, and when I thought about making a scene, all that kept coming to mind was giving the office staff the pleasure of sharing the story about the *Tribune* reporter who threw a hissy fit. I figured I might get a shot at that file if I circled back at some point, and I wanted to keep that option open. Having a tantrum would shrink my chances. I smiled and nodded again.

"Okay, well, tell the deputy chief I'm sorry I didn't get a chance to meet him," I said, trying to wring the disrespect from my voice. "I'll give him a call."

She didn't respond. Mike and I walked out. Something he'd said earlier rang in my head.

"I'm a little bit scared, you might say. I'm up against something a little larger, and I'm not sure I know what it is."

Origins

• • •

THE STONEWALLING receptionist created additional time in Oregon, which turned out to be valuable. It was more time to glean ever-important context. I headed to the library, where the kind ladies behind the desk handed me booklets and a thick file folder of material on Oregon's history. I stepped to a table, pulled up a chair, and started reading.

White settlement of Illinois is considered to have started in the early 1800s. Oregon traces its genesis to 1829. That year, John Phelps, who bears a striking resemblance to actor Harry Dean Stanton with a thick white beard, visited from nearby Galena. Mostly, he wanted to get a look at the pastoral Rock River. He liked what he saw, and in 1834, he was the first white settler to build a house and plant crops in the area.

The place became known as Oregon, a name officially given to it twenty-one years before the state of the same name was admitted to the Union. Origins of the word *Oregon* remain mysterious, although historians' best guesses run along two paths.

It may be taken from a Native American trade route along which *oorigan*, grease condensed from smelt found in the Pacific Northwest, was transported. Or a colorful American who fought for the British in the French and Indian War, Major Robert Rogers, might be responsible. That theory starts with the word *Ouariconsint*, a misspelled French name for "Wisconsin" that later was trimmed to *Ouaricon*. Some historians contend that

Major Rogers heard of the River Ouaricon, which flowed west somewhere beyond the Great Lakes, and then shortened it to Ouragon, then Ourigan. Over the years, people in Oregon, Illinois, adopted a shorthand version of the name and a more phonetic spelling. *Oregon*, they say, is Native American for "river of the west." Perhaps out of sunny optimism for the future, someone tacked "City" onto "Oregon," and on December 4, 1838, the certificate for Oregon City was filed with the Ogle County clerk.

Its most enduring, prominent symbol came seventy-three years later: the contemplative statue of a Native American on a bluff over the Rock River that I'd spotted just north of town. It's not stone, as I'd thought. It's 270 tons of concrete, and it stands forty-eight feet tall, placed atop an eighty-foot bluff. Said to be the second-tallest concrete monolith in the world, it's called *The Eternal Indian* by some, *Black Hawk* by others, and is a symbol of the rich, sorrowful history of Native Americans in the region.

Renowned American sculptor Lorado Taft created the statue, and it is a lasting reminder of another intriguing piece of Oregon history, the Eagle's Nest Art Colony, a thriving group of artists and writers who emerged from the 1893 World's Columbian Exposition in Chicago. After the world's fair, a group wanted to remain in Chicago to nurture each other's creative pursuits. When Chicago's broiling summer rolled around, they escaped to a farm in Bass Lake, Indiana, but a malaria outbreak drove them from there.

They settled in Oregon after Chicago attorney and arts patron Wallace Heckman offered his summer estate on the banks of the Rock. From that summer of 1898 until the last original member died in 1942, Eagle's Nest hosted a steady stream of artists, Taft among the most prominent. Today, it's a 141-acre outdoor education and conference center for Northern Illinois University.

I read about another structure on the other side of the river, also on a bluff. Stronghold Castle was built between 1928 and 1930 by Walter Strong, owner and publisher of a great, now-deceased Chicago newspaper, the *Daily News*. Strong wanted to create a summer retreat, and a grand one he did: ten bedrooms, eight bathrooms, several fireplaces, and at least two secret passages.

He got to enjoy it for only one summer. In 1931, at forty-seven years of age, Strong died. Today, the Presbyterian Church uses the estate for conferences, retreats, and camping. Once a year, the castle hosts the Olde English Faire.

Driving around when I first arrived, I noticed an inordinate number of sculptures. At the library, I found out about the Oregon Sculpture Trail. Aided largely by a local arts group, more than a dozen pieces have been placed in and around town. At Mix Park, you can see Abraham Lincoln crossing paths with Black Hawk. North of the courthouse at the Oregon Coliseum is a four-foot bronze cornball. A human-fish form depicting the life-giving waters of the Rock River stands at the east end of the dam. And here's a juicy trivia tidbit for sports fans: the iconic seventeen-foot, one-ton bronze statue of Michael Jordan outside Chicago's United Center, the one that tens of thousands—perhaps hundreds of thousands—of people have posed with for photos, was cast at a foundry in Oregon.

When I got up from my chair to stretch my legs at the library, I absent-mindedly wandered up to the second floor and found a hidden jewel of a gallery. The space, which Eagle's Nest artists used for exhibitions and lectures, includes an astonishing collection of more than fifty paintings and sculptures the artists donated at Taft's request.

I returned to my seat and paged through more historical documents. Sometime around the 1920s, it appears as if local pranksters attempted to fire one of the two Civil War cannons on the courthouse lawn. Instead, the gun blew to pieces. Civic leaders couldn't find an exact match, which is why when I drove by the courthouse the first time, I saw the pair of mismatched cannons on the front lawn.

A booklet reported that Oregon City's first birth was Lamoil T. Jenkins, son of Jonathan and Rebecca Jenkins. "Born in July 1837, young Jenkins died in 1865 of a gunshot wound received during a political argument," the booklet reported. That's all we know about the relatively short life of Lamoil T. Jenkins. But I couldn't help wondering if he was another Oregon ghost, a ghost of the Civil War, our nation's most divisive political argument, which ended in April of 1865. Was it preposterous to think that the political argument that ended Lamoil's life was about the war?

Shortly before the birth of baby Lamoil, the state legislature tabbed Oregon as the county seat of Ogle County. But community leaders fought over where to build the courthouse, and at some point during the debate, they renamed the city Florence. The reason? A European tourist passing through Oregon said it reminded him of the Italian city. Three years later, everybody apparently thought better of the new name and returned to the original, dropping "City." By February 1843, the official name was Oregon and the population hovered around 200.

Over the decades, Oregon had its brushes with infamy and oddity. In 1876, the history books say, infamous outlaws Jesse and Frank James and company tried their hands at horse racing at the local fairgrounds. After, they headed to Northfield, Minnesota, where they robbed a bank in a very bloody misadventure. About the same time, Oregon resident Henry H. Smith became one of the more famous purveyors of a common household miracle remedy. His King of Tetter was an ointment to treat the skin diseases herpes, eczema, and impetigo. In advertisements, Smith claimed he had cured "scores of the worst cases of tetter" after physicians had given up on the patients. He had "full confidence in its power to effect cure, except in possibly rare cases, which are too long standing; though he would state in all candor that he has not yet met any such."

Oregon had a couple of curious social organizations, too, including the Owls, a bachelor club established in 1870 in part by Judge James H. Cartwright, who later served as Illinois Supreme Court chief justice. They called meetings by blowing a six-foot horn, kidnapped and paddled new initiates in the nude, held annual picnics on an island in the Rock River, and paraded under yellow, red, white, and blue umbrellas. Owls who'd gotten married were fined $5, drummed out of the club, and forced to walk the parade under black umbrellas.

And then there were the Umzoowee, who appear in one reference in a June 19, 1947, article in the *Ogle County Republican*.

"The Umzoowee were a large group of young ladies, who gave out," the article stated. "They scorned matrimony and banded together for preservation of their ideals."

I read about the two Illinois governors who hailed from Oregon. Thomas Ford, in office from 1842 through 1846, was unfairly viewed by some as complicit in the 1844 murder in Illinois of Mormon leader Joseph Smith. That killing drove the Mormons from Illinois to Salt Lake City. Governor Ford also wrote a definitive early history of the state.

Frank Orren Lowden, governor from 1917 to 1921, came close to beating Herbert Hoover for the Republican presidential nomination in 1928 and was a champion of women's suffrage and efficient government. He is best remembered for his love of the land. One state park and one state forest around Oregon bear his name.

The city also has its athletic fame. Landers-Loomis Field, where the Oregon High School Hawks battle on the gridiron, is named for Frank Loomis and Sherman Landers, graduates of Oregon High School who competed in the 1920 Summer Olympics. Loomis won a gold medal in the 400-meter hurdles, setting a world record. Landers finished fifth in the triple jump.

As for commerce and industry, the railroad arrived in 1871, but booming economic prosperity never really materialized. Oatmeal and flour mills, furniture and chair factories, and a foundry sprung up. Most failed. The Schiller Piano Company, established in 1893, became Oregon's largest industry and produced nearly 40,000 instruments. But the factory shut down in 1971.

The one business that has hung on and thrived in Oregon is E. D. Etnyre & Company, founded in 1898 as a manufacturer of automatic hog waterers. In the early 1900s, Etnyre even dabbled in automobile manufacturing but found its core strength in building road construction equipment. It's still in business in Oregon.

Along with this intriguing, quirky history, Oregon had its darker episodes —as any town does—that suggest a place where justice didn't always follow the law.

One was the fight between the Prairie Pirates, also known as the Banditti, and a vigilante group known as the Regulators. The other was a promising county prosecutor's shocking, deadly shooting rampage.

In the late 1830s, a fairly organized group of thugs, the Prairie Pirates, started wreaking havoc on law-abiding citizens in a wide area some historians claim stretched from Texas to Wisconsin and Ohio. The Pirates counterfeited money, stole horses, and murdered. Ogle County—Oregon in particular—was one of their most active areas.

Historical records are spotty, but it appears that at least one attempt by Ogle County authorities to arrest and convict seven leaders of the group around 1841 yielded unsatisfactory results. The sheriff arrested the leaders, but at some point during their confinement, the Pirates' compatriots, still roaming free, hatched a plan to set afire the new Oregon courthouse, next to the jail. In the ensuing chaos, the raiders planned to free their jailed friends.

Half the plan, setting the courthouse on fire, went as expected. They bungled the other half, and the group of seven leaders stood trial. Four were acquitted. Three were convicted but served only a few months in jail before returning to active duty in Ogle County.

These developments provided enough proof to citizens that local authorities were unable to handle the Prairie Pirates and that, unless something more creative was done, the violence and pillaging would continue. Residents responded by establishing the Regulators, which might best be described as a larger, angrier group of thugs with right on their side.

They appointed John Long as their first captain, and he promptly organized a capture, vanquishing some Prairie Pirates and conveying that they were to leave Ogle County. The Pirates responded by burning down Long's sawmill, which led Long to decide he might not be cut out for this captain stuff after all.

Long's successor was Phineas Cheney, who receives little mention in history books on the subject, except that after receiving threatening letters from the Pirates, he too decided Regulator captain was not an ideal fit for his skill set.

Then came John Campbell, the right man for the job.

Challenged to a fight by a Pirate ringleader named William Driscoll, Campbell responded by showing up at Driscoll's house in neighboring DeKalb County with 196 Regulators. After a short standoff, the sheriff arrived and brokered a settlement that called for the Pirates to leave the state. Five days later, the Pirates changed their minds. On June 27, 1841, three Prairie Pirates rode to Campbell's house and murdered him. Several days after that, the Ogle County sheriff arrested John Driscoll, William's father, who also was a leader of the Pirates, and placed him in the Ogle County Jail in Oregon. The next day a group of Regulators broke into the jail, grabbed Driscoll, and brought him across the river, where his sons William and Pierce already had been detained by an impatient group of Regulators and their supporters. They decided this was the perfect time for a trial.

More than 500 people, who one historical reference reported "had previously been drinking at a nearby grist mill," gathered to watch. Things went downhill for the Driscoll clan from there. The judge selected a jury. Witnesses from all over the area testified against the Driscolls. John Driscoll, perhaps in an effort to make peace with his maker, admitted to stealing fifty horses.

The jury convicted all three men but freed Pierce, who was barely a teenager. They dispatched John and William Driscoll a few moments later by dividing a group of 111 armed men into two firing squads. One shredded John Driscoll with bullets while the other concentrated its fire on William.

The Pirates got the message and dropped Ogle County from their service area. A historical marker, placed on the site of the trial and execution, read, "Pastors and scholars, ministers and deacons regarded this terrible example of lynch law as a public necessity."

After returning the materials to the front desk, I asked a librarian where I might look through newspapers from the late 1940s, when Mary Jane and Stanley found each other at the telephone company. Another librarian led me down narrow stairs to the building's microfiche machine, which was broken. She turned and we walked into the dark, tight quarters where the library kept bound copies of local newspapers. I heaved the one marked "1948" from the shelves, set it on a wooden table, and began turning its pages.

The beauty of 1940s newspapers is that they were a little less than nuanced about their political leanings. A century or so after the Prairie Pirates were dispatched, Ogle County was a conservative place in its mores and its politics, at least publicly. That perspective, which remains intact today, was evident in the pages of the *Ogle County Republican*, which called itself "an All Home Print Newspaper," whatever that means.

I found a front-page story encouraging people to vote for a House representative who "is Republican at all times and is always out working for the interest of the Republican Party." Another front-page piece criticized President Harry Truman as a "double talker" for saying that farmers should thank God for the Democratic Party and high prices for their products, but adding that people who have to pay high prices should condemn the Republican Party.

The paper published other, more predictable front-page stories on new businesses, a March of Dimes campaign to fight "infant paralysis," the winner of a national agricultural achievement award, and obituaries on residents "called from life." There were items on new school district boundaries for nearby Leaf River, the Oregon Yacht Club's construction of floating docks, the need for fewer highways and more tillable land, opposition to parking meters, who was visiting whom, and where residents had traveled. "The H. C. Kaspers write of Life in Florida Climate" was one of my favorites.

Two dollars and ninety-nine cents would buy a 100-pound bag of potatoes at the local Piggly Wiggly, and a pound of ground beef was forty-nine cents. Jobs at Kable Printing paid sixty cents an hour. There were ads for the artificial insemination of livestock, Cinderella Frocks for Big and Little Sisters, and Perma-lift girdles.

I gingerly turned the brittle, tea-colored pages. The Oregon Theatre was showing Mickey Rooney in *Killer McCoy*, in which "Mickey battles a tough racket," and *Desire Me*, starring "The New and Exciting Love Team!" of Greer Garson and Robert Mitchum. James Stewart and Jane Wyman were "Lovin' and Laughin'" all the way through *Magic Town*, another feature at the Oregon.

Like any community, Oregon at that time had its more unsettling elements of everyday life, some of which emerged on the pages of the *Republican*.

"Miss Berta Bissell entered the clinic as a mental patient on Saturday" was the headline on one story. Another front-page clip detailed two men killed in a shoot-out during a property line dispute.

Fred Groen, fifty-seven, built a fence that his neighbor Thomas Kersteter, seventy-four, believed was on his property. Kersteter shot Groen with a high-powered rifle while Groen was cutting his lawn. Then, the newspaper reported, Kersteter walked to his garage and "put a bullet through his head" with a .32 revolver.

Looking through more recent newspapers, I came across what, besides the murders of Mary Jane and Stanley, might have been the most unsettling of all the stories I saw among the bound newspapers. Almost three decades after the Reed-Skridla murders, Ogle County state's attorney Richard Caldwell reportedly was in line to become a judge, a position some said he had coveted for years, and a job he may have viewed as a launching pad to higher office.

But his marriage also had unraveled and that, some believe, was the key behind the events of March 9, 1974, when the county state's attorney— the man in charge of bringing criminals to justice—snapped.

It's said he was shocked at not being named a judge, but those who were making the selection had noted in recent months that Caldwell was acting increasingly erratic, which is why they decided he couldn't be trusted as a judge. Later, law enforcement would concede they had been called to the Caldwell home more than a few times for domestic disturbances. Some of those officers admitted to seeing bullet holes in the walls on those previous visits.

When he got the bad news in early March, Caldwell compiled a hit list of those who had wronged him. On March 9, he started to settle the score. First, though, he took out his wrath on his own family, shooting and wounding his ex-wife and killing his thirteen-year-old son, David.

Brandishing a .25 caliber in one hand and pulling his daughter through backyards and streets with the other, a sobbing Caldwell was heard saying, "It's too bad the wrong people had to die." He made his way to the sheriff's office, where local newspaper reporter Kathryn Gelander happened to be checking police reports. Caldwell had a gun in each hand at this point and ordered Gelander to take his statement, she later wrote in a column for the *Oregon Republican Reporter.* He started by stating his name and office.

"I have just shot my wife and killed my son, David, who I loved," Caldwell said. "When I finish my statement I am going to kill myself."

Gelander faintly protested. Chief Deputy Sheriff Mel Messer stepped in the room, trying to persuade Caldwell to put away the gun.

"I have to do this," Caldwell shouted, according to Gelander's account. "Caldwell then uttered a tortured cry. I could not help feeling compassion for him."

"I begged my wife to come back to me," Caldwell continued, "but she showed no charity." He was waving and pointing the gun. Gelander reported that "Caldwell hurled a lot of invective at Messer" and threatened to kill him.

When a second deputy entered the room, Caldwell shot him and dropped behind the counter. Then he turned the gun on himself. Seconds before Messer lunged over the counter firing two shots, Caldwell squeezed the trigger. Gelander managed to escape unharmed. The wounded deputy recovered. Four days after the shootings, joint funeral services were held for Richard and David Caldwell. I never did find out what happened to the daughter and ex-wife.

I kept browsing, stumbled across a reference to something called the Pizza Connection, and was immediately intrigued. A little more noodling and I soon settled in for one of the more infamous organized crime tales in U.S. history, with a very direct link to Oregon.

The Pizza Connection was an estimated $1.65 billion international Mafia network that distributed about 1,650 pounds of heroin in the United States from Sicily between 1979 and about 1984. Cocaine also was trafficked and money laundered. In April of 1984, authorities arrested thirty-one men in the United States, Spain, Italy, and Switzerland on allegations of running the ring. Prosecutors charged that the network used pizza restaurants as covers to distribute the drugs.

One of the alleged leaders was Pietro Alfano, of Oregon, Illinois, the proprietor of a pizzeria three blocks east of the Roadhouse and a few steps south of the Abraham Lincoln statue.

The arrests led to what is believed to be the longest federal criminal trial in U.S. history: seventeen months and twenty-two defendants, prosecuted by Louis Freeh, who would become director of the FBI. His boss, U.S. Attorney for the Southern District of New York, was Rudolph Giuliani, later the mayor of New York City and a Republican candidate for president. During the prosecution, he was known as "the invisible maestro."

Apart from its significance in rewriting organized crime history and playing a key role in the careers of at least two prominent law-enforcement figures, the case was the subject of a 442-page book, *The Pizza Connection*, by columnist, TV commentator, and author Shana Alexander. And, it generated one of my favorite crime-related quotes of all time, from Judge Pierre N. Leval, who presided over the trial.

"Most of the time, it was boring," he told Jeffrey Toobin of the *New Yorker* in 2009. "People also got murdered from time to time in that case."

One of those was defendant Gaetano Mazzara, a New Jersey restaurant owner and alleged heroin supplier. On December 3, 1986, about fourteen months into the trial, his body was found inside a plastic garbage bag in Brooklyn.

Pietro also was targeted for execution, or at least that would be a reasonable inference. While carrying groceries with his wife in New York's Greenwich Village on February 11, 1987, he was shot three times in the back. After that, other defendants asked for their bonds to be revoked and to "go inside" to jail to await trial.

Pietro was paralyzed below the waist. When the trial ended in March of 1987, jurors convicted him and sixteen other defendants. An appeal led to his conviction being overturned in July of that year, but one month later, Pietro pleaded guilty and in October was sentenced to ten years in prison. Last time Oregon authorities checked, he was somewhere in Italy.

Alfano's Pizzeria & Italian Restaurant, however, remains open at the same location and is a popular place that garners top ratings in online reviews. I told myself I'd have to get a slice there.

• • •

I LOOKED UP from my history lesson. Dusk had settled over Oregon, and I had to get back to Chicago. No time for a slice at Alfano's. I'd burned through too much time and would need to return to Oregon to finish reporting, a prospect that made me giddy.

Driving out of town, I found myself wondering how all that history—the bloodshed and art, sinister deceit and natural beauty—fit into Oregon's psyche. Were they mere aberrations? Were they formative? Informative? Were the Regulators the logical response from any community in those years when people felt threatened enough to take desperate measures? Did someone, or many folks, see the deaths of Mary Jane and Stanley—and the mystery of who killed them—as "a public necessity"?

Mike once told me that "Ogle County has been getting away with shit since the days of the Regulators." Tough to say if he was right. To me, Oregon and the area around it seemed to be a beautiful place of escape, creative and otherwise, a place that made up its own rules spontaneously, a place that sometimes didn't play by the rules at all.

Maybe Oregon's distinction was that it could make up its own rules, keep its secrets, compose its own memories, and dispose of unsettling ones. But then, how different was that from everyplace else? Not different at all. You might say it's typically American, in fact. We're famous for re-inventing ourselves and our places.

A big part of my job is to uncover this stuff and absorb it. If I can weave it into a story, terrific. If I can't, mere awareness of it has value in the recognition and appreciation of the timeless importance of the day to day, the everyday quirkiness, the artistry, and yes, even the violence of ordinary people and places. In that context lies the beguiling beauty of Oregon, and everyplace else.

"I Don't Believe in
Chasing Demons"

• • •

I DROVE BACK TO Oregon a few days later, in the still-punishing summer swelter, this time with a little more purpose and a more specific schedule. After some pressed cajoling and Freedom of Information Act requests, Deputy Sheriff Greg Beitel and Ogle County state's attorney Deborah Ellis agreed to let me see the case file. I'd also set up interviews with a former sheriff's investigator and the current coroner.

When I arrived at the sheriff's office that Thursday morning, this time without Mike, an officer led me to a small, bare second-floor meeting room and handed over the file. Copies weren't allowed, he said. I pulled out my notebook and pen, pulled up a chair, and sat at a metal table.

Stuffed in a green accordion folder, the Mary Jane Reed murder investigation file was a mess, clearly picked over. Creased documents had been jammed inside haphazardly. An autopsy report was missing, but parts of other reports were there, lacking any information about when they were written and who wrote them. The paperwork was so ravaged that a clear-cut narrative on the case and ensuing investigation was impossible to figure out. It did contain a shocking photo of what looked to be Stanley—his head blackened—and an obstructed picture of a portion of Mary Jane's body in the weeds where she was found, under thick brush. Only her torso and part of an arm were visible. That was it for crime scene photos. Just two pictures, which seemed ludicrous, even for 1948.

At least one former investigator agreed. In an April 1955 report, Ogle County sheriff Charles B. Allen wrote that he was preparing a new file on the case and was asking for photographs from the nearby *Rockford Morning Star*. He'd found, he wrote, "a file which lacks quite a bit of data."

One report in the folder erroneously said Stanley was found at 6:30 a.m. on June 26, 1948—he was found on June 25—shot once in the chest, once in the right arm, and three or four times in the abdomen. Mary Jane's body had been found at 9:30 a.m. on June 29, another document reported. She'd been shot once in the head. The file mentioned an investigation started in 1986, when an officer received a report of a man who talked of killing two people in Oregon and tossing the gun in the Rock River. The man died in 1972.

And then came two very intriguing observations from separate reports, observations that started to make Mike look a little more legitimate and less like a goofball.

"Report to Sheriff Winnebago County, Rockford, Illinois," the page read. It was dated October 24, 1957.

"Vincent Varco showed no signs of giving me any cooperation in the investigation," the report stated. "Varco was Chief Deputy of Ogle County and the investigation rested solely upon him."

There he was again.

Another largely unedited report said, "The night before the murder Vince Varco slapped Mary Jane in front of her home because she wouldn't go to the Club House with him. On the Fourth of July, he was fishing at Kyte Creed"—I think the typist meant Kyte Creek—"seemingly not interested in the murder."

It started making more sense why material was missing from this file. Maybe it wasn't only from negligence.

I replaced the papers, returned the file to a deputy sheriff, thanked him, and called Ogle County coroner Darrell Cash, who was a deputy sheriff for twenty years before starting in the coroner's office in 1974. Like many people, he was suspicious of Mike's intentions to exhume Mary Jane's body, convinced it would solve nothing. And, he opposed spending money on a fifty-five-year-old crime when resources were scarce and plenty of other crimes needed attention.

"Everybody wants to solve a homicide," Darrell said. "What's the purpose of solving this one? Are we going to be able to prosecute it, and if so, can we get a conviction?"

Most of the people involved in the case have died, he pointed out, probably even the perpetrator, whoever it was. He conceded that Vince might have been Mary Jane's lover, but Darrell wouldn't go any further.

As for theories on the case, he mentioned that Stanley was a gambler. Somebody might have killed him over a debt, he argued, which sounded plausible, but so did an enraged, brutal cop bent on teaching his ex-girlfriend a lesson.

"There are so many avenues that one could travel down and not get anywhere near the truth on this thing," he said. "After fifty years, you disinter this body, is it going to bring closure if you come up with no more answers than you have now? What're your chances of coming up with evidence? Do we want to expend resources that are needed for the prosecution of existing cases, or do we want to spend money on chasing ghosts? I don't believe in chasing demons."

All valid points, but none dismissed the possibility that Mike so adamantly pushed: Vince murdered Mary Jane and the powers that be have a vested interest in keeping her buried, keeping the murders unsolved. If Vince had murdered Mary Jane and Stanley, it's clear that a cover-up of some size had occurred, and it's more than a little likely that a generation or two of law enforcement officers and prosecutors had at least known of the cover-up—maybe a few county commissioners, too. Any of those scenarios left the county vulnerable.

Beyond that, exposing official wrongdoing has a decidedly tangible benefit, no matter how far in the past the violations occurred. It sends a shock wave through present-day officials and puts future leaders on alert. If they fail the public trust, they too could be stung and end up kicked out of office, then land in a place with painted cinder block walls and bars on the windows.

Next I called former sheriff Jerry Brooks, who was surprisingly receptive. Like so many, Jerry clearly was intrigued by the case. It made sense after I remembered that he'd compiled his own personal file on it. He gave me directions to his trim home on the outskirts of town. When I arrived, he welcomed me to sit and visit. He offered me a cold drink. He was chipper, chatty, and a little coy.

Jerry occupied an intriguing place in the story. He told me that at sixteen, he was living on the outskirts of Oregon and was heading into town one summer morning to get some welding done. At the welder's shop, someone mentioned that police had found a body. Jerry, who had an interest in police work, drove by the sheriff's office, where Stanley's car had been moved, and was recruited to push it to a garage. Although a few years younger, Jerry also happened to be Vince's close friend.

Years after the murders, Vince asked Jerry, who'd started working as a part-time deputy sheriff in 1963, to investigate the case.

"He said it'd be a big favor because a lot of people felt he did it," Jerry told me.

So, investigate he did, compiling a four-inch-wide accordion folder worth of material. His theory was that two brothers from Monroe Center, Wisconsin, killed Stanley. Mary Jane happened to be collateral damage. He based that theory primarily on inquest testimony from a tavern patron who overheard two men threaten to use their car to ram Stanley's car.

"I believe they were after him and she just happened to be with him," Jerry said. He also believed that one of the men was still alive. But he wasn't sharing names. He chuckled at Mike's theory.

"He's out in left field," Jerry said. "Oh my."

Vince wasn't the kind of man to murder someone, Jerry said, although he added that others had conceded that Vince was a womanizer who admitted to slapping Mary Jane on at least one occasion, maybe more.

Jerry's theory on Mike's interest in the case was based on the get-rich scenario that I'd heard before. When I asked him what he thought about the presence of spirits swirling around the Roadhouse, Jerry was silent, then leaned toward me. His eyes took on this startled, angry look.

"I don't believe in spirits and ghosts," he said. "I believe in the Lord Jesus Christ."

He didn't believe in letting me take a look at his file, either, claiming privacy and sensitivity to the families involved and to the people he spoke with who ended up having nothing to do with the crime. It was another example of behavior that lent credibility to what Mike was theorizing—not that I'm suspicious, skeptical, or cynical about people's motivations.

We shook hands. He offered to talk again, whenever I'd like. I thanked him and, more confused than ever about this crime, drove back to downtown Oregon.

With time to kill, I ventured to Panheads, a bar in an old building just off the courthouse square and a few steps from the shuttered movie theater. This mini-foray was aimed at what we in the business call Local Color, a sort of person-on-the-street perspective that's desirable in stories like this but always a crapshoot. Random as it was, the encounter I was about to have made me think.

A deep, narrow room with a front window that reached nearly from its pressed tin ceiling to the floor, Panheads was empty except for the bartender and Marv and Kathy, a middle-aged couple seated on stools. In the movies, this is where the hard-boiled reporter orders a scotch or bourbon. I asked for a Diet Coke with a water chaser.

Marv and Kathy lived in the South but were from the Oregon area originally and visited every three or four months. In chatting about Mike's effort to solve the crime, the conversation turned to Mike's push to exhume Mary Jane's body.

"I think it's ridiculous," said Kathy, who added that she had worked at the Roadhouse before it was the Roadhouse. She couldn't recall it ever being haunted. "Come on," she said. "How can something be buried with her? What are they going to find?"

She did, however, remember talk around town that Vince was the murderer. At one point, Mary Jane's sister told Kathy personally, she said.

"That's what I've heard ever since I was a young person," Kathy told me.

Marv said he'd heard pretty much the same thing.

"I heard that the law knew about it and was involved," Marv said. He called Mike "a level-headed guy."

Of the exhumation, Marv said, "I say if something can be accomplished with it, go for it."

Sherrie, the bartender, refreshed Marv's and Kathy's glasses.

"Mike's got to do this," Sherrie said. "He's got to resolve it. Everybody knows who did it, but nobody talks about it."

I had to leave for my next appointment. When I walked into the afternoon sun, heat radiated from the sidewalk. I got back in the Kia and drove to the home of Bill Spencer, seventy-eight, Ogle County sheriff from 1962–66 and chief deputy sheriff until 1970. He, too, had investigated the case and, like Jerry Brooks, was willing to chat.

Seated in a lounger in his small white house outside Oregon, Bill said he had interviewed about thirty people during his sporadic two-year investigation in the 1960s.

"They were just in over their heads," he said of investigators at the time of the killings. "Back in those days, local police didn't have any training at all."

He recalled that somebody pulled a fingerprint from the window of Stanley's car. Unable to identify its origin, investigators sent it to a state police lab in Springfield, where it languished for years and never was identified.

The conversation continued on that theme for a few minutes. I asked him what he'd concluded about various elements of the case. Bill said he couldn't draw conclusions on anything. "A lot of talk, that's all," he told me.

I asked what he thought of exhuming Mary Jane's body. He didn't think it would yield anything. He didn't see how anybody could make a case. We weren't making much progress in our talk. Then he said something that ignited a little spark in my brain.

"It was probably somebody that was jealous."

I paused, hoping the silence would lead him to elaborate. He didn't.

"Do you think Vince could have murdered them?" I finally asked.

He shrugged.

"I don't know if he did it or not," Bill said. He repeated how difficult it was to get solid leads. Then he said something else that caught my attention.

"Some people wouldn't talk at all. They were afraid that they would become a victim, especially the women. They never did ever talk."

Just like that, our conversation was over. Bill didn't want to say more; he said he didn't know anything else to share. I doubted that but kept my mouth shut, and again tried to let awkward silence push him to say something more. Apparently the silence wasn't awkward enough. Bill sat there, not speaking. Then he got up and ushered me to the door. I handed him a card and told him if anything more about the case popped into his head that he'd like to share, please give me a call. He looked at the card, said okay, and closed the door.

Time was running short—and I kept thinking I'd already made one more trip to Oregon than my editors wanted—but I could squeeze in another interview before I hit the road. I searched through a local law directory and found attorney William P. Fearer II, seventy-one, who'd been practicing in Oregon since 1965. I figured he might have heard something over the years and be willing to share.

When I phoned, he acknowledged knowing Mary Jane but he wasn't particularly talkative and wasn't interested in meeting face to face. William sounded a little agitated when I pressed him about the case. A pattern was becoming more apparent. Many people simply wanted the case to stay gone.

Asked what he thought about the Mary Jane shrine Mike had created on the balcony of the Roadhouse, William said that it was "a little eccentric to say the least. I don't know why he would do that, other than it's a marketing thing. Or maybe he's just a screwball. Maybe he's a sleuth. Hell, I don't know."

And then William P. Fearer II hung up.

Distraction, Obsession

• • •

I WROTE THE STORY, but it stayed in the can for weeks until it ran in the features section. A modest but passionate number of readers responded. Most simply found the story interesting. Some took potshots at Mike. Others supported him.

I'd moved on, at least physically, bouncing like a pinball. I covered a vicious tornado that killed eight people in Utica, Illinois, and the placement of the Franklin's ground squirrel on the state's threatened species list. I wrote about a pit bull that snarled rush-hour traffic by scampering along the Eisenhower Expressway, and the dismantling of a nuclear reactor. I reported on a suburb allowing "the hot dog lady" to keep her cart in the downtown area, and I was dropped into the editorial board to write editorials. I covered the grim news of an eighteen-year-old killing his father, mother, and uncle, and I was drawn into coverage of a Catholic priest's child sexual abuse. I even took a field trip to Ellisville, Illinois, to file a story on a great-grandmother who rebuilt the state's tiniest library, which measured about 300 square feet.

But the mysterious Mary Jane Reed-Stanley Skridla murders and Mike's quest lurked in my consciousness, waiting for an opportunity to flow forward.

I realized about this time how little I knew of Stanley. Mary Jane was center stage, largely because she haunted Mike. Stanley was mostly a mystery.

I looked around for relatives and found that he had one surviving sibling—a sister who was incapacitated and living in an assisted care facility—and two nephews. One nephew wanted nothing to do with publicity surrounding Stanley's demise. The other, who'd been in contact with Mike off and on over the years, wanted me to pay him to talk, an offer I declined in a rather animated phone conversation. In the end, their reticence may have had little consequence. Uncle Stanley had died before either nephew was born.

I started digging for documents in my off hours, and with the help of blessed reference librarians found the outline of Stanley's life. He was born May 8, 1920, one of five kids, in Rockford, where he was raised. He attended Saints Peter and Paul School, then high school in Rockford. An ancestry database revealed a Rockford City Directory that lists Stanley as a cabinetmaker from 1938, probably the year he graduated, until 1942. That year, according to his military records, Stanley worked as a machinist at Mattison Machine Shop in Rockford.

He enlisted in the Navy in October 1943 and was placed aboard the USS *Ormsby*, a troop transport in the Pacific, where he served as a machinist's mate third class then second class. The Navy discharged him honorably in December 1945, and he'd worked as a lineman for Illinois Bell Telephone starting in February of the next year. The *Rockford Register-Republic* reported in its evening edition on June 25, 1948, that Stanley recently had worked on lines around Oregon. The paper also reported that Stanley was living with his widowed mother, Amelia, on Loomis Street in Rockford, a neighborhood known for being active, ethnically mixed, but primarily Italian and Catholic. Around 8 p.m. on June 24, Stanley had hopped in his relatively new Buick, left Loomis Street and his widowed mother, and headed for his first, final date with Mary Jane.

That was about all I could find on Stanley, which didn't stop me from continuing to wonder about him, Mary Jane, Mike, and the entire case.

I knew, like I said earlier, that the reason this case stayed with me started with the lure of an unsolved double murder, which might draw anyone. But humans have provided plenty of murder mysteries. I was a little surprised to learn that crime analysts estimate that about one-third of homicides, or nearly 185,000 of them between 1989 and 2008, remain unsolved.

What kept this particular case on a constant loop through my mind was a combination of things.

Apart from the obvious sympathy generated by the murders of two innocent people, the facts specific to the Reed-Skridla killings had the shocking, sad components that would create widespread interest: the ambush of a young, attractive couple probably in a passionate, perhaps carnal, embrace late on a summer night on lovers' lane; Mary Jane's four-day disappearance; the frenzied investigation and prominent coverage from my own newspaper and others from coast to coast; whispers of a cover-up.

Mike's personal backstory and his obsession with the case were also intriguing. During the seventeen years he worked on it, his devotion to Warren Reed deepened, which, yes, was a little peculiar to me, but noble, too. It gave Warren his only hope that his sister's murder would be resolved.

I couldn't help admiring his sensitivity when he would talk about the injustice of failing to solve the murder of a local girl from the wrong side of the river. And when he would talk about cracking the conspiracy, I found that courageous. It was David versus Goliath.

Also, I was convinced something more motivated him: this business about ghosts and his relationship with Mary Jane, such as it was.

He wouldn't come right out and say he was in love with Mary Jane or her ghost, and he understood that sharing anything about the relationship made him look crazy, which he wasn't. But he did let it slip once that he'd arranged to be buried next to her—a move that Warren's children later overturned—and he'd gotten comfortable with her presence in his life.

Watching him struggle to reconcile all that he was feeling with the conventions of normalcy was compelling and a little sad, like watching someone with a burning secret that if shared, would lead to his ruin. He was like some tragic character in a Shakespeare play. As uncomfortable as it may be to admit, I was drawn to that, too. I wanted to keep track of how he was—or wasn't—managing his demons.

The setting had something to do with my interest as well. Oregon felt like this beautiful, largely undiscovered place with its own captivating history. Over the years, on dozens of trips, I'd approach from Route 64 and the town would reveal itself, oasis-like, from the green-and-brown blandness. I always looked forward to crossing the bridge over the Rock River and entering the heart of Oregon. On each visit, I seemed to stumble upon an intriguing nook or cranny—physical, historical, or ephemeral—all presided over by the haunting, contemplative statue of *The Eternal Indian* high on the river bluffs. Oregon, essentially, kept drawing me to it.

And I couldn't help wondering about the resistance I encountered when I wrote the first story and other follow-up pieces about the case. While reporting for almost every article, I'd meet with agitation from someone in Oregon who thought nothing beneficial would come from dredging up the case.

I was always deferential. What real hope is there that the case will be solved? they would ask. Even if it is solved, many would point out to me— as Darrell Cash had—that the killer or killers are probably dead. The greater likelihood is that keeping this case alive merely brings up cheap, voyeuristic gossip, hurt feelings, and confusion, they would say. It smears Oregon.

I understand. Then again, maybe that's the price Oregon had to pay, the unfair consequence it had to endure for bearing witness to the crime and failing to solve it. And, really, how much actual damage is done by this pursuit of Mike's, except to him? Warren supported Mike. At least one of Stanley's two lucid surviving relatives supported Mike's effort, too.

Who else would endure real pain? Would a judgment from a civil suit ding Ogle County? Maybe, but the county's insured. Could criminal convictions result? A highly remote possibility, but if it shook down that way, maybe those convicted had it coming.

Beyond all that, how badly is Oregon's reputation besmirched really? Given that murders happen and go unsolved everywhere, not much would be my answer.

What if Mary Jane and Stanley were your sister or brother, aunt or uncle, or close friend? And what if, somewhere out there, the truth exists and that truth reveals authorities covered up murders committed by one of their own? How safe was anyone in town then?

Besides, isn't there value in pursuing that truth, no matter what? Why should we fear or resist that pursuit? It was that resistance that generated in me, as it would in many reporters, a fairly persistent desire to dismantle it, to find out what was behind it.

But, as I mentioned, I had my distractions, many distractions in the form of other stories that needed telling, urgently and often, as is the case in the news business, and which left no time for all those bigger questions in the Mary Jane Reed-Stanley Skridla case, or questions about Mike, or about Oregon.

Every few months or years, when Mike's quest reached a turning point and I could persuade my editors, I'd parachute in to Oregon—like I did for all my stories in other places—then move on. Many times, even when those other stories were engaging or consuming, I'd find my mind linking some element of them back—tenuously or directly—to Oregon, Mary Jane, Mike, and the entire case.

What was happening wasn't obsession, I kept telling myself. Absolutely not. I'm not the obsessive type, I said, sometimes aloud, even when I was alone, just for emphasis. These were mere similarities that any logical mind would connect. It was synchronicity. Completely rational.

I came to accept that the case was with me all the time, at predictable moments—while mowing the lawn, drifting mentally in church or work-related meetings, taking a shower, driving—and at less predictable times —while having an engaging conversation at a party, listening to a song, watching a movie, sleeping.

Like when I'd heard about the rebirth of Heinous Abe, the little-known world's tallest, creepiest fiberglass statue of our martyred sixteenth president standing in a remote patch of the state. What I thought about was this: Abraham Lincoln and Jefferson Davis, two men who later would stand on opposite sides in one of America's most defining, bloodiest crucibles, fought together in the Black Hawk War near Oregon in 1832. Lincoln was a captain in the Illinois militia, which nearby Dixon, Illinois, has memorialized with a statue downtown along the Rock River depicting Lincoln in military dress. Davis, who has no statue in Dixon but plenty throughout the South, was a U.S. Army lieutenant serving under General Winfield Scott.

Whites started the brief war when Black Hawk, an exhausted sixty-five-year-old Sauk warrior, led several hundred of his people and those from other tribes into northern Illinois to return to land they'd lost in a disputed treaty of 1804. Settlers panicked, the military was called in, and a slaughter ensued. It ended fifteen weeks later. About seventy settlers and soldiers were killed; nearly 600 Native Americans lost their lives. Black

Hawk was captured and eventually placed in an Indian agency in Iowa, where he lived his remaining years under the watch of a chief who'd once been his enemy.

One hundred and seventy-two years later, I found myself 230 miles southeast of that conflict, in Ashmore, Illinois, pursuing the story of a most peculiar statue. It was worth the side trip.

Heinous Abe and a Break in the Case

• • •

NO ONE KNOWS for sure how many historical markers referring to Lincoln exist in the Land of Lincoln, but it's safe to say that number is well more than a hundred, which works out to more than one per county. And, the number is growing. Every town, urban, suburban, or otherwise, seems to have at least one school named for him, including Lincoln, Illinois, home of the Lincoln College Lynx. The state's most compelling honor to the sixteenth president may be his presidential library and museum in Springfield, which opened in 2005. A decade later, nearly four million people had visited, making it the most popular of all presidential libraries.

Few if any of those landmarks and honors are as oddly unsettling as Heinous Abe. Compared to the statue at the Lincoln Memorial, which stands nineteen feet tall and is carved from twenty-eight blocks of white Georgia marble, Heinous Abe was "a presidential Godzilla," as writer Jerome Pohlen put it. Six stories and ten tons of fiberglass and steel, Heinous Abe was brought in the late 1960s to Coles County near Charleston, about 200 miles south of Chicago.

It's a land rich in Lincoln history. Coles County hosted one of the famous debates between Lincoln and his political opponent, Stephen Douglas. Lincoln's father and stepmother resided in the county for much of their lives and are buried there. And, in an odd twist of history, the Coles County Courthouse was the site of a trial in which Lincoln, a young lawyer roving the prairie towns of Illinois, represented a slave owner in a case about the return of the man's runaway slaves. Lincoln lost. The slaves were freed.

On the centennial of Lincoln's assassination, a telling sign, Charleston businessman Andy McArthur hatched an idea for a Lincoln statue in the area, an inspiration sparked by large statues of Native Americans, Vikings, and other folk heroes Andy had seen on vacation road trips. Starting in 1965, he tapped local businesses and residents and raised about $22,000. The statue was to be part of a state park and resort that would surround a planned Lincoln Reservoir about eight miles south of Charleston.

A group coordinating the project contracted with a Saint Paul maker of fiberglass statues and parade floats. In May 1969, trucks delivered the statue in three pieces, prompting Coles County to celebrate with the Lincoln Heritage Trail Festival. Vice President Spiro Agnew wired congratulations.

But concerns arose as quickly as the statue did.

"Chicago has Picasso, and not everybody likes it," a local columnist wrote of the artist's iconic sculpture in the big city's downtown. "Not everybody likes our Lincoln but he was not placed in a spot that would offend the artistic. To see him requires a drive into the country. And, he has brought us a degree of fame."

The issues with Abe were numerous. His head and ears were oversized and his face was locked in a scowl. The index finger on his raised right hand was extended upward, giving the statue its full height of seventy-two feet and making it appear, from a distance, as if Honest Abe was an Angry Abe flipping off the world. Many interpreted it as the president letting Jeff Davis know Abe's precise feelings about the whole secession thing.

"The problem was that once it was unveiled," Illinois's Lincoln curator Kim Bauer told me, "it became very evident very quickly that it was going to be the butt of jokes."

Farmers in the region had more serious concerns. They said the reservoir would exacerbate soil erosion, among other problems. Legislators and other policy makers listened, stalling the state park proposal. It finally died altogether when Governor Dan Walker declined to authorize funding. Abe languished, and in his abandonment drew predictable and dubious distinction.

"It became a place where guys would take their dates to go make out,"

Kim said, "and it also became the spot for some of our locals to go out there and take target practice."

That occasional target practice wasn't enough to discourage nesting animals, though. Once the deterioration led to cracks and other openings in Abe, critters found his largely hollow carcass to be welcoming and cozy.

From time to time, reports surfaced of plans to refurbish Heinous. Seventies comedian Pat Paulson purportedly was interested in acquiring Abe to help promote a show on the president traveling westward. A group from Lincoln, Illinois, considered buying it a few years later but took a look at the finger and decided against it. In 1978, local investors acquired the statue and moved it about four miles east of Charleston to Ashmore, where the group opened Springhaven campground a year later. But Springhaven closed in fairly short order.

I'd learned of Heinous Abe's existence all the way back in the late 1970s, when I was a student at nearby Eastern Illinois University. Sometimes inebriated, many times not, friends and I would drive late at night to its remote location, hop a fence, burrow through the brush, and enter a clearing where we'd stare in wonderment, sorrow, and fright at the presidential monument in the middle of nowhere.

By the time I'd started working at the *Tribune*, I'd largely forgotten about Heinous. But during one of my more anxious story scrambles a few weeks after my trip to Oregon, I noted that the president's birthday was approaching. For reasons I can't explain logically, the statue came to mind. I made a few phone calls and found that hope had sprung from Springhaven's ruins. A few days ahead of Abe's 195th birthday, I turned the Kia on to Interstate 57, drove 200 miles south, turned left, and a few miles later pulled into the parking lot of the local nonprofit restoring the statue.

The organization, Graywood Foundation, served adults with developmental disabilities and had acquired shuttered Springhaven. Graywood was planning to use the statue as a focal point for a recreational center that would attract tourism to the area, train the disabled in vocations, and create jobs. The nonprofit already provided housing for about eighty people in homes around Charleston. The idea for the campground was to offer jobs to some of those folks and others at a place with amenities—a swimming pool, water park, and miniature golf course—that would attract families. Foundation administrators estimated the new campground would employ about 140 people. A gussied-up Abe statue would preside over "Abe's Garden," which would feature waterfalls, reflective pools, and a playground in a landscaped setting.

I entered Graywood's offices and met with three of the organization's leaders. Much like Abe the man rose to legendary greatness from personal and political failure, the Graywood team was hoping the forlorn statue would spark a triumphant metamorphosis for their site.

Work was progressing, the Graywood management team told me. A water-distribution system and water treatment plant had been built. A crew was restoring a barn, converting it to a training center for the disabled who would be employed there or simply use the center for enrichment.

The Graywood folks conceded that their fiberglass Lincoln had a distinctive look but objected to my contention that the statue bordered on hideous.

"It's not grotesque," Chief Operations Manager David Kirsch told me. He seemed to view the statue as a realistic portrayal of the man. "It is not caricature. I don't feel it's obscene. Abraham Lincoln was not a handsome man. His features speak for themselves."

Their next step was to ramp up fundraising. Cost of the entire campground project was estimated at $300,000, $40,000 of which was earmarked for Abe. About $25,000 had been raised so far. Graywood executive director and former Olympic athlete Augustine Oruwari—a national collegiate champion in hurdles while competing at Eastern Illinois—told me he wanted to raise half the $300,000 in the next three to four months. He acknowledged the goal was ambitious.

"We're trying to motivate people to do more than say, 'This is a good idea,'" Oruwari said, "and that can be very difficult."

I wished them the best of luck and drove toward Ashmore, finding the faded, weathered, and vandalized giant in a clearing at the campground. What I thought would be amusement turned out to be largely sorrow. I stood near the base and looked up, pewter clouds passing behind and above the gigantic head, and saw a series of holes had perforated the right side of his nose. A chunk of his left cheek was gone, as if blasted away by gunfire, and green material grew on his face.

My gaze went to his feet, and I walked around the back. A hole the size of two basketballs in Abe's left boot heel appeared to be the entrance that had allowed critters to set up homes throughout the statue. Mercifully, the raised index finger had broken off a few years earlier.

It was a raw, gray afternoon, but I was glad I'd arrived in broad daylight. Nighttime with this Abe would have been a more unsettling encounter than even those I'd recalled from my college days. The wind whipped. The tip of my pen became too cold for ink to flow through it, leaving blank scratches where my red, numbing hand tried to write on notebook pages. I couldn't take my eyes off Abe and started thinking, hoping, that Graywood's plan would work. Sounds ludicrous—reporters are supposed to be hard-boiled cynics—but I thought it could be a wonderful way to rewrite the brief history of ridicule that had hounded Heinous Abe, a way to revise memories and create optimism for this sorry artifact of the 1960s, to take mockery and convert it to honor.

I clenched a fist around my pen tip and blew warm breath on it, which coaxed a few more lines of ink onto the page. I hustled back to the Kia, started it up, and blasted the heat, waiting a few moments for the warmth to penetrate, staring at Abe, wondering if he'd hang on until help arrived.

I headed toward the tree-lined streets and graceful old homes in downtown Charleston, which is blessed with a classic courthouse square that could be a Hollywood film set. Tucked back from one of those streets was the spacious house of Andy and Evelyn McArthur, who welcomed me and were excited to talk about Abe. They pulled out newspaper clippings from scrapbooks and gave me fuller details of the statue's origin. Andy, a spry seventy-two years old, said he was hoping Graywood's plan would be successful.

"It has to be a moneymaker," he said. "I'm happy to see somebody trying to do something with it. The idea behind it was good."

Evelyn had her doubts. Earlier in our visit, she'd told me the nicest thing she could say about it was that from a distance the statue was grotesque. But reviewing all those news clippings, photos, and other mementos, and remembering the community participation and excitement surrounding Abe's arrival thirty-five years earlier, must have softened her. I was pressed for time—a chronic condition in all my field trips—and had to leave. I stood and stepped toward their door. She stopped me.

"We had a great time doing it," Evelyn said. A wistful smile spread across her face. "It'd be great to see the statue refurbished. It's still so grotesque. But it does kind of grow on you."

I thanked them and headed north toward Chicago, trying to dismiss my doubts about Graywood's plan to convert memories of a misfit statue into a worthy venture. Three hundred thousand dollars seemed like so much money.

A few minutes down the interstate, something else surfaced through my daydreams, another statue: *The Eternal Indian* in Oregon, the evocative concrete figure I'd pass every time I arrived in town.

Its history was much richer and more respectable than Heinous Abe's. For starters, sculptor Taft's prolific, highly regarded output includes the elaborate *Columbus Fountain*—a marble masterpiece outside Union Station in Washington, D.C. He also designed the 100-foot-long *Fountain of Time* near the University of Chicago.

Completed in 1911 and placed in such a prominent spot along the verdant river bluffs, *The Eternal Indian* was heralded as much for its mechanics and engineering as it was for its beauty and magnitude. Among its more noteworthy characteristics were a head of solid concrete and a pinkish hue throughout, thanks to granite chips from New England that were mixed with the original concrete.

But, like other stories in Oregon, this one has a mystery or two. Foremost among those is who was the model for the piece. Taft is quoted as saying that he "did not study any one type of race of Indians," that the statue is a composite of physical characteristics from the Fox, Sac, Sioux, and Mohawk people. "In short it represents the Indian personality," he said, according to a 2010 piece in *Historic Illinois* journal.[1] Other sources contend that the model was novelist and Pulitzer Prize–winning biographer Hamlin Garland, an Eagle's Nest Art Colony member, friend, and brother-in-law of Taft, and an enthusiast of psychic phenomena. He also was an ardent supporter of Native Americans. And, more relevant, not Native American.

Beyond that mystery is its name. People have come to call it the *Black Hawk* statue, even though it looks nothing like the Native American leader, and Taft reportedly never gave it a formal name. People also refer to it and Black Hawk the man as the "Chief," though he never was one.

The sure thing is that *The Eternal Indian*, like Heinous Abe, was deteriorating. Struck by lightning in 1939, it was repaired then and in 1945. A third set of repairs occurred in 1973. In 1986, epoxy was applied to deal with spalling and cracks. And, in 2010, an earthquake, of all things, struck and inflicted more damage. A few years after the movement to rejuvenate the fiberglass Lincoln in Ashmore, a nearly $1 million restoration of *The Eternal Indian* began. Private grants and contributions and state money funded that venture.

So, beyond the Oregon area's link to young Captain Lincoln—and Lieutenant Jefferson Davis—the two places and the two stories had connective historical tissue in statue form. By the way, Graywood did end up opening the campground in Ashmore as Lincoln Springs Resort, featuring a lovingly restored Heinous. Renovation of *The Eternal Indian* stalled.

Still, for reasons that may be serendipitous or obsessive, I found their connection intriguing.

• • •

BACK IN MY CUBICLE, I finished the Heinous Abe story and checked my calendar. On it was a reminder of a court hearing in Oregon. Mike's effort to exhume Mary Jane had started officially in January of 2004, when he'd filed a request asking the court to authorize the body's disinterment. In the documents, Mike noted that conflicting reports of exactly how Mary Jane was killed—shot in the head or in the chest—made it unclear who was buried in her plot at Daysville Cemetery.

"Advances in DNA testing will conclusively determine whether the remains are those of Mary Jane Reed," his motion stated. The filing also claimed that "a post-mortem examination will yield clues which may solve or contribute to solving the crime." Mike was willing to pay for the entire procedure—exhumation, examination of the remains, and the reburial.

Most everyone considered his prospects bleak, to say the least, and he faced a reprise of the same personal attacks: people saying he was nuts or that he was trying to exploit the situation for financial gain. But Mike had the crucial support of Warren Reed on this endeavor.

I hustled out to the March court hearing, where the Honorable Stephen C. Pemberton reviewed the documents, listened to testimony, then said he wasn't opposed to the exhumation. Judge Pemberton simply wanted Mike to publish a notice in the newspaper so everyone who wanted to weigh in could. Mike agreed. His hopes rose, and in April, after a very brief hearing attended by a handful of reporters, Judge Pemberton signed the authorization papers.

"I get a feeling that there's a sense of relief that a shadow has been lifted," Mike's attorney Melanie Madsen said in a courthouse hall following Pemberton's decision, "that any regrets could be laid to rest, any possible doubts surrounding the mystery of Mary Jane's death might be resolved."

Mike was a little more direct.

"I'm happy," he said. "It's been a long haul."

The Opposite of Forgetting

• • •

A FEW MONTHS LATER, I arrived at Daysville Cemetery on the outskirts of Oregon at about eight o'clock in the morning on an uncharacteristically cool, clear Tuesday in August. Several parked cars lined the weedy incline of the shoulder. I found a place behind one and talked to our photographer, who said authorities were keeping everyone outside the cemetery, except for those directly involved in the exhumation.

They'd erected a ten-foot-high plastic screen the color of pale green doctors' scrubs around the site, and it billowed and tilted in the summer breeze. Shortly after 8 a.m., a small backhoe cut through the sod and scooped dirt above Mary Jane's burial vault. The tops of the backhoe and a couple of trucks were about the only visible signs of what was happening behind the screen. It seemed like a fair number of people inside were standing around watching. I couldn't find Mike. I pulled a lawn chair out of my trunk, set it up behind my car, and kept an eye on things, making occasional trips to the cemetery entrance to try to get someone from the Illinois State Police or Ogle County Sheriff's Office to say something substantive. I was failing.

By 9:15 a.m., a crew had removed the concrete burial vault from the ground, wrapped it in a blue plastic tarp, secured the tarp with duct tape, and loaded it on a truck. The driver delivered the entire container to a garage behind the sheriff's office, where it was opened to reveal the partially deteriorated casket resting in about one inch of brown liquid. After removing the top of the casket, state police investigators found a black rubber body bag, the zipper of which had become separated from the bag and revealed Mary Jane's remains.

Investigators found that Mary Jane had been clothed in panties. A dress and slip wrapped in a 1948 newspaper also had been placed in the casket. Soon after pulling the body from the casket, authorities loaded it into a van and took it about twenty miles southeast to the Rochelle Community Hospital, where it was X-rayed. Then they turned back to Oregon, to the Ogle County morgue, where a couple of forensic pathologists examined what I was told was her surprisingly well-preserved body. They removed four fingernails from each of her hands, pubic hair, two swatches of her underwear, her left femur, skull, and a few vertebrae. They swabbed her vaginal and rectal areas. All six or so hours of it—from the exhumation to the reburial—was photographed and videotaped.

After the exam, the Ogle County Sheriff's Office received a sample of the brown liquid, the June 25, 1948, *Dixon Evening Telegraph* found in the casket, and Mary Jane's dress and "undergarment," an Illinois State Police report stated. A forensic scientist got the fingernails, a sexual assault evidence collection kit, Mary Jane's panties, and her femur. The developed photographs would be sent to the Illinois State Police and Ogle County Sheriff's Office. Her skull and vertebrae also would be examined.

Somewhere in all of that, Mike hoped, was a breakthrough. He'd purchased a Bible and asked Warren, his son, and a daughter to write something in it. They'd asked for God's blessings for Mary Jane. Mike wrote in it, too.

"May you rest in peace," he said. "See you soon. Love, your friend, Mike Arians."

The Bible was placed in her casket, and before a crew set her vault back in the earth at the family's burial plot, two police chaplains said prayers. I caught up with Mike afterward and he said the whole thing was "kind of a blur," that it was going to take time to sort out. "But," he said, "I'm at a peaceful calm."

This latest foray, like every one Mike had tried and every one he'd undertake in the years ahead, yielded more derision.

"What we need here is for Mr. Arians to come up with something to prove some cover-up so he can get his movie made," the Ogle County sheriff told me. Mike replied by saying his response was unprintable. He noted that his investment in this journey had gone north of $40,000 while business at the Roadhouse continued its southward spiral.

Standing nearby throughout the day's events and watching them unfold was Warren, dressed in a red ball cap, dark gray embroidered Western-style shirt, jeans, and white tennis shoes. The investigators got the forensic evidence. Warren got a gold ring pathologists had removed from his sister's finger. It had been their mother's wedding band.

He told me afterward that he felt the exhumation, forensic exam, and reburial had been handled "the correct way." The examination had been extensive, but the pathologists and anthropologist "were very respectful."

Warren was rail thin, and looked much more worn out than his sixty-two years. But he exuded resilience, a subtle, deep commitment to carry on. I felt that resolve in his handshake. He was, to me, heroic and forlorn.

Sometime after the exhumation, I asked him to breakfast, in part to see if he could shed light on the case and in part because I was so curious about who he was, how the loss of a sister had influenced his personal history.

I'd been on my typical ricocheting path, writing about the closing of an eighty-year-old amusement park and a soccer team of homeless men. I investigated lead in toys and the stubborn, deadly problems of teen driving. Sprinkled through these adventures were the more far-flung travels the *Tribune*'s national desk assigned me. I was dispatched to North Dakota to write about flooding, Minnesota to cover a high school shooting on an Indian reservation, and New Orleans to cover Hurricane Katrina's aftermath.

A troubling subtext had begun. The economy had started to groan under the weight of an insanely leveraged housing market. We at the World's Greatest Newspaper and newspapers everywhere were beset by deep, structural changes in the way people absorbed information. It seemed like we were perched at the top of a stairway. While the house creaked and shifted around us, we peered into the darkness of despair.

Mike's financial situation was grim, too. He talked about walking away from the mortgage on a home he owned near the Roadhouse and taking up residence in the restaurant, which he'd closed for a few months to try to regain his footing.

The cloudy December day Warren and I met, he was unshaven, his gray, wavy hair curling behind his ears and his blue eyes enlarged by thick eyeglasses. Atop his head was a different ball cap, this one red and black with #1 Papa on the front panel. He was living with and caring for his ailing wife Vickie and her two grandchildren in a cramped apartment carved out of a tired, old Victorian house in Rock Falls, about thirty miles southwest of Oregon.

His recollections of his big sister were very different from those I'd heard. To him, Mary Jane wasn't the girl with a number of boyfriends, or a girl who may have been caught in a compromising position with one of those boyfriends.

He remembered only one man driving by the Reed house: Vince Varco.

"Back then, I didn't think nothing of it," Warren said. "But the more I thought of it, after . . . I think he was riding by so he could keep an eye on Mary Jane."

He told me of a big sister who took him to Saturday matinees at the Oregon Theatre to see Western serials starring Hopalong Cassidy, Tom Mix, Roy Rogers, and the Lone Ranger for fifteen cents a ticket. Eleven years older than Warren, Mary Jane would prepare picnic baskets that the two of them took to a scenic park by the dam on the Rock River. Sometimes sister and brother simply would take long walks together. She took him shopping and to Sunday services at the Church of God, where, beginning when she was about fifteen years old, Mary Jane taught Sunday school, Warren said. She'd even enrolled in Oregon Bible College and earned a certificate of completion.

"I was her baby," Warren recalled. "She loved me, watched over me because there were times when Ma didn't feel good. You know what I mean?"

Ruth Reed suffered with rheumatoid arthritis, a condition that became so debilitating that Mary Jane left Oregon High School her junior year to care for her mom and the home, Warren said.

"They were good times. I don't know how to explain that, but I mean, I knew she loved me. She told me all the time, 'I love you, Lee,' 'cause it's my middle name, Warren Lee. She just . . . called me Lee. I can remember falling asleep a lot of times, listening to the radio or something, and she'd carry me up, put me to bed."

He was six years old when his big sister disappeared, and during those few days before the two detectives in suits came to the door of the Reeds' house, Warren kept asking his mother if Mary Jane was coming home. Ruth's response was unwavering: she'll be coming home. She'll be coming home.

Warren was standing at his mom's hip when she greeted the detectives that day. They asked if she was Mrs. Reed, and then they said they had bad news. Authorities had found her daughter.

"Mother says, 'Well, when is she coming home? When are you going to bring her home?'" Warren recalled. He remembered his mother sliding her hand over his at that moment and squeezing, a memory that still choked him up decades later.

The detectives clarified that Mary Jane wouldn't be coming home. She was dead.

"And I'll never forget that feeling," Warren told me, stopping. His blue eyes grew more intense, wider. "I could feel vibes going through my mother's body. I don't know how to explain it, but I could just feel the draining, like she was going to pass out."

He remembered the detectives grabbing Ruth to prevent her from falling.

"That's when everything started," Warren said. From that day forward, his mother slowed down considerably and was scared that whoever had killed Mary Jane was going to do the same to little Warren or the entire family.

One of the first things she did was pull the curtains closed on all the windows in the house. Then she moved the family's worn maroon couch a few feet from the wall, tossed a blanket and pillow in the space, and forced Warren to use it as his play and nap area. If he needed a toy, she brought it to him.

"I wouldn't stay behind constantly," Warren said. "I'd come out, monkey around in the living room, as long as she was keeping an eye on me. But at night, prior to it getting dark, that's where I went, and right now, I can't stand it in a closed area."

She stopped sending him to first grade. Even when the school principal came to the house, Ruth was adamant: Warren wasn't going to school that year. When he finally did return, months later, he'd fallen so far behind that he had to repeat first grade.

About a year after Mary Jane's death, Ruth Reed had a mental break-down, Warren recalled. She continued to believe her daughter was going to return home. Warren's father decided to place Ruth in a state mental institution in East Moline, about eighty miles west, on the Mississippi River.

Warren, the only child at home, moved to another sister's house while his father seemed to bury his grief in work at the local silica plant. Ruth returned more than a year later but wasn't the same. Warren said she'd been given shock therapy, and even though the family never discussed Mary Jane's killing to avoid stirring up Ruth's emotions, she kept lapsing into the belief that her missing daughter soon would walk through the door. Warren, dealing with his own wrenching grief, kept correcting his mother, and she kept insisting.

The family limped along. Warren continued in school, but as a kid from the impoverished east side of the river, he was stigmatized, targeted, a magnet for fights. He dropped out of high school his junior year and got a job in a printing company about ten miles away. A few years later, an ambulance came for Ruth.

"I can remember them taking her out of the house," Warren told me. "She came out on a gurney. I can remember walking over to it, reaching out, and she grabbed my wrist. She said . . ." His voice cracked. "I can remember her looking me right in the eye. First, she called me honey. She said, 'Warren, I will not be coming back, but there's one thing I want you to do for me. Would you do me a favor, please? Will you please find out who killed Mary Jane for me?'"

"I said, 'I'll try,' and they took her out."

Ruth Reed died the next day. She was sixty-four years old. Mary Jane's murder, Warren said, took fifteen years off his mother's life.

Warren was twenty-three then. Clifford Reed died a few years later, at eighty-four.

Over the decades, Warren found work as a welder in Oregon, then at a factory that made automobile coils, and that's where he stayed until retirement in about 2000.

As stable as his work life was, Warren's personal life was rough and ragged for years. He'd been married four times and had five children. Two of those wives had drinking problems, he said. Two of them cheated on him. He'd taken another man's wife. There had been fistfights with brothers-in-law and confrontations in bars.

But, by the time he'd reached fifty, he seemed to have put all that turmoil behind him. At the automobile coil factory where he worked as assistant foreman, he started chatting with a kind woman who also worked there. Vickie and he became friends. Warren asked her to dinner. Two years later, in 1997, they married, Warren said.

Now, sitting in a booth of cracked green vinyl at a diner a stone's throw from the interstate, he was a seventy-year-old man, the lone survivor of Clifford and Ruth Reed's six children. Warren was happily married, settled but exhausted.

Vickie's health was in serious decline. A diabetic, she had suffered at least one severe stroke, was virtually blind, and could barely get around using a walker. Soon she'd be in a wheelchair.

Warren was a tender, dutiful caretaker, getting her in the shower, administering something like thirteen medications a day, and giving her shots. He checked her blood pressure, took her to dialysis three times a week, cooked for her, cleaned the house, chauffeured her two grandchildren to school and activities, and did the grocery shopping. Most mornings, he said, he'd wake at four o'clock, have a cup of coffee, smoke his pipe, fire up the computer, and shoot pool online. Then he'd check newspaper websites, listen to the radio for a while, and begin waking up everyone to start their days. He took the kids to school about 7:30 and continued on various errands and tasks until about 5 p.m., when he'd pick up sandwiches at the local Subway. Once in a while he and Vickie went out to dinner. Other times, he said, she'd get a craving for Chinese food and he'd run to a local buffet for her.

When I asked him how he was able to handle everything he was doing for Vickie and the kids, he said he didn't know how to answer the question.

"I gotta do it," Warren said, annoyed. "It's a revolving door that I keep going in and out. I just automatically do it."

"That's a helluva lot you're doing for her," I told him. "A wonderful thing."

Warren looked at me and didn't say a word.

• • •

SOMETHING ELSE might have strengthened the bond between Warren and Vickie, something in their history that they shared. Depending on one's perspective, that shared something could feel like evil shadowing Warren or a weird sort of grace, a serendipity that placed him in Vickie's life.

About ten years after they were married, Vickie's daughter was murdered.

Heather Muntean had been in trouble for a while, and drugs seemed to be at the core of it. Warren told me that when he'd met Heather the first time, she was heavyset. The last time he saw her, she was emaciated. Years before her death, Heather had relinquished control of her two children to Vickie and Warren. She'd been living in central Illinois for some time, running with a degenerate crowd, possibly scratching out an existence as a prostitute.

Heather would visit Rock Falls occasionally, and Warren and Vickie would try to persuade her to stay and get cleaned up. She refused every time. On one visit, she'd gone to sleep and left a small square of tinfoil on the bathroom floor. Warren suspected drugs had been wrapped inside.

After the murder, investigators had told Warren that the man who'd killed Heather had been fighting with her over money. "Whether it was or not," Warren said, "we don't know. He ended up throwing her off some part of a bridge."

News clippings on the case reported that authorities concluded Heather and her boyfriend, Curtis Lee Collins, were on a pedestrian bridge in Urbana, Illinois, late on May 15 or early May 16, 2007, arguing over whether to spend $80 on liquor or drugs. Collins shoved her and she fell, striking an I-beam running along the bridge before landing, probably unconscious, in Boneyard Creek, where she drowned. Heather was thirty years old, the papers said.

Fifteen months later, Collins pleaded guilty and was sentenced to twenty years in prison.

"We didn't even get a chance to go to the trial," Warren told me. "We wanted to go there, look him in the eye, but all it was, we got a call, said it was over with."

He fell silent again, and after a while I asked about the grandchildren, neither of whom are Collins's offspring. Both were doing well. I asked about what Warren did with any free time. Except for early mornings, he said, he didn't really have free time. He'd given up fishing, which he said he loved, to take care of Vickie.

"In fact," he said, "I got a $175 rod and reel set that I don't even use."

The waitress came over and asked if we wanted coffee and dessert. We declined. She scribbled the total on the bill, set it on the table, and thanked us.

I asked Warren if he ever dreamed of Mary Jane and he said no, that he had dreams of his mother, "just weird dreams," he said—her sitting in a chair talking to him, her walking in the kitchen or in another room—dreams he couldn't interpret.

"When she's talking," I asked, "does she ever talk about Mary Jane?"

He couldn't remember.

Some nights, Warren said, he'd step in his bedroom, lie down, close his eyes, and try to visualize his parents and siblings because, he said, he wants to remember everyone. He's able to see his parents, brothers, and two sisters, but not Mary Jane.

"I can't bring her in," Warren said, " . . . and I don't know why."

Warren told me he was convinced Vince killed her based on conversations he'd overheard all over town and "based on feelings, vibes, the way he was riding by when we were out in the yard all the time. He'd stop. Why would he want to stop? I can remember the old squad car, you know, the black and white . . . (him) with his suit on. I can remember Mary Jane looking over there, but she never said nothing. It'd happen more and more."

We talked about his thoughts on the investigation, about Mike, whom he liked and credited for keeping him going on his quest to honor his mother's dying wish.

"Why do you think he's doing it, truthfully?" I asked Warren. "Do you think he's hoping for a settlement? Do you think he's hoping to cash in on some of this stuff?"

Warren paused.

"Between you and me?" he asked.

"Well," I said, "I just want you to tell me the truth."

He was silent for a couple seconds.

"Yeah, I think he's looking for a settlement, too. I told him I'm going to offer him something, okay? It depends on what we get."

I was surprised by Warren's take. The prospects of a judgment against the county always had struck me as extremely remote. For Mike to have poured as much money, effort, and heart into this endeavor as he had on

the chance that he might get a piece of a large cash judgment seemed ludicrous. Yes, Mike had tried to collaborate on a book and a screenplay, but
both those projects never got off the ground.

For his part, Warren wasn't too concerned about a cash judgment
against the county, at least that's what he told me. He simply wanted the
court matters to be cleared up and hoped that once that had occurred, he
could talk with somebody in law enforcement or in the coroner's office or
with the state's attorney without Mike, someone who knew the full story,
would share it with him and admit that Varco had killed Mary Jane. He
thought Jerry Brooks might be that person, or Mel Messer.

"That's what I'm hoping," Warren said. "Whether it's going to happen or
not, I don't know, but I don't think it will. I don't think they'll really want
to come out and admit that they've been wrong all this time."

He asked whether he'd helped me at all, and I told him I couldn't thank
him enough, that it was so interesting to be able to talk with him for two
hours. He was a central character in this ordeal.

We talked a little more about the childhood hassles he and his friends
had endured from kids on the west side of the river. I told him I should let
him go, that he had a lot of other things to do. He wanted to talk more. I
asked if there was anything he thought he should add that I hadn't asked
about.

"I can't think of anything right now," Warren told me, "but I got so
much in my mind all the time that sometimes my mind overflows and I'm
an empty basket for a while."

• • •

PROGNOSTICATING ON HOW the pain from a murdered sister and
daughter plays out in a family over more than a half century is a tricky
endeavor that can easily veer into cheap psychoanalysis. But there it had
been, sitting across the table from me for a couple hours.

Warren's life seemed to have been set on a tumultuous course early. That
course may have had much to do with being born in a part of town that
many viewed as shabby and depraved. Certainly, dropping out of high
school played a part. But how can you assess the damage done to a little
boy who lost a loving big sister, someone who likely would have watched

over and guided him? That, coupled with a wrecked mother and Warren's inability to get answers for her and for himself, seemed to be obvious factors, particularly in his stormy personal life—perhaps in his relationships with women.

It was an unassuming life, easy to dismiss for people with college degrees, two-car garages, and spring vacations at Disney World or Cabo. But Warren was hanging in there, demonstrating his love and commitment to his wife in the daily, messy, thankless grind of caring for her, stabilizing a pair of kids from infancy who weren't his and probably would have been lost without him—and not complaining.

That's what some might call walking the walk. As rocky as it might have been for all those years, Warren's walk was authentic now. I admired his priorities.

The Earnest Grave-Finders
Exhume Reconciliation

• • •

ABOUT THIS TIME, millions of people and businesses across the country
—and across a fairly significant swath of the planet—were in the depths
of a historic financial hardship. Many were teetering on the brink of economic doom.

The very wealthy—some of whom were responsible for getting us into
this mess—were the exception, of course. They made sure their millions
were cozy, well fed, and getting fatter. The one-percenters, those at the very
top of the income scale, managed somehow to tough it out, helped a bit by
their income jumping by what a University of California economist said
was more than 30 percent from 2009 to 2012.

Meanwhile, sparked by the implosion of the inflated housing market,
the rest of us working stiffs were dropping into the worst economic reces-
sion since the Great Depression of the 1930s. Nearly nine million jobs were
shed while unemployment soared to more than 10 percent. Depending on
who was crunching the numbers, $11 trillion to $16 trillion of the nation's
household wealth was disappearing. On a larger scale, the gross domestic
product of the world's advanced economies would decline by what the
International Monetary Fund called an "unprecedented" 7.5 percent in the
final quarter of 2008 alone.

Mike's experience in that near-universal vortex manifested itself in several disheartening ways. He and June divorced after sixteen years of marriage, citing the usual "irreconcilable differences," although their unconventional relationship barely changed. She kept working at the Roadhouse and, for the most part, living with Mike. He continued referring to her as "a wonderful person."

The reason for the split, Mike told me, was to protect them financially —mostly to shield assets from a farm June owned in southern Illinois. The economy started tanking, and the couple foresaw creditors circling them like vultures. Mike and June took a preemptive approach.

Also, Mike stopped talking about walking away from the modest green house down the street from the restaurant and in fact did it. He remodeled a section of the Roadhouse's north dining room, converting it into an apartment, and moved, saving what he figured was about $1,200 a month. He'd been sleeping in the restaurant consistently for the past six months anyway and said he might as well make the setting a little more comfortable. He sealed the deal by taking in a stray smoky gray cat and having June join him. Besides, Mike didn't exactly need the space for customers. Business was so bad that he and June talked about selling the Roadhouse for the first time since we met.

He told me he was "so far over the dam" financially that he wasn't sure how he was going to pull out of the nosedive.

Mired in a protracted court fight with the county over costs and evidence related to Mary Jane's exhumation, Mike also grew increasingly weary of the case. Prospects were collapsing around him. Key people in his exploration of the murders—Vince's widow, the guy who found Mary Jane's body, another man who worked on her original autopsy, and an attorney for Ogle County—had died recently.

"People are dropping like flies," he told me. "Some lady who gave me information just died."

Still, he couldn't give it up, as much as he tried. His conscience and Mary Jane wouldn't let him, Mike said. I could relate.

"I think about the case every day," he told me in a phone call on a sunny spring day. "I'm a prisoner to it, really. And when you're a prisoner, what do you do all day? You think of every single angle on a case all day long."

The weird, unexplained noises and bumps continued at the Roadhouse, Mike said, and he'd simply gotten used to them.

At the World's Greatest Newspaper, it started to feel as if we were in a free fall. Buyouts and layoffs had started and continued every few months. The cluster of cubicles where I sat—once at capacity with seven reporters —had dwindled to just one: me.

Almost overnight, the World Wide Web seemed to snare all the classi-fied ads that had been the backbone of newspaper advertising, while it also managed to aggregate content from newspapers and give it away gratis. Digital versions of stories and photos were becoming easier and easier to access, and the digital platform's capacity to provide a video interpretation of a story made it that much more attractive.

Advertisers started wondering why on God's green earth they were spending so much money on newspaper advertising when fewer and fewer people were reading newspapers and the country was plunging deeper and deeper into the economic abyss. Newspapers were scrambling to find the answer to that question, and it wasn't going well.

Into the mess rode real estate multibillionaire Sam Zell, an iconoclastic lover of Ducati motorcycles who called himself the Grave Dancer. The nickname was an allusion to his penchant for taking over unappealing, moribund businesses and real estate and turning them profitable.

On December 20, 2007, Zell closed on an $8.7 billion deal to take over the Tribune Company, including its eight major newspapers and dozens of TV stations. Less than twelve months later, the company filed for Chapter 11 bankruptcy protection.

Between those dates, it felt like the *Tribune* was on the back of one of his motorcycles while he took us on a wild ride through a Halloween haunted house.

It was kind of exhilarating, even encouraging, for the first few weeks. I certainly could appreciate that the staid *Tribune* needed an electric cattle prod to the derriere at that point, and I think many of my brothers and sis-ters in the trenches felt the same way. Sam looked to be an ideal candidate for the job, a man who could change culture in a hurry.

Brash, salty, and irreverent, he embodied the antihero that resonates with many journalists. Sam was a Chicago guy, born here, and he had achieved staggering financial success—a fortune estimated at $4 billion.

After he took charge, Sam brought in a former radio executive, Randy Michaels, to be CEO, and Lee Abrams, who migrated from satellite radio, became chief innovation officer. Randy—whose birth name was Benjamin Homel—had a reputation for decisiveness and freethinking, what Sam called "real-time creativity."

The atmosphere changed quickly. Sam and his team placed pinball machines in the cafeteria and lounge areas and issued new employee badges featuring a photo of Frank Sinatra and the words "the best is yet to come." Within days, the corporate managers traded their suits for blue jeans, an amusing manifestation of chameleon survival instinct. In one lobby was a new statue, *Bureaucratic Shuffle*, depicting a squat six-legged man running in circles. In a nearby display case was an illustration of penguins standing on melting icebergs, meant to remind everyone, constantly, that the company and industry were undergoing dramatic change.

To keep the emphasis on urgency, Sam's crew rolled out a new acronym, AFDI, for "actually fucking doing it." No, I'm not kidding. In addition, Randy recommended a number of changes, including the end of front-page stories that jump inside, the creation of a feature called "Knuckleheads in the News," and a new section titled "Strange."

Those never took hold, but other initiatives did. A tabloid version of the paper, under consideration for years, was produced and became a temporary success. Ad reps were pushed to sell print and digital ads while working in a commission format. Every week, we'd get a companywide email from Lee that tried to rally us around thinking outside the box, questioning the status quo, being the new rock 'n' roll radio, or something like that. The leadership team was all over the map, which confused lots of smart people, which may have been what Sam and company wanted. We joked that white smoke floating from the top floors of the Tower might have come from something other than cigars.

But the excitement and urgency devolved. As chronicled in fascinating, exhaustive, and illuminating coverage by *Chicago Tribune* reporters Michael Oneal and Steve Mills, the new management team's style was viewed as too often stepping over the line, too coarse, too focused on change without much regard for the human beings tasked with carrying out the orders or without much understanding of the company's fundamental strengths.

"There was always a right way and a wrong way to do things," a former *Tribune* editor told reporters Oneal and Mills. "And they always chose the way where they could break the most windows."

Resentment percolated when Sam called editors and reporters at the Tribune Company's Washington, D.C., bureau "overhead" and got caught on tape saying "Fuck you" to an *Orlando Sentinel* photographer who pressed him on his views of journalism.

Randy was criticized internally, Michael and Steve reported, for placing friends and former colleagues in top positions despite their lack of relevant experience. The reporters also noted that he became "noticeably prickly about being questioned" during management meetings. In short order, the merry band of grave-dancing, rogue power entrepreneurs became less than enamored with their authority being challenged.

Their cause wasn't helped much by other unsettling conduct. Randy had a reputation for being a little too freethinking when it came to decorum, particularly among females. Michael and Steve reported on his penchant for crude jokes and sexual innuendo in business meetings. I witnessed it at an employee town hall gathering, where Randy approached a young woman dressed in tight-fitting clothes. Ogling her and grinning, Randy said something about instituting a new dress code. She squirmed and smiled, a look of uncertainty under her blush. I cringed.

There was more. Randy held a cigars and beer poker party in the hallowed and stately upper floors of Tribune Tower. Sam said it was acceptable for employees to watch porn at their work stations.

It doesn't take much to lose credibility among journalists, and when that happens, we can behave like jackals. The atmosphere can turn dangerous in a hurry, the relations toxic. I think in this case, a perception took hold that the new guys' original, fresh, invigorating energy shifted into disregard and animosity toward employees in response to well-grounded resistance. The tanking economy and structural change in the newspaper industry of course contributed.

It all began to feel like an inflating balloon. Frontline soldiers started mocking the leadership crew, viewing their brand of innovation as clueless bullshit in disguise, and ill will radiated throughout the staff. Every new initiative was greeted with a new AFDI chant: "Another fucking dumb idea."

The situation finally blew up in October, when the *New York Times* published a front-page story on Randy's role in creating an allegedly hostile work environment and what the paper termed "frat house" conduct at the

Tribune. A few days after that, Lee sent an employee email that linked to a purportedly humorous video containing profanity and nudity—a stunt that yielded a protest letter from staff and an embarrassing story we were honorable enough to run in the *Chicago Tribune.*

Soon, Lee was gone. Then Randy resigned, and a new executive council purged the company of several of his administrative hires, as well as his projects. Sam departed as chairman. Editor-in-Chief Gerould Kern led a redesign that added news pages and offered a more sophisticated layout.

"Over the last year," Sam said in prepared statement around the time of the bankruptcy filing, "we have made significant progress internally on transitioning Tribune into an entrepreneurial company that pursues innovation and stronger ways of serving our customers. Unfortunately, at the same time, factors beyond our control have created a perfect storm— a precipitous decline in revenue and a tough economy coupled with a credit crisis that makes it extremely difficult to support our debt."

I remember thinking we'd been knocked on our keisters and now would get back on our feet. Not so. The bad news kept hitting the company like exploding winter waves on the Lake Michigan shoreline.

A few weeks after the bankruptcy protection filing, wire services filed stories saying the Tribune Company was laying off 300 people at the *LA Times,* including seventy people in the news department, or 11 percent of that workforce. Rumors of course swept across newsrooms throughout the entire company. A few months later, the rumors proved true.

It happened to us on a spring morning, and through the miracle of the hyperkinetic gossip that crackles in news organizations, everyone seemed to know the exact day, even though management tried to keep a lid on information.

Getting ready for work, nauseous with anxiety, I kept checking the email inbox on my cell phone—making sure the ring tone was activated, waiting for some official notice of the bloodletting, and hoping I wouldn't get an electronic or telephonic pink slip. Nothing came across.

I even delayed my drive to the office, and when I pulled into a parking spot at work, I shut off the ignition and just sat in my car. Again, no word. I figured the threat of layoffs had passed for that day. The tiniest blip of relief lit inside me.

Turns out the information was solid. Layoffs must have started while I was making my fifteen-minute drive to work. By the time I entered the cubicle farm newsroom, the slashing was over, at least in our bureau. Three people from our office were let go—all hardworking, smart, collaborative, enthusiastic, highly capable journalists. They stood at the center of a cluster of about six others offering condolences. I walked up, expressed shock, dismay, and sympathy, and probably placed a hand on a shoulder, but it wasn't nearly enough.

It felt a little like the seconds after being punched in the jaw—dizzying, disorienting, knees wobbly—but without the physical pain. We all stood there awhile, awkward and silent, repeated our condolences, shock, and outrage, then fell silent again. None of us wanted to dwell on pity, and the vibe was morphing into that. We peeled away and returned to our cubes.

I'd been spared for the time being and was grateful and relieved. I even tried to convince myself that the newspaper had bottomed out—again—and was ascending. I was wrong, of course. The fact that the nausea and sorrow refused to subside was probably telling. Over the next few hours, our former colleagues packed and left. I deliberately don't remember the details of our good-byes.

By the end of the day, the *Chicago Tribune* had cut a total of fifty-three newsroom employees, followed by an official statement from Editor-in-Chief Kern that spoke of focusing our efforts on local news and investigative projects and changing the structure of the operation to adapt to people's digital habits. Over the months that followed, at least 5,000 employees were let go throughout the Tribune Company.

Later, reporters Oneal and Mills would reveal infuriating facts: that Sam made what amounted to a 2.4 percent down payment and yoked the company with $13 billion in debt; that the top thirty-eight managers at the Tribune Company got nearly $150 million in payments when Sam's takeover was consummated; that a court-appointed bankruptcy examiner concluded it was "somewhat likely" that Sam's buyout of the Tribune Company represented "intentional fraudulent conveyance," a suggestion that the company intended to defraud creditors.

It was a foreboding chapter in *Chicago Tribune* history.

Seemed like the ideal time for a field trip.

• • •

THE OPPORTUNITY arose via the veteran story-finding strategy I like to call OME, for "opening my email."

Whether they drop in my digital inbox or on my desk via the U.S. Postal Service, sparkling story ideas occasionally drift down from unexpected places and I snatch them like a poor man would grab a $100 bill floating from the sky. It happened in the Mary Jane Reed-Stanley Skridla case, and it happened in July amid all the turmoil.

I received an intriguing email from a friend who'd heard about a college instructor leading an exhumation in Herrin, a town of about 12,000 in deep southern Illinois. I immediately thought of Mary Jane. Then I recalled another factoid: Mike had lived near Herrin while in college.

But this exhumation had some distinct differences, too.

For starters, it dealt with upward of twenty sets of remains, and it was about 360 miles south of Oregon.

Yet, like Mary Jane's exhumation, the Herrin version had its roots in violence that many there would prefer to forget.

Known as the Herrin Massacre, it took place on June 22, 1922, in Williamson County, a wild region of Illinois where, at the start of the Civil War, citizens gave serious consideration to seceding from the Union. Particularly in the 1920s, "Bloody Williamson" was the scene of violent, armed family feuds that featured, among other shocking innovations in mayhem, bombs dropped from a plane. Gambling, prostitution, and bootlegging were so rampant in Williamson that the Ku Klux Klan emerged as something of a law enforcement regiment that ended up spilling more blood and fomenting more chaos.

A central part of Williamson County's identity throughout all that turmoil was coal mining and people's fierce, wide union support of the men who worked the cold, dark ground. In the spring and summer of 1922, coal miners across the United States were on strike, forcing the shutdown of mines. In southern Illinois, though, mine owner William J. Lester decided to break the strike by bringing in non-union workers—who may have been unaware of what they were getting into—and armed guards from Chicago. It was a textbook example of poor executive judgment.

On the night of June 21, several days of gunfire and dynamite attacks in and around the mine culminated in the deaths of two union miners participating in the siege. The next morning, hundreds of angry and heavily armed supporters, including many from out of state, took control of the mine and reached an agreement with those running it. The non-union workers and guards would cease operations and be escorted from Williamson County.

But mob mentality took over while they marched the estimated sixty strikebreakers from the mine. In a wooded area near a barbed-wire fence, armed union supporters opened fire.

Accounts of the massacre differ. What's clear is a shocking display of brutality. The strikebreakers dashed madly from the gunfire. Some were caught in the fence and executed there. Others were tracked to nearby woods and shot or hung. Six were marched through town—forced at some point to crawl while being harassed by people who'd gathered along the route. The workers were yoked with rope in a single-file formation and led to Herrin City Cemetery, where they were shot. Afterward, one person walked among the fallen men, slitting the throats of each. An Associated Press reporter, Donald Ewing, wrote that he observed a woman holding a baby move from the crowd, approach the bodies, and press a foot on one of the dead men's wounds, forcing blood to ooze from it. A total of twenty-three men were slaughtered.

At a morgue set up later, people were allowed to view the bodies. Some spat on them. Some stuck cigar and cigarette butts in the dead men's mouths. Parents brought their children to take a long look at the bums who tried to take their food from them.

News of the massacre spread fast, and outrage erupted across the country. An investigation was mounted and indictments announced. But two trials of those arrested in the massacre ended with acquittals. The entire ordeal remains perhaps the ugliest event in U.S. labor history.

Over the decades, Herrin's anger morphed into shame then silence. People tried to purge the episode from their memories. One consequence— deliberate or not—was that they lost track of where the massacre victims' bodies were buried.

Until nearly a century later, when a radio talk show host in the area, Scott Doody, took a listener's phone call urging Scott to visit the massacre victims' graves. It was a joke, but Scott didn't know that. He went in search of the graves and couldn't find them.

Scott started researching the massacre and its victims, and most of what he found pointed to the bodies being buried somewhere in the twenty-five-acre Herrin City Cemetery. He also discovered that five of the men were military veterans and one, Antonio Mulkavich, had served valiantly in three significant campaigns of World War I—the Second Battle of the Somme and the Saint-Mihiel and Meuse-Argonne Offensives. Mulkavich in fact had received medals for his service in those conflicts.

In a word, Scott was pissed, pissed that this military hero was murdered by a crazed mob and that his final resting place was unmarked and generally forgotten—like Mike Arians's anger that Mary Jane's murder had been dismissed. Scott became obsessed with the mystery of where they'd been buried—which also sounded familiar.

Like Mike, Scott dove in, enlisting a Southern Illinois University professor, hiring crews to conduct ground-penetrating radar sweeps, and orchestrating two excavations. He came up empty handed, except that the SIU professor had brought to the second dig a geographer, geologist, and geospatial scientist named Steven Di Naso. He too had gotten hooked by the story.

A few days after that second dig, Scott was moping around, thinking he'd failed, when his phone rang. It was Steven, who worked at Eastern Illinois University. "What's your next step?" Steven asked Scott. The collaboration between scientist and talk show host was born.

Scott, lean as razor wire, had the more fiery personality, one that a city official later said "pushed the envelope." Scott is "a very aggressive person," the official told me, although he also grudgingly credited that personality as vital to accomplishing the hard work that needed to be done.

More courtly and professorial in his thick, dark goatee, Steven's extensive research and practical experience gave him immediate credibility and lofty status, and he was shrewd enough to keep all that discreet. Modesty can be a very powerful thing, especially in places like Herrin.

Their effort, which they personally funded, lasted four years, and they worked nearly every day on it. As word spread, offers of help materialized. Someone thought he could find the graves by "witching," a practice similar to dowsing for water: someone carries a stick or rod and is physiologically directed to the grave. In addition to that offer, a psychic proposed to hunt for the graves. It reminded me again of that other odyssey being undertaken by a former mayor 360 miles north.

Scott and Steven respectfully declined those offers of help and relied on more tangible approaches. They ended up pulling together an impressive team of volunteers that included retired Washington County sheriff, former coal miner, and history enthusiast John Foster, Eastern Illinois geography professor emeritus Vincent Gutowski, forensic anthropologist and Southern Illinois University professor emeritus Robert Corruccini, and Grant Woods, a genial and hardworking graduate student in geography at Eastern Illinois.

Their individual strengths and the mostly collaborative personalities—Scott and Steven were known to occasionally test each other's collegiality—made the Earnest Grave-Finders one very effective unit.

Scott had a formidable information processor between his ears and proved to be a diligent, thorough archival investigator, once driving six hours to the Chicago History Museum to review its records. He later wrote and published *Herrin Massacre*, an exhaustive, engaging 334-page book on the massacre and grave-finding expedition.

Steven brought a casketful of crucial technological expertise that may have made the difference. He and the team collected everything they could on the massacre, its victims, and the Herrin City Cemetery. Then he took that mountain of information, including old maps, charts, graphs, and numbers—including 9,600 interment records from the cemetery—and ran it through Geographic Information System (GIS) software. That blending and crunching was like the information technology version of several food processors, except this process didn't yield goop. It allowed Steven to store, manipulate, analyze, and present all the information, as well as various slices of it, on a computer. It's what someone back in the 1960s might have called far-out, mind-blowing shit.

The result was a very informed best guess at where the bodies of the Herrin Massacre victims were buried: a paupers' field measuring about twenty by forty feet in the city cemetery. Scott and Steven believed that the remains of around a dozen victims were still in the ground. The team's earlier research suggested that family members had claimed the others in the months after the slaughter.

Winter approached, but the grave finders were anxious to test their theory. Finally, on a chilly November day, a backhoe loaned from the city dug a trench that Scott, Steven, and Grant Woods stepped inside. They scooped and scraped at the cold mud and found the end of a wooden burial vault that looked like those used for the massacre victims. Scott managed to slide his hand between the vault and coffin, grab something metal, and yank it from the mud. It was a handle, and it was a perfect match to those that the team's research indicated were on the victims' coffins.

Scott and Steven looked at each other, then at the mud-caked handle in Scott's mud-caked hand, then at each other again. They smiled.

"I could have hugged the guy right there," Steven later told me. "It was a moment."

Steven plunged a hand into the mud, felt around the outside of the coffin, grasped something, and pulled. Out came an aluminum plate, the words *At Rest* etched on it, which also was significant. The crew's research indicated those plates were used on the victims' coffins.

They continued digging over the next two weeks and found five more graves, all of which bore unmistakable signs that they held the remains of massacre victims. Thrilled at their discovery but frozen to their marrow, the grave finders decided to shut down for the winter and resume when the weather and overall conditions were more civilized.

I got word of what they were doing the next summer and drove all the way down to Herrin, arriving at the gently contoured cemetery on a hot August afternoon. The crew was in the middle of digging for more bodies —or at least the bodies' very sparse remains. Moderate to highly acidic soil in the area and the cemetery's high, fluctuating water table had so thoroughly deteriorated the bodies and caskets over time that much of the evidence, besides the metal handles, memorial plates, a few teeth, and bone fragments, had disappeared.

While I was there, Steven, Scott, and their band located the remains of two more graves, discoveries that I figured would generate joy, or at least relief, throughout town. I was wrong.

Unearthing those bodies forced Herrin to reexamine itself, revisit memories, and confront some of the past's uncomfortable details. Many found those exercises unpleasant.

Other complications arose. The team found that some burial plots above the massacre victims' remains were occupied by bodies that had been buried there in the decades after the killings—deliberately or inadvertently. In addition, the cemetery had sold other plots above the victims to people who were still among the living.

The reaction from Herrin mayor Vic Ritter and others was to discourage the exhumations. He contended that the massacre had taught its lessons of civility. In his view, the shame and anger that Herrin residents felt after the massacre had led to reflection and favorable change, which future generations had embraced. Stirring up the entire mess again was unnecessary and would inflict more harm than good, he told me. Besides, he said, the city was strapped for funds. It didn't have the money to spend on this excavation.

"I believe in rest in peace," Mayor Ritter told me when I asked for his thoughts on the digging at the cemetery. "That's the way those people should be. They've been laid to rest. They should be left alone."

It was a perspective eerily similar to what some folks in Oregon told me. Don't stir up ghosts from the past. They may haunt you with more vigor, cause more pain and mayhem. And really, what value is there in getting to the bottom of all this? Everybody who had anything to do with it is dead.

My thoughts in both scenarios were the same, only a little more strident on the Herrin Massacre exhumation. Letting two murder victims rest with unanswered questions is one thing; deliberately pushing aside and willfully neglecting the ugly, historically significant mob slaughter of twenty-three men—and burying them in anonymity—is a little more serious.

Many in Herrin ended up sharing the position of Alderman Bill Sizemore, a lifelong resident who ran Teddy's Sports Bar & Grill. He told me people never talked about the Herrin Massacre, that he thought they had hoped it would just go away. Not Bill.

"I don't think we should ignore it," he told me while we stood near the trenches on that afternoon, sweat bees buzzing around us. He supported the exhumation and would visit once in a while to see how the dig was going. "I think we should grow from it, learn from it, and become better people. We are much better, and we need to pay our respects to these men."

A few feet away was Villida Moore, watching in silence. She'd purchased two lots—one for her husband and one for herself—that were among, and a few inches above, massacre victims' graves.

She told me she had mixed feelings about what she was seeing, that she didn't know what to do.

"Have you ever owned a piece of history?" Villida asked. "Me either, until now."

But she was sure that finding the victims' bodies was a healthy thing.

"These men weren't any different from union men," said Villida, who was seventy-three years old. "They probably just needed those jobs. It's a dirty mark for Herrin, but it happened. It's part of history, and they ought to be recognized."

I was getting ready to leave. Much as I wanted to stick around and see what else the grave finders drew from the earth, an impatient, cruel deadline loomed, as always. I asked Scott and Steven what would happen next.

They weren't sure how much more digging they'd do. They said they were certain this site was where the men's bodies were buried. Now, they figured the most respectful gesture would be to erect a graceful, understated memorial at the site for all the victims and a separate marker for Mulkavich. They were thinking about creating markers for the other veterans, too. What to do about the unrelated graves and lots remained an open question.

Steven said a lot of good had come from the dig, despite how long it took and the resistance the team encountered.

"It's time to recognize it actually happened," he said, "and who these men were, and just rewrite the history on it."

Scott said the "horrible story" had a "good ending because the right thing" had been done.

"But," he said, "you had to go back to visit the past."

Back in the office the next day, rushing to finish the story, I found in my notes the phone number of the grandnephew of victim Ignatz Kubinetz, a Slovak immigrant and steam shovel worker from Chicago's far south side. I debated whether to call. I had three editors waiting to read the story so they could get the hell out of the office. *Shit*, I thought, *time always rushes past me.*

I picked up the phone and punched the number. A phone in California rang, and Ken Kormanak answered.

He was happy to talk about his great-uncle's death. Ken told me that Steven had contacted him and told him a more complete story of Ignatz, which Ken, himself a fan of history, found fulfilling. Until then, he'd only gotten a vague outline from his parents. Ken said it was reassuring that Steven and Scott had found Ignatz's remains.

But, he said, the remains should stay right where they are.

"The sadness that I have is not only with my granduncle," Ken told me, "but with everyone who went down there. There's no real value in returning him to Chicago, and from a historical perspective, he should stay there with the rest of the people he was buried with."

I hung up, dove back into the story, and missed my deadline, but what the hell. We're not robots. And guess what? The paper still came out the next morning.

Driving home that night, I started thinking again about revisiting painful memories, coming through shame, fear, and what's on the other side if you make it there. It's more than closure, whatever the hell that means. Maybe it's reconciliation, which also has its ambiguities and ambivalence.

Owning it, that nouveau buzz phrase, came to mind, and I figured that idea might start to capture what I was trying to name. Owning the messes of our past and moving through them yields something resembling light. It makes us wiser. It gives us a healthier, if heavier, bearing. Embracing those memories brings sadness, but firmer footing, too, a grounding in where we are, who we are, and what a place is.

• • •

THREE MONTHS AFTER that other exhumation I'd been following—Mary Jane's—the state police sent results from tests on Mary Jane's remains and other materials in the casket to the Ogle County sheriff. Nothing significant was found. At the same time, Mike's agitation did more than piss off local authorities. Late that year, Ogle County sheriff's captain Rich Wilkinson was directed to undertake a new investigation. Three months later, on a Friday afternoon in February, Sheriff Mel Messer announced the findings.

The timing made me suspicious. News released on Friday afternoons is known in the business as a Friday Dump. It's timed precisely to coincide with the moment most human beings are paying little attention to news and more attention to cutting loose by getting a couple of drinks with friends, clearing out of town, collapsing on the couch, or stalking former classmates on Facebook. Those activities are followed on Saturday and Sunday by other activities that pull one even further away from the near-constant feed of mayhem and unsettling developments that are your daily news stream.

By the time Monday morning rolls up, bleary-eyed citizens have at best a foggy notion of what happened in the news on Friday afternoon, and they need to muster energy for the upcoming week.

The sheriff's conclusion was that a now-deceased man from Waterloo, Iowa, probably shot Stanley while the perpetrator's brother, who had lived in Oregon and now also was dead, watched, in what looked to be a robbery attempt. But the sheriff's office had blacked out names and so much other copy in the publicly released version of the report that it was difficult to follow. And, authorities declined to state definitively that the two brothers—Lloyd and Perry DeShazo—were responsible for killing Stanley and Mary Jane. They merely were "persons of interest."

They reached that opinion primarily from conversations Captain Wilkinson had with a couple of sources whose identities were blacked out. According to the scenario these two unnamed sources laid out, on the night of the murders Lloyd and Perry had seen Stanley flashing money around town, including at the restaurant that five decades later would become the Roadhouse. They planned to take it from him. The brothers followed the couple to lovers' lane and confronted Stanley. Perry pulled a gun, surprising his younger brother. Not as much as he surprised Stanley, I bet.

Apart from that murky conclusion, Captain Wilkinson did report that he "found almost nothing in the investigation that would support the local opinion which suggested that Vince Varco was involved." In fact, a source told Captain Wilkinson that Mary Jane—not Vince—may have done the slapping hours before the murder when Vince showed up in the parking lot of a bar and tried to persuade her to go to a dance with him at a local country club.

But even the highly edited version included dubious observations. Captain Wilkinson noted a number of inconsistencies in early police reports on the case, including the number of shell casings found on lovers' lane, references to different guns used as the murder weapon, confusion over

Stanley's and Mary Jane's wounds, the disposal of interview records with a key person, and no contact with a man who "appeared to have been a very strong lead." Captain Wilkinson used the word *negligence* to describe the original investigation.

He wrote four sentences that were particularly troubling. About midway through the report, he stated, "I did find suggestions throughout [a] report and during [Wilkinson's later] investigation that pointed to political, as well as social connections, appearing to have some influences on this [the original] investigation. It also appears as if the information that had developed in the case was not documented and passed on between administrations. Evidence also appears to have been either lost or been destroyed over the years."

Then came this sentence, Captain Wilkinson's final one in his report: "This investigation, in my opinion, was corrupt and mishandled from the start," he wrote, "and nothing I am aware of can possibly change those facts."

It felt to me like Wilkinson's investigation was made to look just serious enough, but not too persistent or probing, the kind of investigation intended to make the case go away without real answers. Mike said investigators closed this review too early and other evidence was out there.

For an investigation meant to clarify, this one left more questions than answers.

But I didn't have time to explore them. Editors' interest in the Reed-Skridla case evaporated with the rushed filing of my story for the largely ignored Saturday paper. They wanted to know what else I was working on, what was next. As always, the famished news beast needed something fresh on its plate.

I'd have to circle back to Oregon sometime down the line, whenever the hell that would be. For now, although I didn't know it yet, an invasion of fat, flying marauders needed my attention.

Rivers of Fate

• • •

ASIAN CARP were supposed to be our friends when they arrived in the southern United States in the 1960s, brought by fish farmers and researchers to enhance water quality by eating algae and parasites that had gotten out of hand. They're well suited to the task. Asian carp can eat up to 40 percent of their body weight a day and grow to more than 100 pounds.

The strategy yielded mixed results until August of 1993, when heavy rains in the upper Midwest led to the most costly and devastating flood in modern U.S. history.

The Great Flood burst levees and destroyed farm fields, towns, roads, and railways along the Mississippi and Missouri Rivers. It covered more than twenty million acres in nine states, completely inundating at least seventy-five towns. Forty-seven people were killed, about 54,000 were evacuated, and 50,000 homes were destroyed or damaged. The U.S. Geological Survey estimated losses at nearly $20 billion.

That vast deluge of rogue water expanded and expedited the Asian carp's southern waterways, setting the prolific gluttons on a ravenous trek up the Mighty Miss. By the early 2000s, they'd invaded Illinois. The rich, historic artery that bears the state's name took another vicious hit.

The Illinois River valley once was an abundant, beautiful ribbon of prairie and woodland, dotted with Native American burial mounds. In the late 1800s, the river and its backwaters supplied 10 percent of all the country's fresh fish. But the entire ecosystem started devolving in 1900, when the city of Chicago reversed the flow of the Chicago River away from its natural mouth near the tip of Lake Michigan. Through a canal and tributary, the water flowed into the Illinois. Why the reversal? The Chicago River was the city's open sewer and Lake Michigan was—and is—the metro area's drinking supply. Separating the two was a shrewd, if disingenuous, move for the city.

But reversing the flow, considered an engineering marvel, sent a near tsunami of untreated domestic sewage, industrial waste, and assorted goo into the Illinois River. The surface area of the river doubled, and it grew deeper. Oxygen virtually disappeared from a stretch between Chicago and Peoria. For a few years, aquatic plants in the river disappeared, too. People were pulling fewer fish from the Illinois, and many of those were deformed. At the same time, aquatic bird populations declined. Sediment levels rose.

"They had overflowed the land," former congressman Guy L. Shaw told a House committee in 1924. It's unclear who "they" were, but it sounds like he was referring to Chicago leaders. "They had killed thousands of acres of timber . . . They have almost destroyed some of the villages and cities along the river, and the supply of fish and animal life in the river has been destroyed; the conditions have become intolerable."

A University of Chicago doctoral student named William B. Philip drew a more damning conclusion in his dissertation in 1940.

"The magnitude of the pollution of the Illinois River was unprecedented in the nation," he wrote.

Since those dreadful days, wastewater treatment plants, federal limits on the amount of water Chicago can send downriver, and, most important, the Clean Water Act of 1972 have improved conditions on the Illinois. Remarkable species diversity and productivity have been able to hang on, too, proving that Mother Nature can be one tough old broad.

But what the U.S. Army Corps of Engineers calls 150 years of "intensive human development" has inflicted significant damage, and the river's ecosystem continues to decline. Here as throughout the country, urban development and modern agriculture swallowed up land and fostered channelization and problems with runoff. The Illinois became a highly degraded river. Its history and people's memories of it have been forever changed.

Now the Asian carp were arriving en masse.

The fear was that the fish, known as the piscatorial poster child of invasive species, would scour the waterway of food that other species need, starving out those native populations that had managed to survive the preceding century. Continuing north and east up the 273 miles of the Illinois, then through the Des Plaines River, Chicago Sanitary and Ship Canal, and finally, the Chicago River, the carp would enter Lake Michigan. Within a few years, they would decimate the Great Lakes, rendering barren bodies of water that—among other natural and recreational wonders—sustain a $7 billion a year fishing industry.

"We know the Great Lakes would be very receptive to these species," Illinois Department of Natural Resources fisheries chief Mike Conlin warned the *Tribune*. "If they get in there, basically the whole ball game's over."

It was one part ball game, one part water war, and one part aerial fish fight. In addition to their unseemly eating habits, Asian carp have a bizarre behavioral quirk: they fly. That's right. When spooked by vibrations in the water from boat engines, the corpulent lunkers soar through the air.

To put it mildly, that's something midwesterners are unaccustomed to in their fish, especially those that tip the scales at three figures. We like our fish to comport themselves with the respect and modesty that are trademarks of our character. An occasional, brief break from the water while trying to spit out a hook is fine; a quick splash when lunging for a bug on the surface? Okay. But spontaneously leaping ten feet in the air and soaring a few feet horizontally? Unacceptable. Horrifying.

Stories quickly spread about the havoc the fish were wreaking on unsuspecting—and suspecting—river travelers. A jet skier on the Illinois was struck in the head by a fish near Peoria and knocked unconscious. Occasionally you'd hear about concussions or a broken jaw. Talk of contusions and scrapes was routine. Biologists and fishermen wielded garbage can lids as shields. Fearful, trembling boaters held folded lawn chairs in front of them while coursing the river. The slimy, painful experience of being violated by a fish slap was made that much more humiliating by laughter from boat mates who witnessed it.

This invasion was a serious problem, one that led the White House to appoint a "carp czar" and establish an $80 million assault on the fish to keep them from getting anywhere near Lake Michigan. Extensive research was done, and experts came up with a multipronged attack. It started with underwater electric barriers about thirty-five miles southwest of the lake in the Chicago Sanitary and Ship Canal, the channel that essentially links Lake Michigan to the Illinois River via the Des Plaines River. Crews also built a thirteen-mile concrete and steel mesh fence on low-lying land separating the Des Plaines River from the canal to prevent carp migration from one stream to the other when the area floods. State officials dumped more than 2,000 gallons of fish poison in the Chicago Sanitary and Ship Canal in what may have been the largest deliberate fish kill in Illinois history. Then they did it again six months later in a section of an Illinois River tributary. Commercial fishermen and state workers dropped nets along more than five miles of another canal that feeds the Des Plaines—the Cal-Sag Channel—for several days, scooping up fish in a hunt for the carp. None were found, but scientists remained skeptical.

All of that fascinated me, and while flailing about during another desperate story scramble early one fall, I wondered, *What's happening with the Asian carp?* I browsed online, made a few phone calls, and ended up finding Jim Garvey, a Southern Illinois University fish ecology expert who was helping with the state's research, control, and marketing of the Fish That Was Eating the River. He told me about "Carpe Carpio" (rough translation: "seize the carp"), a one-day symposium in the Peoria County Courthouse on how to turn the perceived scourge of the waterway into an economic boon. Could this gathering be the spark that led to Illinois's version of the tilapia phenomenon, in which an invasive species became a culinary rock star? I knew one way to find out. "Carpe Carpio" was scheduled for a few days later.

The story-idea bell rang like a lovely wind chime in my head, a sound made all the more sweet by the vision of a field trip.

I persuaded my editors that an expedition to the Peoria region was necessary, and a few mornings later, I found myself sitting in a downtown Peoria fourth-floor meeting room packed with about seventy-five people listening to earnest business leaders and consultants discuss the potential $40-million-a-year benefit of the Asian carp.

The goal was to generate economic bounty from harvesting the thug invaders in big numbers, thereby creating the proverbial win-win. Experts talked about the Asian Carp Value Chain, which included carp pituitary extract and carp collagen.

At the heart of the strategy was a rather nifty revenge exacted on the carp's own gorging: people would eat Asian carp in mass quantities. *Brilliant in its simplicity* was my immediate thought. *Gag me with a spoon* was my next.

Shortly after the Asian carp invasion, the hope had been that China and other Asian countries, where eating carp is relatively common, would be hot markets. But the Chinese suspected that Asian carp in the United States were tainted.

On top of that public relations challenge, the fish are very labor-intensive to harvest and they spoil quickly, posing shipping problems.

Some in the audience suggested government financial help to grow markets, a step that leaders in the great, nearly bankrupt state of Illinois were reluctant to take.

"The problem is they're carp," Steven McNitt told the group. "And in the U.S., nobody under the age of forty would eat carp. They think the fish is dirty." He suggested leaving off the fish species from food product labeling. "You need to get the word *carp* out of there," he said.

Steven held a position of respect in the room. He was a sales manager for Schafer Fisheries, which processed truckloads of carp every year in a plant near the Mississippi River in northwest Illinois. Schafer, family owned and operated since 1955, had come up with some creative twists, including carp bologna and salami, even carp hot dogs. But creativity hadn't transformed the invasive fish into an economic boom.

The consultants in the room decided they could take an immediate step right then and there to attack the stigma Americans attach to ingesting carp. Seminar leaders asked the audience for a more palatable name for the fish.

Someone shouted, "River dolphin," which sounded lyrical but also brought visions of gutting a beloved mammal. "Silver fin," another audience member called out, which I thought sounded promising, as did the next suggestion, "river cod." A guy close to me muttered, "Another white meat," and all of us within earshot snickered.

Over the next couple of hours, the group dynamic turned optimistic. Steven said they needed to promote the view that Asian carp were "more a resource than a problem because the problem is never going to go away." Jim Garvey told the group that, in addition to having as much of the healthy omega-3 fatty acids as salmon, Asian carp had very low levels of contaminants. More mercury is found in tuna, he noted. Jim also said tests at the Illinois State Fair and Taste of Chicago showed that people are willing to try Asian carp if it's free.

"Carp Czar" John Goss, who'd come all the way from Our Nation's Capital to attend the conference, kept a low profile until the end, when he stood and did his part to rally the troops.

Commercial fishing is "a key part of the strategy" to overcome this invader, John said. He talked of a "market-based solution" and told the group, "You're on the right track." And repeated, "There is an absolute need for this to be part of the national strategy. Please stay on track. This could very well stimulate a model that could help many communities in the Midwest."

Seminar leader Jim Haguewood, echoing Steven's sentiments, wrapped up by reiterating that the carp is a great natural resource.

"We have market demand sitting in the room," he told the group. "We have the fish in the river. We have the capacity to get the fish out of the river, but we need additional capabilities." That was one of the goals of the conference, he said.

"We build collaboration. There'll be new business relationships that come out of this meeting today, and I hope that there are dozens and dozens of them. There's no reason it can't happen in Peoria."

The meeting broke up, and clusters of attendees chatted. Fishermen met with owners of area freezer warehouses. A few locals spoke with a Florida couple who had a fish preservation business that used salt.

Someone or something will need to kick-start the Asian carp economic boom, Jim Garvey told me.

"Otherwise, we're just going to have these things flipping and flopping around everywhere, and they're going to be in all our waterways, and it's going to suck."

Much as I love economic development conferences, the flipping and flopping was what I was most interested in observing. A couple days earlier, I'd arranged to see it firsthand. So, after stepping from the courthouse in the afternoon sun, I hopped in my car, drove thirty miles upstream —dodging various roadkill—crossed a bridge on the outskirts of charming Lacon, Illinois, and met Nathan Wallick at a landing on the Illinois River next to a hot dog stand named Mr. Mike's.

A former college football running back—he was Millikin University's all-time leading rusher, most valuable player for three consecutive seasons, and team captain his senior year—Nathan now was a Peoria firefighter and EMT who had gone out on the river a few years earlier and seen it explode to life with flying carp for the first time. "I said, you gotta be kidding me," Nathan told me.

That sight ignited the entrepreneur in him. He sank thousands of dollars of savings into a twenty-one-foot aluminum deck boat, the *Carpocalypse*, which had a two-stroke, 115-horsepower engine. It was an ideal package for maximum water vibration. For protection, Nathan had erected volleyball netting that extended eight feet in the air along all but the stern of the boat. He also rigged seven bows with arrows attached by neon string. That was the essence of his business, Peoria Carp Hunters, which took clients out for search-and-destroy missions on the Illinois. Now he was known as "Captain Nate." His videos had become internet sensations, but he hadn't quit his day job.

That brilliant September afternoon, Captain Nate wore a camouflage floppy hat, tight-fitting silver-rimmed sport sunglasses, and shorts. On his muscular torso was a black T-shirt adorned on the front with a white logo of a carp head and skeleton impaled by an arrow. He was taking three gents from a national cleaning company on the river for a bow fishing expedition and team-building exercise. They'd agreed to let me tag along.

"It's all about the vibration," Captain Nate told me as we pushed from the dock and moved at a modest clip through the wide stretch of brown-green water. Exhaust fumes and the odor of fish cut into the fresh air. A blue heron stood along the wooded shoreline. High above, a bald eagle perched on a branch.

We were going to seek the enemy, engage his slimy, sorry, scaly ass, and terminate him. I began to relate to Robert Duvall in *Apocalypse Now*. I love the smell of diesel and fish in the morning. Smells like victory.

Not three minutes into the search-and-skewer expedition, a carp flew from the water a few feet behind the boat. Then, Captain Nate swung his vessel to a quieter stretch of the river and slowed the engine. He was looking for what he called a fish "cloud." We found one.

The surface erupted with dozens of them, as if the boat had sent an electric shock wave through the water. We were under attack, outnumbered maybe five or six to one. Carp flipped and flopped, slashed through the air, some just a few inches from the surface, others a few feet; some eight inches long, most much, much bigger.

The three cleaning service friends—Duke, Scott, and Mark, all experienced bow hunters—opened fire from the stern. Scott bagged a fish quickly. Then someone else drilled another. Every time one of the guys nailed a carp, Captain Nate sprung from the pilot's seat with the agility honed by avoiding linebackers. He skipped around buckets and other impediments, grabbed an arrow with a fish on the tip, and shook the bloated, hemorrhaging creature into a garbage can before returning to his post.

Water splashing all around us, the hunters hooted and guffawed while they fired away. Carp glanced off them or walloped them squarely. Fat flying fish were banging against the boat with thuds and pops. They sprang off the volleyball netting like it was a vertical trampoline. Here and there, a fish would leap into the boat from the rear. I laughed like a madman.

After we passed through the cloud, relative calm returned. I sat next to Captain Nate, who over the years had grown to dislike the fish that contributed to his livelihood.

"They're really, really slimy, and they bleed easily," the captain told me. "Plus, they poop all the time. That's pretty much all they do when you get them in the boat, and they like to break things."

We navigated into another cloud, and the pandemonium repeated itself. A fish landed near Scott's feet.

"It's crazy, isn't it?" he said. "It doesn't make any sense. Dumbest fish out there and they're the most plentiful."

Duke told me he loved it. He and Scott called it awesome, an adrenaline rush way outside the normal realm of fishing, the normal realm of anything. Mark said the same thing. Scott joked that it's 10 percent skill and 90 percent luck. Then one of the valiant hunters smiled and extended a bow to me.

The theme from *Pirates of the Caribbean* swelled in my head as I grasped the weapon, stood, and found my footing on the rear edge of the vessel a few inches from the hulking, loud black Mercury motor. I adjusted my floppy hat, which in an earlier life had been my sister-in-law's gardening bonnet. Over the next hour or so, we plied the Illinois, traveling through open water and side channels, finding three or so carp clouds. I shot arrow after arrow furiously and missed every single time—until our final run through a cloud.

Firing about twenty feet behind the boat into an explosion of carp, I nailed one maybe a half inch below and in front of his dorsal fin. I shouted like a bloodthirsty savage, or maybe a basketball player after a dunk, and started reeling in the poor sap. Then, too late, I saw something white glint on my left. Before I realized what it was, I was ambushed.

A stout compatriot of the guy I'd struck flew up eight feet in the air, made an aerial maneuver that would be the envy of a circus acrobat, and whacked me on the jaw and neck. I shrieked like a ten-year-old girl in a haunted house. The creature slammed against my upper leg and fell to my feet. My left eye twitched. My line slackened. My prey had wriggled free. I looked down and thought for an instant that the slimy bastard on the boat floor smiled at me. I nudged the fish with the toe of my boot. He didn't move. I turned to my fellow hunters.

"That counts," I shouted, wiping something slick from my jaw and pointing my bow at the kamikaze. "I bagged this one. You saw it. That counts." Captain Nate, Duke, Scott, and Mark stared at me, a hint of pity on their faces.

We had to return to the landing. A Japanese TV crew was waiting. On the ride in, Captain Nate was conflicted. He appreciated the fun the fish brought to his clients and the revenue his side venture was generating, and he enjoyed getting out on the river. But he was concerned with how rapidly the carp were proliferating, a trait that earned them the nickname River Rabbit, and he was convinced they'd made their way to the Great Lakes already. Captain Nate was skeptical that Americans would eat carp in great numbers, and he was tired of getting attacked by them.

"It's funny getting smacked once in a while," he told me, "but after a few years of this, getting smacked sucks." He said he'd soon have to erect a steel cage around his boat.

We neared the landing, and I could see the TV crew unpacking its gear from a car. Captain Nate eased his boat to the dock. I thanked him and thanked the affable trio of Duke, Scott, and Mark.

"I'd take these fish being gone over running my business any day," Captain Nate told me. "It's that bad."

I looked in the garbage can. A pile of more than twenty sizable fish, motionless and bleeding, stared back at me. Captain Nate told me he would bury them. His clients aren't interested in eating carp.

I stepped off the boat, and the TV crew boarded. Captain Nate guided the vessel onto the river for another hunt. I walked to land, grabbed a map from my car, and ordered a hot dog and pumpkin shake from Mr. Mike's. Sitting on a picnic bench in the shade of a massive tree, I plotted the scenic route home, the one that would take me along two-lane highways through small towns and the harvest gold and emerald prairie for as far as I could delay the interstate. I shook my head at the marvel of Mother Nature and looked over the river. Soon I was drowsy, too tired to hit the road. It was around three o'clock. By the time I got to the outskirts of Chicago, I'd be in the teeth of a punishing, hot rush hour. The shade felt cool, the breeze a gentle caress. I walked to my car, pushed back the seat, opened the windows, and closed my eyes. Drifting off, my mind wandered to another river in another place that was in some ways vastly different from the Illinois, and in others, very similar.

• • •

THAT OTHER TOWN, eighty-one miles north of Lacon, was Oregon, the other river the Rock.

Known as the Hudson of the Midwest, the Rock River starts in the pristine, internationally acclaimed Horicon Marsh in south central Wisconsin and flows directly south into South Beloit, Illinois, before coursing through Rockford and heading southwest to meet the Mississippi River at Rock Island. It's a narrower, longer, pastoral river that, despite some issues with agricultural runoff, remains far less damaged than the Illinois.

"My image would be of the Illinois River as a big, strong brother, contrasted with the Rock, which is a gentler sister," Greg Farnham, coordinator of the Rock River Trail, told me. The trail is a mix of water and land routes along the river. After the Asian carp story ran, I'd called Greg to find out more about the Rock and its place in Oregon's psyche. I thought I might squeeze from the conversation a lead on another story for the *Tribune* that would involve a field trip.

The beautiful stretch of the Rock River in Oregon—many say it is the most scenic section of the river—was where, on the east bank, Mary Jane would take little Warren for picnics. It's also where, about 2,000 feet from its west bank, she was abducted. I'd even heard that the killer had tossed the murder weapon off the Oregon bridge into the Rock.

The river's 318-mile run includes a number of places with historically intriguing significance: A. G. Spalding, whose company became the mammoth sporting goods manufacturer, was a member of Rockford's amateur baseball team, the Forest Citys. John Deere revolutionized farming by developing a "self-polishing" plow in tiny Grand Detour, the same town that gave the world Dick Welles, a gentleman innkeeper whose son Orson found a fair amount of success in Hollywood, and the place where Chicago Cubs legend Stan Hack ran a restaurant after retiring from baseball. A few miles downriver from Grand Detour is Dixon, where Ronald Reagan spent his childhood and, while working as a lifeguard during his high school and college summers, reportedly saved seventy-seven people from drowning in the Rock. The second-largest whiskey distillery of the mid-nineteenth century was on the Rock River near Sterling. At the mouth of the river in Rock Island once stood a compound for upward of 12,000 Confederate prisoners.

"What I like is the sense of continuity and the sense of linking thirty-seven independent communities in two states and eventually joining the grandfather of all rivers in Rock Island," Greg told me. He loved the Rock's capacity to pull together a variety of landscapes, too—farmland, rolling fields, urban centers, exposed cliffs, bluffs, and open prairie. To him, the river was a powerful way to connect with Mother Nature.

It's hard to deny the beauty and mystery of the Rock's passage through Oregon. Sheer limestone cliffs emerge from wooded shorelines. Tall bluffs, one of which is the spot where *The Eternal Indian* monument gazes over the valley, rise on either side. On some nights, the moon shines so bright, the valley looks as if it's bathed in afternoon sun.

Apart from all that, it's a place infused with creativity. This was, after all, the setting for the Eagle's Nest Art Colony, which flourished for nearly a half century.

Greg and I talked about that. Then he recommended that I reach out to local character Frank Schier, founder of the Rock River Trail.

When I got Frank on the phone, he said he was really busy, about to go from one appointment to the next. Since 1992, he'd been editor, publisher,

and owner of the *Rock River Times*, a free weekly regional newspaper established in 1987 that "strives to be the Voice of the Community, repre-
senting all viewpoints," its website announced. The *Times* did, however,
have an editorial agenda: "We continue to fight for historical preservation
in Rockford, the richness of many cultures, fairness and loyalty in commerce, protection for the environment, the use of alternative energy, true
and affordable justice in the courts, equality and honesty in politics and
support for the arts."

Frank talked with me for a half hour, which struck me as very generous
for such a busy guy, so generous I soon realized I was going to be late for
my next appointment. Before then, Frank spoke of the Rock River's pastoral ambience, its rich Native American history, the high number of burial
mounds near Oregon. He gave me his mini autobiography, which included
an English degree, graduate work in international service at American
University, various publications of poetry, a black belt in Shotokan karate,
a Reiki Master degree, and forty years of canoeing and boating on the
Rock River.

"I was in the restaurant business for a while," Frank said, "but fired
myself for bad attitude." He had set out to become a college professor but
ended up running a newspaper. "So go figure."

He'd lived in Washington, D.C., Boulder and Telluride, Colorado, and
Seattle before returning to his hometown of Rockford in 1982—the same
year he published a book of poetry, *Splitting Hairs*—and settling in the
1870s Victorian where he'd spent his childhood, raised by a single mom
who was a teacher and watercolor and china painting artist.

It was one of the most densely packed thirty minutes of conversation
that I've experienced. Before it ended, Frank told me something that made
the back of my neck tingle: the Oregon area has a bit of a reputation for the
occult. I told him about the talk of ghosts that I'd heard.

"There's a boatload of them out here," Frank said, mentioning that it
was common knowledge that the ghost of former Illinois governor Frank
Orren Lowden haunts the Oregon Public Library.

He told me of Conover Square, the former piano factory converted to a
shopping mall, where reports of a little girl's giggle, piano playing, spec-
ters of men and women walking about, even tugs on clothing have been
reported. He also spoke of a phantom lady, tall with long blond hair, who
roams the roadside just north of Oregon on Kennedy Hill.

Fueling some of that ghost talk was the presence of upwards of thirty Native American burial mounds along the river in and near Oregon, including what Frank described as an altar the Potawatomi had made. The slab of rock was about six feet tall, three feet wide, and two feet thick, and had been mounted in a base of stones but now rested in the river. Frank believed vandals had shoved it into the river sometime between 1900 and 1950. The river itself is thought to act as a path for Native American spirits to travel, Frank told me. *Maybe white folks' ghosts were drawn to the same spirit path*, I thought.

More ghosts may be hanging around Oregon than other river towns for another reason. The city's notorious low-head dam creates a strong, nearly inescapable downstream flow known for catching boaters and canoeists by surprise as they approach. That powerful current draws vessels to the dam, flips them over the structure, and traps them and their occupants in a deadly churn of rushing water. The result has been far too many drownings in Oregon.

"It's creepy-crawly," Frank said of the ghosts. Then he chuckled. "Because it's kind of understandable."

The presence of burial mounds made me wonder about other similarities shared by the Rock and Illinois Rivers. I hadn't heard talk of ghosts along the Illinois, though I'm sure they exist—or at least the legends of them do.

I took a look at a detailed map of both rivers and found something that surprised me: they're connected by a now-shuttered canal that played an important part in one of the world's most well-known canals but has been largely forgotten.

Shaped like an inverted uppercase T, the Hennepin Canal diverts water from the Rock River a little south of Oregon and directs the water south on a thirty-mile leg that connects to another section of the canal. That lower main channel runs east and west, connecting with the Illinois River near Bureau Junction and with the Rock River in the town of Colona, about sixty-five miles west. The two flow west as one for about nine miles before the canal branches off again and enters the Mississippi near the mouth of the Rock.

Also known as the Illinois and Mississippi Canal, the Hennepin was designed as a shortcut for barges headed to the Mississippi River from Chicago, and it cut more than 420 miles from the route those barges had taken. Just as the Chicago Sanitary and Ship Canal had an impact on the Illinois River, the Hennepin was expected to influence the Rock, but in a much more favorable way.

Except that by the time the first boat traveled on the Hennepin in 1907, the canal had been rendered obsolete. It was too small to accommodate increasingly larger boats. And, the cost of moving material on the iron horse, otherwise known as the railroad, was dropping, making railcars a preferable choice for moving goods. The Hennepin turned out to be one of the last canals built in the United States, and its primary users soon became recreational boaters. It closed in 1951.

Before it did, however, the Hennepin had become its own engineering marvel, like the Chicago Sanitary and Ship Canal. The Hennepin made at least two crucial and largely unheralded contributions to canal technology, Gary Wagle, president of Friends of the Hennepin Canal, told me. It was the first canal to use concrete instead of cut stone, and it carved a feeder canal from a man-made lake. Both concepts were incorporated into the Panama Canal.

Today, the Hennepin's new place in history is as a 104-mile linear park with trails, campgrounds, canoe runs, and fishing spots. It's on the National Register of Historic Places but remains unknown to many.

A trip along it reveals the evolving, forlorn, beautiful portrait of nature reclaiming the remains of humankind's ambition and will, the melancholy beauty of modern ruins. Rusted steel bridges and deteriorating locks, large broken blocks and cracked walls of concrete, decaying wood pilings banded together—all of it abandoned and being swallowed by the slow, inevitable advance of vegetation that is revising the landscape and history, creating new images and memories.

"I've frequently referred to it as the hidden treasure," Gary said.

I started wondering about another possible similarity between the two rivers: If they were connected physically, then could they be connected biologically? I asked Greg, Frank, and Doug Blodgett, the Illinois River coordinator for The Nature Conservancy, the same question: Are Asian carp invading the Rock River?

Frank said he hadn't seen them yet, "but it wouldn't surprise me if we've got them."

"If they're not there already," Doug said, "it's almost inconceivable that they won't soon be."

And Greg? He said no technical reason exists that would spare the Rock from the invaders.

"I'm not looking out my window seeing Asian carp jumping out of the river," Greg told me. Then he paused. "But I'm sure they're here."

So maybe the Illinois and Rock Rivers were closer than I'd thought. Not that it mattered in my day-to-day existence as short-order cook in the kitchen of the news beast. I never did squeeze a story idea, with or without a field trip, from my newfound knowledge of the Rock River. But I considered myself an improved human being for expanding my understanding of the world around me.

• • •

ALL THIS TIME, Mike had continued to grind away at the mystery of who killed Stanley and Mary Jane, and one day, his grinding yielded a bizarre twist.

Near Christmas, when news seems to trickle as slow as water off an icicle, he called with a shocking development. Investigators who'd examined Mary Jane's remains eventually had given some bones to Warren, who'd turned them over to Mike, who'd sent them to a forensic anthropologist, who with an associate had analyzed the remains and sent Mike a report.

The anthropologists' conclusion: the skull in the casket wasn't Mary Jane's.

The cold season for news had experienced a sudden heat wave. I was back on the case.

Send in the Ghosts

• • •

I DON'T REMEMBER exactly how Mike told me what he told me—that the skull in Mary Jane's casket belonged to somebody else—other than it was over the phone.

But I do remember my eyes fluttering in a kind of sustained twitch while my mind tried to grasp what he was saying and my hand tried to take notes. I was thinking, *This can't be.* Then, in staccato bursts, I would repeat something like, "Well . . . well . . . but . . . wait, what?"

He offered to send me, via email, the report from the pair of experts who'd examined Mary Jane's remains, and I accepted. It arrived a few minutes later. The final two paragraphs said it all.

The top two cervical vertebrae, known as the atlas (C-1) and the axis (C-2), "do not belong to the same individual," wrote Linda Klepinger, PhD and author of the book *Fundamentals of Forensic Anthropology*. It's considered an essential text in the field. Her co-analyst was John Moore, a professor of anatomy, pathophysiology, and forensics at Parkland College. What they were saying was that C-1 fit the skull but did not fit with C-2.

"In other words," the report stated, "C-1 and the skull are from one individual while C-2 through C-7 are apparently from another individual of similar age."

My eyes fluttered again. I read it one more time.

"There is no obvious explanation for this impossible articulation" other than the explanation they'd offered, Dr. Klepinger and Professor Moore wrote. The pair went on to say that cut marks were absent from the vertebrae, although they did notice "small scratch marks" on a surface of the atlas "that might have resulted from knife or scalpel cutting."

Apart from the bombshell, their three-page report was unremarkable and its observations aligned with what somebody would think of as Mary Jane's remains. Vertebrae C-2 through C-7 "articulated well into a cervical column," Dr. Klepinger and Professor Moore wrote. The skull probably belonged to a teenage white girl who was older than fourteen, they stated.

One detail did stand out to me: trauma to the skull indicated that this victim, whoever she was, was shot near the left side of her nose. That differed from news reports in 1948 that stated Mary Jane was shot at the base of the skull. Then again, this wasn't looking like Mary Jane's skull.

I called Dr. Klepinger, who elaborated with a formal, technical conclusion.

"It's wacko," she said. "It's just weird . . . very weird."

So weird, Dr. Klepinger said, that she had never come across anything like it before in more than forty years of forensic experience and anatomy research.

"Neither one of us had seen anything that fit so poorly together," she added. "If I had found this in archaeology, in a museum, I would have thought this was boxed up wrong."

Dr. Klepinger went on to say that if those vertebrae and skull were inside the same person, that individual would have suffered serious health problems, including neural damage and arthritis. Mary Jane's lifestyle suggested the exact opposite.

"The only thing I could think of," Dr. Klepinger told me of the mismatch, "is that it had to have been purposeful."

We'd spoken for about twenty minutes. She couldn't offer much more, other than to say somebody might take another look at the case now and that the circumstances might have made for an episode of *The X-Files*.

I didn't know what else to ask, but didn't want to end the conversation. After a few seconds of awkward silence, I sensed that Dr. Klepinger was growing anxious, as was I. I had a story to write. Deadline loomed. She was a busy woman.

"It is a little disquieting," Dr. Klepinger finally said, "when you wind up with something weird like this." I expressed my agreement, thinking, *More than a little disquieting.* Then I thanked her for her time.

My next call was to Mike, for whom I had plenty of questions.

"Why would anybody have severed the head in the first place?" I asked.

He said it probably was done at the time of the original autopsy in 1948, possibly to extract the bullet from the skull, or for a trophy.

"A trophy?!" I said.

Mike explained that he'd found research by a criminal profiler who'd reported that killers sometimes kept skulls as trophies. Criminals with that grisly penchant often had psychological issues—you think?—or "desired an individual way to capture or keep that person," Mike said.

Then where is Mary Jane's skull? I asked.

"If in fact this is not hers, we have to go back to the trophy theory," he told me, "which would mean that someone has it, buried it, destroyed it, or tossed it in the river."

Okay, I said, then whose skull is the one found in Mary Jane's casket?

"There were a lot of skulls floating around during that period of time," Mike said, which I found hard to believe at first. But his explanation sounded plausible. He said that trophy skulls were somewhat common at the time of Mary Jane's murder, a result of poaching that had occurred on the battlefields of World War II. Mike added that it was "very common" for doctors to have skulls and bones at the time, too.

"One thing it means for sure," Mike said, "is that it [the investigation] was bungled from the beginning, in 1948. Something was done dishonestly, whether it was the authorities or the undertakers, at that time." He went on to say that the Illinois State Police further bungled the case and that people in town are "scared to death to say anything" about the killings.

"We've got a sixty-year-old problem here that began getting bungled and bungled and bungled, and it's time to get somebody on this who knows what they're doing."

We talked a while longer. Mike was hoping to get FBI personnel and their sophisticated, high-tech investigative tools involved. He also wanted to get an accurate artistic rendering of the face that at one time covered the skull. But expenses were piling up. He said he'd spent more than $50,000, and the meter continued to run. It was becoming more and more irresponsible to keep funding his obsession and fighting this fight, he said. But

Mary Jane was hanging around. At the same time, Mike couldn't shake his indignation or his commitment to Warren.

Warren.

What an agonizing twist this must be for him, I thought. He was certainly someone I needed to talk to for the story. I ended the conversation with Mike.

When I got Warren on the phone, he kept repeating how confused he was now. "There's been a screwup somewheres along the line," Warren said. "I just want some answers."

He recalled that while observing the autopsy of his sister's remains, he was shocked and confused to see that the skull had already been detached. For months after, Warren said, he had to fight with authorities to gain possession of the skull, vertebrae, and other remains. The coroner wanted to cremate all of them, Warren said.

"I think it's probably a real good idea" to get the FBI involved, Warren told me. "Maybe they can do some further DNA testing and determine whether it really is her skull or not."

Deadline pressing down on me, I had to close our conversation and squeeze in one more phone call. I dialed the number of Greg Beitel, who'd become Ogle County sheriff.

My call was the first notice he'd received that Dr. Klepinger's skeletal analysis report existed. He was disappointed that Mike failed to share the conclusion with the sheriff's office before notifying the media.

Sheriff Beitel said he found the conclusions "interesting" but didn't know anything about the qualifications of the people making them. He rejected Mike's assessment that the investigation had been bungled or a cover-up had occurred—at least since he took office. What had happened before? Sheriff Beitel was unwilling to go into much detail.

"There probably were things that could have been done that weren't," he said of previous investigations. "But we can't do much to change that at this point."

I was surprised when he said he'd welcome an outside agency's investigation of the case. He said he wanted the public to have confidence in his office, "that we'll do a complete and thorough investigation. We don't have anything to hide."

I'd run out of time. I thanked the sheriff, hung up, and started writing the story. One question nagged me, and I was surprised Sheriff Beitel failed to mention it: Could Mike have found a substitute skull and sent that along with the box of bones to Dr. Klepinger? Could he have orchestrated this "purposeful" collection of evidence? There was no time to explore that now. I needed to bang out the story.

In the weeks and months that followed, I stayed in more frequent contact with Mike. Instead of waiting for him to call me, I'd call him to check on his odyssey, and one of the things I asked was whether he'd placed a different skull in the items he sent for analysis. He didn't like that question, and he let me know it.

Mike asked if I knew how hard it was to obtain a skull these days. I didn't. And, as proof of his integrity, he offered a $25,000 reward for the return of Mary Jane's skull. He also said he'd allow any legitimate law enforcement forensic anthropologist to examine the remains and how he'd handled them. Both those measures seemed to demonstrate his credibility but didn't unequivocally disprove the doubts, which Mike's critics would continue to point out to me.

Lingering doubt or not, I could tell that the skull discrepancy had energized Mike with righteousness.

A few months later, he showed how energized he was. Mike sent a letter to the U.S. Attorney in Chicago asking the office to investigate, and he called a press conference to announce the move.

"I truly believe the county coroner, the sheriff, and the state's attorney are fine, upstanding people," Mike told the handful of reporters, photographers, and cameramen assembled at the Roadhouse on a Wednesday afternoon. "They got caught holding the bag for something that happened sixty years ago."

I looked up to make sure it was Mike talking. For years, during various court battles with Ogle County, Mike had used less-than-flattering characterizations of county officials. Now, he was downright magnanimous. It made sense from a strategic point of view. Mike was trying to clarify who the bad guys were and build empathy with current law enforcement officers and administrators in Ogle County.

In his letter to the U.S. Attorney, Mike reiterated an earlier contention that according to federal law, Warren was a victim of a violent crime.

"Acting now as an advocate for the victims of violent crimes as recognized by state and federal statutes," he wrote in his letter to the U.S. Attorney, "and after receiving two death threats to my person, I beg your intervention into my inquiry for closure and justice for all concerned parties."

He alleged a corrupt investigation in 1948, violation of Warren's civil rights as a victim of a violent crime, desecration of human remains, and "willful nondisclosure of material facts and evidence." In addition to the U.S. Attorney's Office, Mike sent copies of the letter to the FBI and the Vidocq Society, a Philadelphia-based group of criminologists and other experts who solve cold cases.

"This is no longer a whodunit," Mike told me and any other reporter who'd listen. "It's now a question of why did Ogle County authorities back in 1948 switch out the skull of Mary Jane Reed."

He followed that move by hiring a forensic artist to compose a facial image of the skull in Mary Jane's casket. The rendering resembled an Asian of unknown gender. About the same time, Mike sent a letter to Ogle County demanding it pay $1.5 million to Warren for violating his civil rights, and he filed a lawsuit in a neighboring county making those same claims against Ogle County. He contacted U.S. Senator Dick Durbin's office for help, and he started talking to me about his planned surprise attack: exhuming Stanley's body.

Mike said Mary Jane's skull might be in his casket. It sounded like crazy talk; then again, after what had happened with Mary Jane's remains, I thought it might be best to keep an open mind. Still, to pull off Stanley's exhumation, Mike would need to engage in a rather delicate dance with Stanley's extended family, which had to approve the dig before a judge would.

Overall, it looked like something was going to burst forth simply from the sheer force of Mike's exertion.

While all this was churning, business began to rally at the Roadhouse, a development helped largely by the installation of video gambling machines. But, like many other people's experience in the supposed post-recession economy, the residue of Mike's earlier financial struggles remained. One day, while scanning the Oregon newspaper, I'd seen a blurb that the house he'd walked away from had been foreclosed and was to be sold at auction.

At the *Tribune*, we emerged from bankruptcy four years after filing for it and were moving toward what would be a split into two companies:

Tribune Media, the broadcast operations that included forty-two TV stations, and Tribune Publishing, the company's newspapers and digital outlets. In the breakup, Tribune Media took ownership of the Tower. The *Chicago Tribune* became a tenant in the landmark skyscraper it built about ninety years earlier. Our suburban crew moved a couple more times.

All in all, it was a consistently unstable existence, a condition made more painful by ongoing media reports of said instability, including comprehensive coverage in the *Chicago Tribune*.

Perceptions weren't helped by the September report that a former Tribune Company executive charged with stealing $264,000 from the company had plead guilty and was sentenced to two years in prison. A day after that item popped up, news circulated that Tribune CEO Peter Liguori was calling on managers to find $100 million in cuts. That report was followed about eight weeks later by Tribune Company's announcement that its profits were up but revenue was down, an accomplishment achieved largely through staff cuts and lower newsprint costs.

You didn't need a degree in finance to see that those moves were short-term fixes. A few days after the profits and revenue news came this: the Tribune Company was cutting nearly 700 more jobs across the corporation, including positions at the *Chicago Tribune, Los Angeles Times*, and six other papers the company owned. A dozen newsroom employees lost their jobs in Chicago, some who'd been with the paper for more than two decades. Two loyal, hardworking staffers got tossed from our suburban outpost.

I was deliberately losing track of what round of layoffs—fourth or fifth —we'd endured over the years while advertising continued to decline along with readers' interest in newspapers. Each wave of cuts was scarier than the last.

The common threads through at least the latest rounds were the sadness and anxiety, sometimes ascending to nausea, that seemed to wash over everyone, whether they kept or lost their jobs. Layoffs were coming so regularly that employees at the Tower had instituted an efficient ritual to show their empathy and gratitude. As their recently former colleagues left the newsroom, everyone would stand and applaud. This last time, I was told, when the staff gave its ovation to a pair of people walking from the newsroom, one of the former employees broke down sobbing.

Journalists being human beings, sadness and anxiety usually ushered in bitterness. A bizarre mix of sensations and emotions took hold in me—the aforementioned sorrow and anxiety-induced nausea accompanied by short-term relief, persistent pessimism, and, yeah, a dash of bitterness. In one way, I almost envied those let go. They had the benefit, grim as it may have been, of a certainty that I imagined might feel liberating. For better or worse, they were moving on.

We remainders still had jobs that we viewed as a calling, jobs we loved, despite all the doom-filled prospects, absence of raises, and shifting duties that felt like desperate human experiments.

Every day we knew the swords were poised over our heads. All of us had the acute awareness that it didn't seem to matter much how hard or smart we worked. We too might be liberated on any given morning. One thing was certain: we all were learning the valuable life lesson of dealing with constant instability.

My conversations with Mike and others involved in the case became a respite of sorts, something to take my mind off the precarious, largely gloomy existence I was living in the news business. Better to examine their obsession than to question my own commitment to journalism.

One of those "others" involved in the case was crime novelist Jack Fredrickson, author of five books chronicling the exploits of private detective Dek Elstrom. Jack had followed coverage of the Reed-Skridla case and had become so intrigued that he went out to Oregon to chat with Mike three times and pore over stacks of documents and other material. The result was *Silence the Dead*, Jack's fictionalized treatment of the crime in which a supporting character is a forlorn, fairly pathetic newspaper reporter. Who inspired that persona I'll never know. British publisher Severn House released the book, an engaging, fast-paced read.

A lovable rogue, Jack had an earlier, very successful life as an efficiency expert at various corporations, then as the owner of an office furniture and interior design company. He "made a damn fortune, plus ate really well" in that venture but became bored out of his mind, started selling parts of the company, and then closed it. When he left the corporate world, Jack's plan had been to "indulge in frivolous pursuits" that included building a banjo, making a Windsor chair using 200-year-old tools, obtaining an advance rating in scuba, and reading, which he'd always loved. After pursuing those adventures for three years, Jack would return to business.

He'd written a couple of business books and dabbled in writing fiction while still working in the office furniture world. He even ended up finishing a novel but dropped it in a drawer and left it there. Writing wasn't on his frivolous pursuit agenda, but Jack found that the experience of placing words on the page relaxed him and focused his mind unlike anything else. He took a short-story writing class and a novel-writing class, and one New Year's Eve he sent a short story to *Ellery Queen Mystery Magazine* without telling his wife and kids. It was published. Jack then began concentrating on writing humorous crime fiction and indefinitely postponed his return to the business world. A few years later, he'd published his first Dek novel.

When Jack and I met, he was in his mid-sixties and had been on sabbatical from the business world for nearly twenty years. He stood six feet, four inches tall, had wavy, slightly unruly brilliant-white hair, and could tell a great story. He also had whip-snapping analytical skills and routinely displayed a self-deprecating, witty, charming demeanor. We became fast friends and would meet at various coffeehouses to chat about our shared disorder.

"You've got the same disease I do," he told me while we sat one afternoon at Brewed Awakening, an eclectic, neighborly café near the tracks in a western suburb of Chicago. "The Mary Jane Reed unsolved murder disease."

Jack believed it was very likely that Vince, with or without help, killed Stanley.

"I think only a cop could have gotten him out of that car to stand on the road to get killed, okay?" Jack told me. "Only a badge could have gotten him out. Who else? Somebody with a gun? Sure. Okay, but I think if somebody comes up waving a gun, the move might be to start the car and drive the hell out of there."

Jack said he'd seen the scenario unfold hundreds of times in his mind. "I can see the moon. I can see him coming up on foot, hoofing it from the Roadhouse, coming over the overpass, coming in there, flashing his badge, 'Get out of the car,' and killing him. I see that," Jack told me. "I know that."

After Vince shot Stanley, Jack said, Vince could have abducted Mary Jane and kept her in a secluded cabin near the Rock River—one of Mike's explanations for why she was found four days after Stanley was killed despite the vast, frenzied hunt. While there, Vince could have tried to coerce Mary Jane into keeping the romance alive, Jack said, or at least remaining quiet. She probably was firm in her rejection, which prompted Vince to kill her, Jack said.

Apart from having a motive, Vince instilled enough fear in the community to keep a lid on people's intentions to step forward, Jack deduced. Vince also was in a position to exert influence on the investigation.

"All of these things winnow away certain key players, okay?" Jack told me. "But the one who is always left standing is Vince."

He was convinced that if an investigator were to track down Vince's old farm and search a few posts where he shot target practice, he or she would find bullets that matched those pulled from the bodies. Remember, Jack noted, all but one of the shots to Stanley's body were in the groin. Doesn't that suggest a crime of passion?

Again, that wild set of events was plausible, but huge gaps existed, and closing those gaps seemed impossible. That quandary was ideal for two people suffering from our mutual disorder.

When our conversations turned to ghosts, spirits, and related topics, Jack was skeptical. I was intrigued and scared. Over time, Mike had told me of various psychics and mediums he'd brought to the Roadhouse or spoken to on the phone. One told him Mary Jane's skull was buried at the base of a pole in Vince Varco's backyard or beneath a flagpole in Jerry Brooks's yard. Another psychic said Mary Jane's skull had been tossed in the Rock River. One visited the basement of the Roadhouse, grabbed her neck, and said she felt as if her throat had been slit. That concept—Mary Jane or some other young woman being killed in the Roadhouse basement—seemed to be common among psychics. At one point, Mike held a séance that he videotaped from the balcony. A heart-shaped light appeared on the video, pulsing when Warren spoke at the séance.

Based on my talks with him, Mike was pretty certain these supernatural elements existed, and he dabbled in the spiritual hereafter; one might say he immersed himself waist-deep at times.

"The best way to describe this relationship," he once told me, "is you don't really have somebody talk to you. It's almost like you just feel their presence. You actually can carry on a conversation, but it's more through your thoughts."

The most unsettling conversation on the topic was one I had with Doug Oleson, who'd written a five-part series for a local paper on the fiftieth anniversary of the murders—the series Mike had read that set him on this course.

"This is a strange case," Doug told me over the phone. "This is a weird freakin' case. I saw something once that scared the hell out of me."

What he saw, he told me, came to him as he'd finished the series. He was at home and stepped in the shower.

"I just kind of glanced, and for one second, I swear I saw her," Doug said, meaning Mary Jane, "and I don't see things like that."

He said whatever he saw "was just a flash." He told me again that he's "not that way": he's not the kind of person who sees ghosts or experiences psychic phenomena. But he couldn't deny that he'd experienced something.

"God, I've never felt anything like that before," Doug said, "and I hope I never feel that way again."

I had my own difficulty reconciling all this talk of spirits. Apart from my chickenhearted avoidance of the topic, I wondered if Mike's sensitivity to Mary Jane's plight was so strong it created his belief without any actual proof that something weird was happening in the Roadhouse. I wondered if his empathy somehow had morphed into certainty, if his mind was playing tricks on him.

Was Mike delusional? I doubted it. He may have been a little eccentric, but he was many cerebral zip codes away from someone who, say, believes chickens speak Mandarin or signposts dance, or whose internal dialogues are louder than most everyone else's.

The other possibility, of course, was that everything Mike was saying about these spirits was true. Lots of people agree that Oregon has its ghosts.

As with other aspects of his life, though, Mike had an uncomfortable, inconsistent, and nuanced relationship with the realm of the otherworldly. He acknowledged the existence of spirits and that they represented a heartbreaking injustice he was trying to make right. At the same time, Mike clearly understood that many people, especially in a publicly conservative, small midwestern town, could perceive his acknowledgment as loony, even satanic. He didn't need to encourage those perceptions. So, he was guarded.

I'm guessing he also saw an economic opportunity in ghosts, a chance to draw customers. And he may have seen this as a moment to capture a slice of the limelight, which might be alluring to someone who produced and performed in community theater.

So maybe Mike was talking up spirits for personal gain, or maybe it was to draw attention to what he saw as an injustice. Maybe both. They aren't mutually exclusive.

Pondering all this could set my brain on spin cycle, which is why, in search of clearer understanding and personal growth, I accepted Mike's invitation to a séance.

On a crisp Saturday night under a crescent moon two days before Halloween, I drove out to the Roadhouse. I was creeped out enough to carry a Greek Orthodox icon in my breast pocket, right next to my pen.

I arrived to find six people sitting at a table in the main lounge and about the same number milling around the place. It was organized by Kathi Kresol, who told me she'd arranged paranormal events throughout the area. She got the idea for that night's event after stopping by the Roadhouse and hearing its history, including that involving Mary Jane.

"I was hooked," Kathi told me.

For this séance, she brought Ed Shanahan, who had a fairly prominent profile as a psychic and "spirit feeler" in the Chicago area. He's authored a couple books—*Taking the Paranormal and Spiritual World Seriously* and *My Letter to God*—been interviewed by various media outlets, offered private readings, and even worked as a spiritual and intuitive coach. Ed sported a gray goatee and was dressed in black shirt, sport coat, and pants. Attendees at the night's event paid $30 each to watch him and his team stir up ghosts.

I found Mike, also dressed in black, who told me he'd arranged the séance to get some answers. "There are certain characters that come with this place, like any place that's been around as long as this place," he told me. "The one that's most frustrating is Mary Jane Reed."

He was introduced to the group at the table. While the rest of us sat on bar stools a few feet away, behind a low dividing wall, Mike gave the backstory of Stanley and Mary Jane's date—even mentioning a shocking theory that after Stanley's murder, the killer or killers brought Mary Jane to the Roadhouse basement then raped and murdered her. Mike gave a brief personal bio, spoke about how he came to own the Roadhouse, and explained how he became involved in the case. He told the anecdote of a

mysterious young woman who visited three times while he was remodeling the restaurant right after he'd purchased it, saying the place reminded
her of what it had been in its glory days. She'd become rather annoying,
Mike said. After she walked out the door on her third visit, Mike told the
group, he followed her to see what car she drove. But when he got to the
lot, it was empty.

He shared other coincidences, some he'd told me: the jukebox spontaneously playing "After Sunrise," the letter he'd received from the Illinois
Environmental Protection Agency signed by a Mary Reed. Once, he said,
he was driving up to a vacation spot in Wisconsin and playfully invited
Mary Jane to come along. He noticed his cat was acting strange and took a
photo of it. The picture showed a shadowy blur next to the feline that may
have been an apparition of Mary Jane. People have told him the Roadhouse is haunted, Mike said, adding that bartenders have quit because they
sensed something eerie about the place. Waitresses have said they'd caught
glances of a woman walking around after closing.

"I'm still on the fence," Mike said, "but I'm leaning in one direction."

In my opinion, he'd hopped the fence.

Kathi asked Mike a few questions and while he answered, Ed snapped
a photo using a cell phone and then shared it. Next to Mike in the image
was something that looked like a human form.

"Holy crap," a woman sitting next to me said.

Ed had brought two "spirit feelers" and a couple more assistants who
were working with electronic devices, including a "ghost box," an AM/
FM scannable radio designed to pick up and lock on the voices of spirits.
Before the formal start of the séance, he walked through the Roadhouse,
calling to people on his team then calling to wake up the spirits. He started
with Vince.

"You know I don't like authority figures," Ed shouted, pacing around the
place. He said that Mike was investigating the case and then called out, "Is
that you, Ruth?"—a reference to Mary Jane's mother.

"Mary Jane . . . Is that you?" Ed said. "We've got a group here tonight
[to] see if we can raise somebody tonight, get some answers for Mike . . .
Stanley?" Ed called again. "Is that you?"

Nothing.

At 11:45, Ed rang a bell to call each member to the séance. Two more people joined the six already at the table in dim golden light near the center of the cleared-out lounge. Ed paced more. Mike set a drink on a table, lit a cigarette, and sat down. He said he was feeling agitated. Someone nearby said she was feeling cold.

"Definitely something going on in the room right now," Ed said. "I feel Ruth's presence. Ruth is the strong one . . . "

Ed asked the group at the table to read the séance invocation, which he said he'd pulled from a 1901 weekly newspaper, *The Spirit Speaks!*

> *There is a land where we all go,*
> *Hence neither the frost nor cold wind blow,*
> *And friends remembered reunite,*
> *And those who hate, forget their spite,*
> *In glow surround these gentle beings,*
> *We call you now to bless our meetings,*
> *Heaven's promise, our spirits thrive,*
> *So now for the living, let the dead come alive.*
> *Greetings spirits,*
> *Speak thee to us?*

With that, Ed blew out three candles in a candelabra on the table and asked that the séance attendees hold hands, take a deep breath, and tell themselves to open up.

"We feel you," Ed said to whatever spirits could be felt and were interested in floating forward. "We know you. We ask you to join the circle." He paused, then said, "To all you spirits, allow this to be your playground. This gathering is part of your remembrance. The one we're interested in is Mary Jane."

As he would for most of the séance, Ed resumed pacing around the lounge. He called out to one of his assistants, or it may have been to Kathi. I couldn't tell.

"Anything?"

"She's here," the person said. "She's kind of shy with this many people. She's afraid that the one who hurt her is here."

"Feel free to join us, Mary Jane," Ed said. "I feel your presence. Nothing to be afraid of. Nobody's going to hurt you. Mike, the owner of the place, is actually working to help you. He's willing to help you . . . Tony, anything?"

Tony, who stood nearby and looked as if he was trying to tune one of the gadgets to the right frequency, answered no.

"Mary Jane," Ed continued, "this world's looking for who killed you and . . . how it went down. Stanley was killed first. I get the impression that they were angry at Stanley for a few reasons . . . that he was the winner and that he had a young girl . . . "

I was scanning the room, looking for signs of ghosts and starting to feel a little tingly, when my stomach growled. I was afraid someone might think it was a spirit making itself known. I'm pretty sure it was a couple slices of frozen pizza making themselves known.

A member of Ed's team said Mary Jane's spirit was frustrated, that when she was alive, she couldn't get help. "It was a cover-up," another member said. Someone else said, "It's freezing in here," and Ed called out to Ruth with no discernible response. He moved to Mary Jane.

"Ain't that what happened, Mary Jane?" Ed asked. "You just came in here . . . "

Kathi, who apparently had tapped into some otherworldly wisdom, said Mary Jane felt that Stanley treated her differently, "that there was a future." And Ed followed that up by asking Ruth's ghost if she heard that Vince murdered Mary Jane.

"He was like the bully with the badge, wasn't he?" Ed asked.

Kathi said, "I think she feels angry at herself—Ruth does—not protecting her daughter."

It was now about 12:15, and Mike stood near the bar.

"Mary Jane," he said, "I'm going to make you a drink."

Which he did, setting it on the short wall separating the bar from the lounge and lighting two cigarettes—one for her, one for him.

Kathi said Mary Jane was too afraid to talk about what happened in the basement, and after the murders, Ruth feared others would come for Warren.

"Is that why they locked you up, Ruth?" Kathi asked. "To keep you quiet?"

I was trying to tune in to whatever might be out there, calling on whatever keen powers of observation I may have honed through years of being a professional observer of humankind, but I was coming up empty. No chills or breezes, no flashes or strange sounds. No Sergio Mendes & Brasil '77—or '78, for that matter.

Ruth had one other thing to say, Kathi mentioned.

"She says before you go, she wants to know why Mike doesn't talk to her as much anymore."

Mike didn't answer.

At this point, Ed decided to focus on Vince again. He invited Vince's ghost to join the party. It wasn't a friendly invitation.

"You were the bully in the neighborhood, with a badge and a gun . . . and Vince, instead of protecting the people, you were involved in it . . . some say you killed Stanley . . . you had a gun, badge, you could direct the investigation."

Kathi said Ruth wants Vince to attend, that she's not afraid of his badge.

"Come out, Vince," Mike suddenly called out. "You're a wuss. You're a big wuss."

Kathi said Vince is angry at Stanley, and Ed said Vince was jealous of Stanley.

"Was he more of a man than you?" Ed asked. "Was Stanley a better gambler than you, Vince? Stanley was a good-looking guy. You were just a bully of the neighborhood. The more I know of you, Vince, the less of a man you seem like. What, did Stanley stand up to you? You're not that powerful. I don't feel that here. Why am I feeling Stanley call you, Vince? He says that you were a blowhard."

I missed a few words in there, but I know I heard the word *jag off* emanate from Ed's lips in reference to Vince. I thought that would have brought out his ghost, but it didn't—at least not that I could tell.

Ed continued taunting Vince, repeating that Ruth was not afraid of Vince. Then Mike stepped in again.

"Vince," he called out, "you got a problem with me?"

This was the moment when I could feel my chest tighten and my eyes widen, the moment of The Confrontation between what I might consider Mary Jane's most passionate suitors. I fiddled around in my breast pocket for my mini-icon, pressing my thumb, forefinger, and middle finger on it.

"He says he doesn't have to worry about you because he got away with it," Kathi said.

"But Mike's digging deep," Ed said.

"I think he's afraid of you, Mike," Kathi said.

"What about Jerry Brooks, Vince?" Mike said. "Was Jerry Brooks with you?"

Kathi said Vince doesn't like Ed, who responded by saying that Vince was picked on as a kid.

"Vince wants to know if you have a daughter," Kathi said to Ed.

"Did you have a sister, Vince?" Ed called out to the semidarkness. "Did you mess with her, too? Momma's little boy. You were pretty stupid, too, in school."

Mike interjected, "Vince is going to be pissed with me tonight."

Ed was building on his momentum: "Your mom was probably an alcoholic, huh, Vince?" he said.

If spiritual entities were awakened, floating around and communicating, I was unable to sense it.

"Can you shift it back to Mary Jane?" Mike asked. "I feel like somebody's saying, 'You'll pay,' like Jimmy Hoffa in the death of Bobby Kennedy, and I'm feeling that Mary Jane might come forward, or Ruth."

Kathi shifted and said Ruth wanted Mike to know that she appreciates that Mike hasn't exploited Mary Jane and hasn't exploited this case.

But Mary Jane's spirit, wherever she was, stayed put.

And then, at 12:45, it was over. Apparently ghosts have deadlines, too.

The circle broke. Ed thanked everyone, and Mike turned on the lights. I stepped forward to talk with attendees. One young man said he didn't feel a thing. An older woman said she "felt really cold and had the shakes." She said she was sure something would have happened if Ed had kept badgering Vince's ghost. Another woman told me she could feel how angry Vince was. Others said they heard the voice of a young girl floating from a corner. Kathi hugged Ed.

It had been a long day and strange foray into the dark, and it was nearing 2 a.m. I still had almost two hours of driving ahead of me. Mike was busy chatting with people, escorting guests to their cars. I decided to head home.

I got in the car and sat for a moment, half expecting Mary Jane's ghost to materialize in the passenger's seat, like a genie appearing through a cloud of smoke. It didn't. For the first half hour or so of my drive, especially on the dark, deserted two-lanes, I was a little twitchy, throwing glances to the backseat, looking for her. She didn't show up there, either.

Which got me revisiting the bigger question of whether ghosts exist. I tend to believe they do, regardless of what had occurred—or hadn't— that night in the Roadhouse.

If you're a person who believes in a higher power, and I place myself in that category, it doesn't seem to be a big leap to believe that spirits, angels, ghosts, or whatever one chooses to call them float among us.

So what if Mary Jane had appeared in my passenger seat? For whatever reason—probably based on having attended a ghost party and come out of it intact and calm, even sleepy—I realized I wasn't afraid, which surprised and relieved me. Maybe I would have had the courage to ask her a few questions.

I guess it's like the old truism that walking straight into one's fears usually dissolves them. Of course, that evening's experience hadn't exactly been me confronting my fears one on one. It was more like I was in the studio audience of a TV show.

The stronger, more enduring conclusion I'd come away with is that some people are better tuned in to those spirits than I am—frankly, just about everyone seems to be—and that some people might not be tuned in at all, but they like to pretend they are for motives that aren't all that hard to figure out.

My trouble was determining which ones were which.

• • •

I SPOKE WITH MIKE again a few weeks later. He'd taken the séance in stride, accepting that some people felt what they felt; others, including him, did not feel much of anything. He said he thought the event might have been too cluttered with gadgetry and people to make the atmosphere welcoming to ghosts.

We drifted back to conversation about the mismatched skull, and I again expressed my shock and wonder. Mike mentioned something else that piqued the conspiracy theorist in me.

"Have you ever seen video of the autopsy?" Mike asked.

No, I said.

"Well, there's about a fifteen-minute gap in the audio that no one can explain."

"What do you mean?"

Mike said that while pathologists were working through the glop and bones of Mary Jane's remains in the examination room, they'd stopped and gotten into a discussion over something. That discussion escalated into a dispute, and then the audio cut out and remained silent for the rest of the examination and Mary Jane's reinterment.

"You're kidding," I said.

"Nope," Mike said. "I can send you a DVD copy if you want."

I wanted.

Memory and Silence

• • •

A FEW DAYS LATER, the DVD arrived in the office mail. I slid it in my computer. After some whirring and clicking, an icon appeared. I clicked my cursor on it and there it was, with its digital time stamp of 7:43 a.m. on August 23: the opening shot of an orange backhoe in a verdant cemetery bathed in bright morning light. The camera panned to Mary Jane's gravestone, then zoomed in on the engraved words: her name, years of birth and death, and the word *daughter.*

Digging started about fifteen minutes later, and a few minutes after that, the vault was exposed. The workers slid cables under it, and the backhoe lifted the container from the earth and set it on the ground. One of the workers swept off brown-gray caked-on dirt. The pale green screen that prevented people on the outside, including me at the time, from watching what was happening billowed in the summer wind.

I was riveted by the video. Something about being behind the screen and watching the exhumation felt closer to the truth, a truth that some people didn't want to get out. And that gave me a small, voyeuristic, energizing buzz. It satiated my curiosity—some might call it my obsession—for the time being.

At least eight people were watching the exhumation. A photographer was shooting pictures. Four guys wrapped the vault in a blue plastic tarp and secured it with duct tape. A few minutes later, a lift on a powder-blue truck hoisted the wrapped vault and placed it on the truck bed.

I moved the cursor to the control buttons at the bottom of the screen and saw that the video was almost four hours long, which meant I had more than three more hours of viewing. I didn't have three more hours—not at the office, where editors who'd gotten an update on the Mary Jane Reed story a few weeks earlier had little interest in the latest twist. They instead were expecting me to carry out the primary responsibility of a general assignment reporter: get them something different, now.

I'd in fact found something very different one morning. Story antennae up, begging the idea gods to drop something on me and trying not to think about that fifteen-minute audio gap in the autopsy exam, I stood in my bedroom, attempting to slip on socks while listening to the radio. I heard the last seconds of an interview with a gentleman who had a lilting southern drawl, a manner of speech I've always found hypnotic, especially because I'm immersed in Chicago's nasal-tinged whine. I sat on the bed.

The interviewee, Michael Verde, was talking about an endeavor he'd brought to some of Chicago's toughest public schools. Called Memory Bridge, it matched individual teenagers in the schools with elderly dementia patients at a nursing home. It was an effort to generate empathy and, by extension, peace in schools where kids entered through metal detectors, teachers struggled to control classrooms, and tension crackling below the surface routinely erupted into fights.

It sounded crazy. It sounded like a story.

One sock on, I walked to my notepad on the dresser and scratched out the words *Michael Verde/Memory Bridge*. When I got to the office, socks and shoes properly assembled, I used the modern miracle of Google, found contact information for Michael, called him, and set up a time to chat in his office a few weeks before the school year began.

I arrived at the second-floor space on Chicago's north side to find it mostly empty and dark, except for Michael and a young man named Philip Kendall, a music teacher at a city high school named Bowen Environmental Studies Team, or BEST. Michael was about to place Memory Bridge at BEST, and by doing so, give Memory Bridge its toughest test. It also was something of a last gasp for Memory Bridge in Chicago Public Schools.

One of Chicago's most violent, forlorn high schools, BEST was in a ravaged section of the city's South Chicago neighborhood. In the past year, five teenagers had been killed around the campus, an area that gangs had brought under siege. The most recent figures from Chicago Public Schools, which were sixteen months old, showed that 95 percent of BEST's students lived in poverty; 7 percent had passed state competency exams.

At one point in its five-year history, Memory Bridge had $250,000 in annual funding, mostly from the state. Overall, it had reached more than 100 Chicago Public Schools and more than 2,000 kids since its inception. Then the recession hit, funding dried up, and within months, the Memory Bridge staff of five, including Michael, was out of work. A final federal grant was carrying BEST's program.

My idea was to watch an entire semester of Memory Bridge unfold at BEST and write about it. I was able to persuade a skeptical editor that it was a worthwhile endeavor.

In his early forties, with wavy brown hair and intense hazel eyes, Michael was a charismatic, well-read, independent thinker with a deep, clear understanding of what he was trying to do. He could communicate it in very concrete terms. Philip, twenty-seven, resembled actor Daniel Day-Lewis's younger brother and seemed like the quintessential young idealist willing to get his hands dirty.

During a handful of breakfast conversations at an artsy hangout called the 3rd Coast Café & Wine Bar in Chicago's Gold Coast neighborhood, I learned more about Michael. A Texas native, he was raised in tiny Hamshire, about sixty miles east of Houston, where he played football and then enrolled at the University of Texas at Austin. That giant public university overwhelmed him and he left, embarking on a quest of self-discovery and a dream of becoming a writer. He moved to Paris—the one in France, not Texas or Illinois—and began reading eleven hours a day and meditating for one. That inward journey led him to return to Texas about a year later and make fifteen hours of audio recordings of his grandfather telling stories. When Grandpa Leonard later died from Alzheimer's complications, Michael played the tapes at a family gathering and found them to be revelatory.

"His self was in everybody in the room," Michael told me of his grandfather. "All of the love he had given to these people was in them. Alzheimer's wasn't getting to that."

Michael graduated from college, earned master's degrees in theology and literary studies, created curricula at a high school in Wisconsin, followed a girl to Boston, and ended up submitting a paper to the Smithsonian about folk practices as memory triggers. That paper included the bones of Memory Bridge. From there, Michael took a high school teaching job in suburban Chicago and started bringing students to a senior living center to engage with residents afflicted with dementia.

"The facility coordinator said she'd never seen anything like this before," Michael told me one morning at 3rd Coast. "See, the residents start to get love from these kids, and they just wake up. The cool thing is the kids got to see it in real time. It's goofy cool. I believed at that point. I just knew this would work for kids."

That led to a Memory Bridge pilot program at a junior high, and momentum built from there.

While Michael was reinterpreting fundamental societal roles and mores, Philip Kendall was growing up near Kokomo, in north central Indiana, on a farm that had been in his family for about two centuries.

The Mennonite faith and music were two dominant themes in his life. Philip's parents sang to him as a child and started him on piano lessons at seven years old. He took violin lessons and sang in his church choir. At Goshen College, a small liberal arts institution affiliated with the Mennonite Church and focused on peace, social justice, service, and prayer, Philip majored in music education. While at Goshen, he lost a grandmother—afflicted with dementia—to pulmonary complications and pneumonia.

He graduated and moved to Chicago in search of a teaching job. Eight months later, he was hired at BEST as a music teacher one week before classes started. Placed in a windowless classroom, given no instruments, no stereo, not even a chalkboard, Philip was overwhelmed. Textbooks were from the 1980s. Students were very unruly. It was an emotional battle to come to work every morning for at least two years. But Philip also was very committed to figuring it out.

In his fourth year of teaching when we met, Philip was no longer the scared young instructor, but he also hadn't sunk into the morass of cynicism.

"I think I'm finally beyond just surviving," he told me one late afternoon in his new classroom—one with windows and a piano. "Now, I just understand it much more."

He understood the bloated, byzantine Chicago Public Schools system and the role that poverty played in his students' lives. He knew that members of two rival gangs attended BEST but that most fights broke out over the pettiest things: someone's foot touching someone else's desk or a few poorly chosen words.

"All of a sudden there's this yelling match," he told me. "And once they cross that line, they're going to fight unless they're physically kept from fighting. It's that whole pride, earning respect thing, that if someone challenges you to fight, you have to carry it through."

Social standing in the school, Philip said, depended greatly on an individual's reputation for being someone you can't mess with. Sounded like prison to me.

And that led him to another topic during our conversation: all students at BEST suffered from constant anxiety.

"Someone getting shot down the street outside the school is not shocking at all," Philip said. "It's sad to them, maybe, a little bit, but it's just another day. It's just another shooting. Their thought isn't about who got shot but how they're going to get home, how they're going to avoid getting in the middle of it. It's crazy, just unfathomable."

I asked him what kept him at BEST, what could he possibly like about the experience. He said he was too emotionally invested, and he was deeply troubled by the notion that education is supposed to be where these kids can turn their lives around but BEST had become "a kind of holding place for the kids who can't." Higher-performing students were continuously leaving for other schools, he said.

"The system is messed up when the kids who can't be successful are all put into one place to not be successful together," Philip said. "Then it's our job to transform them and work miracles. It's ludicrous when you think about it."

He'd first heard of Memory Bridge a year earlier, when he'd seen a presentation on it at a conference and thought it might help his students. Philip reached out to Michael.

In creating BEST's first Memory Bridge program, the two men were applying one of the hottest concepts in education: social and emotional learning, defined by *Educational Leadership* magazine as "the process by which people develop the skills to recognize and manage emotions, form positive relationships, solve problems, become motivated to accomplish a goal, make reasonable decisions, and avoid risky behavior."

It was hot for a reason. The Collaborative for Academic, Social, and Emotional Learning (CASEL), based at University of Illinois at Chicago, had analyzed 213 social and emotional learning programs and found that they improved achievement scores by 11 percent. They also significantly enhanced social and emotional skills and decreased anxiety, depression, and misconduct.

"In other words," Michael said of BEST students, "the person they would need to be for that person with dementia to come out . . . those attitudes, aptitudes, and ways of communicating are also precisely the things that they would need here in BEST High School and in their homes to make those communities more habitable."

That's the symmetry of Memory Bridge's unique mission, Michael said. "This thing is not just about people with dementia. It's about what we're all forgetting. And what these people are not only remembering, but what they can teach us about being human."

Talking with Michael, I often told him over our breakfasts of oatmeal with blueberries and brown sugar, was a mind-stretching experience.

The timing of all this was prophetic. My mother—a vivacious, smart, accomplished, profoundly generous octogenarian, and the person who has been the strongest influence of love and integrity in the lives of many, including me—had begun to show signs of memory loss.

She'd gotten lost on her drive to church a couple of times, and then I heard from my wife and siblings that she was making other erratic driving decisions—spinning a U-turn in the middle of a busy street, driving way too fast, and getting lost to destinations other than church. She was misplacing her supplements and medications, and repeating herself more frequently—asking the same questions and retelling the same stories from her childhood. I denied anything was wrong. So did she, and she probably was hiding it, too. But what was happening was plain to my wife, sisters, brother, their spouses, and even my mother's siblings. We had to start making practical, sad choices.

• • •

A FEW WEEKS AFTER meeting in the vacant Memory Bridge office, I sat in Philip's classroom at BEST. He and Michael, both white, stood at the front. Staring back at them were ten black teenage faces and one Latina— Antonio, August, Dejah, Dominique, Ericka, Jacirby, Kayla, Natalia, Taylor, Tina, and Vance. Philip had recruited them for the class.

Memory Bridge was an after-school activity at BEST. On that warm, clear October Tuesday afternoon, classes were ending and the hulking, 100-year-old building was clearing out. At the metal detector inside the main entrance, a security guard shouted with boys who wanted to reenter school. Outside, five Chicago Police officers took positions around campus. Across the street, three young men clustered under the flashing blue police surveillance camera atop a light pole.

Michael opened the session by telling the kids that he believed they could create magic.

"And not the kind that makes people disappear," Michael said in his Texas drawl-twang. "I'm talking about the kind of magic that's just the opposite, the kind of magic that makes people appear."

He explained the difference between sympathy—"feeling for" somebody —and empathy—"feeling with" somebody. "That means you're getting into the same space with them," Michael told the students. "If you feel with someone, some very extraordinary things begin to happen."

He asked how many had heard of Alzheimer's disease. Five hands went up.

He explained that people with Alzheimer's have "confusion taking place in their brains but emotionally, they're just like you and I are." The difference, Michael said, is that "people start disappearing from their lives."

"But," he added, "when you get into their world, something in their world starts to come out. They start to respond to you in ways people around them think they cannot."

After Philip showed a video about Memory Bridge, Michael spent a half hour answering questions. Was it okay to correct their Alzheimer's buddies on facts? Was it okay to talk about Alzheimer's with their buddies? Are students going to have the same buddies every time? What should they do if their buddy becomes angry or violent?

"It's never happened and it won't," Michael said.

They finished the class with an exercise called "I-Lands." Gathered around a table, each kid received a large sheet of paper on which they drew symbols and pictures and wrote words that reminded them of who they are underneath it all.

"It's about capturing your memories, aspirations, your dreams, your fears," Michael told them. Like many classroom exercises, "I-Lands" was designed to strip away the layer of coarse street persona that is particularly thick in the kids.

Philip went first and talked about being "really overweight in high school," something he deflected attention from by trying "to be really good at other things" like academics and music. He pointed to a drawing of a mask to show "I want to figure you out before you figure out me." He said something about being "not always happy" and having "layers."

Antonio spoke next, his right knee bobbing, his voice shaky and soft. Hunched over the table, he pointed to sketches of a radio with a microphone and notepad with lyrics on it to convey that he likes to rap and write lyrics.

After him was Dejah, who pointed to a picture of a chicken wing and a park bench. She told an allegory of sorts about sitting on the bench in a white dress when a bird carried her off and dropped her in the mud, infuriating her mother.

Tina pointed to sketches of a Chicago Cubs logo and a bear and talked about sports being a religion in her home. She pointed to a boxing glove and said people think she's violent, which she rejected.

"I'm not that good with feelings," Tina added. Trust is another problem, she said.

Jacirby made a drawing of an infant in a crib and told of falling out of her crib at that age and of the scar on her eyelid that remained. The crib represented bars, she said; her mother was jailed when Jacirby was still in the crib.

Two weeks later, the group rode a school bus through the drizzle to Montgomery Place, an assisted living center in the teeming anthropological lab that is the Hyde Park neighborhood, home of the prestigious University of Chicago. The students were looking over two-page biographies of their buddies, complete with color photographs of them, that each had received a week earlier.

When they arrived at Montgomery Place, Natalia blurted out, "I'm scared." Antonio asked why they'd been chosen for this.

Michael stood. Raindrops popped on the bus roof.

"You're the future," he told them. "Specifically, Mr. Kendall thinks in you is the best of the future. You have something in you that this world is counting on."

If anybody else had made that statement in my hearing radius at any other moment, the cynic in me would have rolled his eyes and smirked. But Michael was a very smart guy, and I came to realize over the months I got to know him how much he'd put into building and honing this program. He knew what he was doing, and he was one sincere dude, fully consumed by sincerity.

The BEST crew spilled into the lobby. August said her heart was beating "really, really fast." They shushed each other in the elevator. One girl said she had a sister born in an elevator and that Montgomery Place reminded her of a Hyatt.

Silent and tentative, they entered the third-floor lounge. There, seated at tables, on couches, and in wheelchairs, were the buddies. The contrast was striking. Nearly all of them were white and frail. All of the students had the untamed, electric vivacity of youth, and all were black or Hispanic.

Students shook hands with their buddies then sat with them.

Tina was with Rupert, who had a perennial grin on his face. She recalled he spoke Spanish and asked if it was hard to learn.

"My parents went to the West Indies, and I had to learn Spanish," Rupert said. "I went to a Panamanian school. For me, the English part was easy."

He was chatty about not having much education beyond eighth grade in Central America. They talked about different dialects, about Rupert's graduation from the University of Panama, his job as an engineer with the city of Chicago. I detected the non sequiturs—he had to learn Spanish, was in a Panamanian school, but learning English was easy? He didn't have much education beyond the eighth grade yet graduated from university? But I didn't think Rupert was in an ideal mindset to clarify, and Tina had the wisdom to simply go with the flow.

"I built a whole lot of bridges," Rupert told Tina.

"That sounds cool," she replied.

Across the room, buddy Jean asked student Antonio where the kids were from.

"Bowen High School," Antonio answered. "On 89th Street. You know where 89th is?"

"No," Jean said. "But it doesn't matter."

Antonio asked if she had a lot of relatives, and Jean said she had enough. Then she handed him a piece of chocolate, which Antonio accepted but didn't eat.

"Afraid of the candy?" she asked. Jean laughed. Antonio did too.

In another area of the lounge, Vance and Taylor visited with William, a former teacher who used to play the violin and had traveled to the South Pole. Taylor asked if he had siblings, and William answered yes. When Taylor asked if he was close to them, William started to weep.

Students guessed the names of their buddies' children and talked about their buddies' favorite food. They'd ask a question, which often was answered incoherently or met with another question. Sometimes the residents were lucid and engaged. Other times, they rambled nonsensically, muttered incoherently, or became intensely agitated.

I was a little surprised at how sincere the students were, how unfazed they seemed during the odd, sweet exchanges, and how they embraced the silence when it came.

At 4:20 p.m., Michael closed the visit, asking each student to introduce his or her buddy to the group. That's when things hopped off the tracks.

"What grade am I in?" buddy Jean interrupted one student. "I'm in first grade. Ha, ha. Kindergarten."

"Is everyone here?" buddy Eva called. "Has the meeting been called to order?"

Somewhere in the room I heard an elderly woman sing loudly, "Boo boo bee doo."

On the bus ride back, the students laughed and goofed, saying they loved the experience and were surprised the older folks weren't grumpy. But the kids also weren't above poking fun at their buddies' memory lapses, their repetitive statements, their drool.

Over twelve weeks, the students made five trips to Montgomery Place, interspersed with classroom sessions aimed at processing the visits and stripping away the students' harsh exteriors.

At the same time, my three siblings and I were deciding whether to keep my mother in her condo and bring in a helper, to move her to one of our homes, to encourage her to live with her best friend and older sister—who already was staying with her at the condo a few nights a week—or to place her in a senior residential center. The sisters didn't want to live together. They wanted their independence. One thing was clear: my mother soon was going to have to surrender some of hers. We started interviewing helpers.

• • •

THE LATER Montgomery Place visits were as jumbled and unpredictable as the first. Students would be nauseated by their buddies' appearances or exasperated by their responses. Other encounters unfolded as if student and buddy were a couple of chatty neighbors.

Music helped, as it did when, gathered in a loose circle with Philip at the piano one afternoon, the BEST students and buddies sang "You Are My Sunshine," "Amazing Grace," "He's Got the Whole World in His Hands," and "Hava Nagila."

They were awful, thoroughly unpolished, out of sync, and clueless about some of the lyrics. The BEST soloist, Kayla, was hoarse.

But everybody smiled and sang along—some clapping, some waving their hands in the air.

After, the students and buddies returned to one-on-one visits. The mood was electric, if not altogether coherent.

Two weeks later, the students brought drums, and a music therapist coordinated activities. One buddy refused to leave his room and covered himself in a blanket. Another woman called the session stupid and walked out. A third buddy kept trying to escape to have dinner with her husband, who had died years earlier.

But those who remained provided a beat for student Vance, who danced, spinning and pop-locking. The teens laughed, shaking their heads. The buddies beamed.

Later, in BEST's lobby, Vance said he was shocked by his buddy Seymour's enthusiasm. I asked if Vance felt that he'd gotten anything from Memory Bridge.

"Yeah, I feel like I got to entertain, which is what I wanted to do," he said. "Basically, make them laugh, making them feel good. It made me feel good too, you know, like I accomplished something.

"I think I have more patience now," he told me, "as far as dealing with them and getting them to open up."

Less than halfway through the term, two homicides had occurred within a week of each other near BEST's campus; one victim was a sixteen-year-old boy walking home from the school. At Montgomery Place, William, the former teacher who had wept at the mention of his siblings, died. Three students had stopped coming to Memory Bridge. Michael worried that the experiment was failing.

On a bone-chilling, dark January afternoon, students made their final visit to Memory Bridge. They brought yellow roses to their buddies. The buddies gave their students personalized bracelets with letters spelling out the name of the student and that of his or her buddy. Montgomery Place staff had baked a cake. "Thank You Memory Bridge" was scripted in white icing.

In the lounge, Eva, so agitated two weeks earlier that she wanted to leave in the middle of a visit, asked August to come to her room and place the rose in a pitcher. A little later, Eva tapped one of her manicured red fingernails on her cheek and directed August to "give me a kiss right here." August grinned and complied.

Tina told Rupert she wanted to be a lawyer.

"My brother's a lawyer," Rupert said. "How often do you come here, about once a year?"

"Yeah," Tina said, "just about."

Sitting together near a counter, Vance noticed a ring on his buddy Seymour's finger.

"It was my wife's," Seymour said. "She gave it to me right before she died. She said wear it for her. I wear it for her."

When Michael gathered the group to sing, Vance, who'd joked a few weeks earlier about slapping a mouthy senior, helped Seymour to his seat. During the singing of "Amazing Grace," Vance took a solo, but his voice was shaky. Seymour bowed his head close and the two sang a lovely, imperfect harmony. Vance's voice gained strength.

Minutes later, the kids said good-bye and tumbled out of the lounge. An eerie, lonely silence flowed into the room behind them.

"They're a great bunch," Eva said, beaming in her wheelchair. "A great bunch."

A resident assistant rolled her past the cake. One word of icing remained: Memory.

• • •

I'D LIKE TO SAY THAT Memory Bridge brought sweeping change to BEST, but it didn't. Far too many factors were working against that.

But I did see compelling flashes. It was uncanny how the Alzheimer buddies sprang to life when those kids entered the room and stayed that way until their young friends departed, when a catatonic state seemed to lower like a blanket over the old folks. As for the teenagers, anyone could see the impact—brief or otherwise. It was so startling, in fact, that the kids were unsure what was happening and how to describe it. But after the final visit, they all conveyed the same things: they loved the interactions and they found them sublimely fulfilling. Goofy cool, as Michael put it.

Philip told me he got to know the kids and the kids got to know each other better after a couple weeks of Memory Bridge than they had in entire semesters or years.

"So many of our students couldn't tell you one thing that they're good at or one thing that they feel good about that they've done in school their whole lives—or it would be a very short list," Philip told me. "The fact that they can give of themselves in such a basic way is pretty significant, and it doesn't take intelligence or an outgoing personality. It just takes the ability to sort of relax."

Montgomery Place staff noticed the impact, too.

"I call it taking them from a state of ill-being to a state of well-being," program director Rebecca Reif said of her geriatric charges one afternoon while we watched them interact with the teens. "It's a beautiful circle of knowledge, emotion, and life force." The visits, she said, were "better than any pill."

Several of the kids said they wanted to return to visit their buddies, and a few did come back when Philip brought a chorus there a few weeks later. He planned another installment of Memory Bridge, if he could find funding, and kids who participated in the first version wanted to sign up again.

Then it evaporated.

Michael's work caught the attention of a professor at Indiana University who wooed Michael to pursue a PhD in empathetic education there. He managed to keep Memory Bridge alive as something of a one-man traveling show.

Philip took a job at a different high school, one that still struggled with poverty but had a little more administrative and community support than BEST.

I walked away from BEST and Memory Bridge feeling a little heartbroken and a little hopeful. Something about the class sparkled with promise and rang true, even to me, a skeptical pragmatist. I couldn't help being moved by Michael's and Philip's willingness and persistence in trying something so startling, so laughably different, because they believed it works.

What they and the Memory Bridge participants were doing on a higher level, I think, was redefining and repurposing memory, personal history, and identity. All of those components were transformed when these raw teens surrounded by violence, poverty, and hopelessness merely sat attentively with fragile, addled seniors in the fading glow of their lives. These kids, who some might disregard in the same way Mary Jane was disregarded, restored lives darkened by the loss of self, and their elders presented a new future to the young people.

It showed mortality in unvarnished, slightly frightening ways *and* showed our power to better navigate all that sorrow and fear with simple, authentic, humane presence. It was sad and beautiful, unsettling and reassuring.

• • •

WE DECIDED to place my mom in a retirement community ten minutes from my brother and me. She resisted. We asked her to visit for two weeks to see how it felt. Lucky for us, she liked it and ended up moving to a top-floor unit with a surprisingly engaging view of sunsets over flat suburbia.

The socialization—hundreds of people in more or less similar life stages whom she could hang with—made an enormous difference for her. The days were filled with activities that included lectures, dancing, workouts, field trips, card games, and arts and crafts. The place served three hearty meals a day in a clean, elegant dining room, and we set up a schedule in which one of us kids visited her every day. Many weekends we took her out.

. . .

IN THE MONTHS and years after Memory Bridge left BEST, I found myself recalling something Michael said at one of our 3rd Coast oatmeal breakfasts.

"This cultural move to prevent memory loss is very admirable in one scientific way. But it's also missing the point: that the point of living is not to keep living longer so you can keep living longer. The point of living at all would be to be with people in emotionally meaningful ways, to have a kind of communing, an intimacy. So one way you can fight Alzheimer's is by taking the actual time that you have to go and put yourself into things that are going to survive forever, like other people."

He leaned across the table and lowered his voice.

"You want to save yourself? Give it away, 'cause our bodies are disappearing."

I've wondered what would happen if an entire struggling high school or several schools like BEST adopted Memory Bridge for a few years. Maybe it would surprise people, even the skeptical pragmatists and cynics among us.

But the most powerful notion that stays with me is a mix of melancholy and ludicrous optimism.

I can't help thinking that these two discarded groups of people—teens from violent neighborhoods in distress and old folks who seem to have lost their identity and their minds—can rescue each other.

. . .

AS CONSUMED AS I was by Memory Bridge—and it may be obvious at this point that I was fairly consumed—the ghosts of the Reed-Skridla case continued hovering in the spaces of my mind, always. One Saturday morning they woke me before dawn, and I walked down to my cold basement, fished out the exhumation DVD Mike had sent weeks earlier, and slid it in my laptop. While it whirred into position, I pulled out a notebook and pen.

Again, I saw the opening shots of the orange backhoe, Mary Jane's gravestone, men standing around watching other men dig, the vault, wrapped in a blue tarp and duct tape, being placed on the back of the powder-blue truck.

The next scene was in an expansive county garage where the vault had been placed on the ground and opened, revealing the casket, which then was opened. More photos were taken. Two people lifted a tattered black body bag from the casket and placed it on a table. I could see people covering their noses. Warren approached with two people who looked like his adult son and daughter. He peered into the casket. I could see people holding roses. Ogle County sheriff's police looked on as an official-looking man in a white shirt snapped pictures. Ogle County State's Attorney Ben Roe watched while talking on a cell phone.

The body bag was opened, and the camera panned the brown remains. They looked remarkably well preserved. I could make out the tops of the legs, the hips, and a concave rib cage. For the first time, I saw the skull with its top shaved off, placed at the body's left shoulder. Someone pulled a newspaper and what appeared to be a balled-up dress from the casket. The newspaper, a June 25, 1948, edition of the local *Dixon Evening Telegraph*, featured a top headline about a highway in Ogle County. The balled-up clothes included what looked like a slip. The items were placed on the table.

The old body bag was slid into a new, white version, and that was placed in another white bag.

The video cut to an examination room, and the first sound, which was very clear, was the unzipping of the bags.

"Do I need some calcium on this?" a woman in scrubs asked. "I need the exhaust," she added quickly, "as much as you got." The exhaust fan was activated and filled the room with white noise, but at a volume that left enough space to hear voices. Still, I could hear only shreds of sentences, a word or two.

A man said, "What they normally do is . . . cotton." I saw more flashes from cameras and thought I heard someone say the skull "is a lot farther along than the rest of the body," but I couldn't be sure.

" . . . trauma to the head . . . focus on that . . . we just had one a few weeks ago."

By this time, two people wearing blue plastic gloves had peeled away the two white bags and opened the original body bag. One of the people examining the body pulled something gooey from an area on the right upper thigh while the other examiner pointed with tweezers at two spots on the left side of the body. An investigator shot photos. The examiners removed more material from the body's right side and placed it on a paper towel to be photographed. An examiner removed a ring—I remembered that Mary Jane was buried with her mother's wedding ring—and continued working on the body. For the first time, I saw Mike, on the left side of the frame, dressed in jeans, cowboy boots, and a white collared, rumpled short-sleeve shirt. He was wearing glasses and peering intently at the examiner.

I was a little queasy. An examiner moved to the right side and rooted around in more goo, which made me queasier. I felt an ache budding on the right side of my head. I took a sip of water from the glass I'd brought with me. The examiner used longer tweezers to remove solid pieces of the body about the shape of bite-sized Tootsie Rolls. A photographer took a few shots, and the examiner began to root around in there with his fingers, then wiped goo off them. He reached and plucked what appeared to be pubic hair, then swabbed with cotton on a stick a body cavity that I'd rather not think about.

My stomach regretted the decision to take a sip of water. An examiner used scissors to snip and pull away clothing. The female examiner grimaced while lifting the body to turn it from its right side onto its left. I couldn't hear much but the slow churn in my stomach and the slightest throbbing in my head. I kept watching, jotting in my notebook.

The body oozed something, and the examiners needed more paper towels. They pulled off cottony material that reminded me of wall insulation, then removed the skull in two pieces. The male examiner took both to a table and then returned and extracted the lower jaw from the muck. He rooted around more, and I couldn't stop watching, but my stomach and head needed a break. I hit the pause button and pulled away, rubbed my eyes, walked from the basement. I was hungry but wasn't about to eat a thing. Even taking a drink of water was out of the question.

When I came back a few minutes later and hit "play," I saw Mike holding a Bible. Someone handed him a small plastic bag containing what looked like the ring. The two examiners continued digging through the upper half of the body, slicing away cloth and unidentifiable material to get at the backbone area. I didn't know how much more of this I could take, but my curiosity pushed me.

I heard someone say, "There's a three-ring binder over here." At least three people left the room. Someone said, "Thanks, Dwayne." The rooting around continued. Someone reentered the room, and I heard, "You forget something?"

I'd been watching for nearly three hours when I saw the first gap, this one only a few seconds of blue screen—I'll chalk it up to technical difficulties—before the video feed resumed to show the female examiner slicing open the chest. She poked and grabbed and pulled and sliced, creating a wider opening, pulling back the ribs, or at least that's what it looked like through the fog of a headache and nausea that were taking hold in my mind and body. I heard somebody say, "Are you serious?"

Lots of talk was going on, in fact. "Investigative side . . . shit yeah . . . we're here . . . I subscribe to it . . . now my son's starting . . . freshmen . . . "

It sounded like they were talking about high school sports, but it was hard to be sure. Whatever the subject, it was like they were standing around engaging in the common bullshit that colleagues offer while waiting for the staff meeting to start. The difference was that a couple of people were in front of them slicing, pulling, prodding, and rooting around in a brown mass that was a human body buried more than a half century earlier. I hit "pause" and took another break.

When I resumed watching, someone in the room said "parquet floor . . . beautiful . . . I don't see how . . . X-rays are going to show." I heard, "Rochelle High School . . . you guys 4A or 5A?" an apparent reference to the school's sports classification. One of the examiners removed a bone that looked like a femur, and somebody said, "Tougher team." I heard the phrase "offensive line," so yeah, they seemed to be talking about high school football.

About three hours and eighteen minutes into the video, someone called out, "Rich?" I heard the words "muscles" and "pretty decomposed . . . makeup of the body . . . that's a question." The examiners stopped working on the body. "I've been at your side the whole time," somebody said. "Joel. Hey Joel? Got a question . . . I didn't see . . . " I heard a word that sounded like "Jesus," then the words continued to pop up amid the exhaust fan noise: " . . . fracture . . . scenario . . . I didn't see an exit wound . . . I'm not 100 percent convinced that that's . . . " A woman said, "I didn't see any either . . . " I heard the words "external . . . and what better way," and then two utterances caught my ear and made me hit the pause button.

"There are some abnormalities in there . . . I want that redemption."

I rewound it a couple seconds and played it again. I jotted notes, stopped the video, and replayed it one more time to be sure I heard what I thought I'd heard.

With all the errant snippets of words I was catching, it was tough to discern what anything meant, but "I want that redemption" sounded like somebody with an agenda, somebody pushing for a certain result. I wasn't sure who said it because many of the voices were floating from outside the camera frame, which was trained on the examining table for the most part but also included a few feet of a counter.

On that counter, I could see two or three people examining the skull. One of them asked, "Who is going to get a picture?" Someone said, "They've just finished cleaning the skull." A man poked at the shell. One man said, "On the other side, there are some bones broken around the inside of the head . . . through the neck, from the back. That would do it."

They got another close-up of the skull and somebody noted, "This beveled area here, all right."

Another man responded, "All right, what are you concerned with now?"

A man in a blue shirt pointed with a scissor-like instrument and said, "This appears to be some kind of defect right there." Another photo was taken. Somebody called for a ruler.

Then I heard this: "You don't want to, trust me . . . " and "I've never seen anything like this . . . the family, they were basically, and I told them . . . that in order for me to write a report . . . saying, well, if I'm going to write a report, I need . . . That's kind of . . . I like to . . . "

I couldn't make out if the same person was saying all that, but I'm not sure it mattered. I won't pretend to know my autopsy conversational etiquette, but it sounded like a few gents were having a fairly intense discussion, gents who looked like investigators. But I couldn't make out much of what they were saying.

Mike later told me he was in the room at the time but the conversation had just started to heat up when Warren, who was not in the room, came in and asked Mike to talk in the hall.

Then, at three hours, twenty-nine minutes, and fifty-six seconds, the sound cut out. As Mike said, the remaining twenty-seven minutes of video are silent: a troubling gap.

I didn't see anything shocking in that time, but it's certainly curious at the least. For reasons I can't fully explain, those twenty-seven minutes were more poignant than anything else. At one point, no one was present in the frame for about three minutes; eventually, an investigator picked up the skull from the counter and carried it off screen.

A few minutes later, the picture cuts abruptly to a couple guys rolling a gurney through the garage. On it was the white body bag containing Mary Jane's remains. They hoisted the bag into a casket on a wheeled cart. Warren, accompanied by people I thought were his two daughters and a son—they'd been by Warren's side much of this day—stepped next to the casket, placed a Bible inside, stepped toward Mike, and shook his hand. Mike was clearly shaken, walking and staring at the casket as it was wheeled out of the garage.

The scene cut again, this time to the same garage where the vault was opened originally. The casket had been placed in a new vault. Mike and Warren took photos. Then the scene cut to the cemetery, this time bathed in softer afternoon light. A truck backed up to the grave, where a crane lowered the vault into the ground. Two sheriff's officers and two guys in suits watched. The camera panned the site and took in a total of eleven men and two women who watched. Warren shot another photo. Mike gestured with his hands, talking to the women I thought were Warren's daughters while the young man I presumed was Warren's son stood nearby. Mike took a deep breath. The camera panned back to the grave, providing a close-up of the nameplate on the vault. The backhoe scooped brown dirt on the nameplate and the vault. In a few seconds, it was covered completely and the screen went blue.

I looked at the clock. It was near noon—much later than I'd thought. The nausea had passed, but the headache lingered, as did fatigue. Noon on a Saturday when you're a father of three little kids and a husband places you about four precious hours behind schedule. Bathrooms needed cleaning. A lawn needed cutting. Somewhere, children needed feeding and clothing. I pulled the DVD from its cradle, slid it back into its plastic case, and hustled upstairs.

It's tough to say the exact moment when the mystery of this case prompted me to do what I would do months later, but watching nearly four hours of video after observing this entire ordeal unfold for more than a decade might have been that moment. I needed to do something that, at the very least, would make this case leave me alone.

13

Our Shared History, Revised

• • •

MIKE, OF COURSE, was highly suspicious and cynical about the audio gap in the autopsy video.

He started working with a sound expert to try to clear the exhaust fan noise and isolate whatever was being said in the minutes leading up to the silence. He also prepared a four-page report, ostensibly for use in court or in some investigative capacity.

His conclusion was that, while making copies of the video, somebody dubbed out portions of the audio at the exact moment investigators in the examination room were speculating about Mary Jane's murder.

The report also included a time line analysis in which Mike broke down what happens at different points on the video, an analysis that includes a couple of intriguing tidbits that I hadn't heard in my review. First, Mike noted that while he was standing in the examination room, the cameraman said, "Just so everyone is aware, I cannot shut the audio off on this camera. I want to inform everyone in the room of that. You may want to be careful of what you say."

Second are slight differences between what I heard and what he heard. For example, where I heard, "All right, what are you concerned with now?" Mike heard, "Are you concerned with them?" But those differences seem insignificant. The core issue is the gap of silence. Neither one of us heard the complete discussion in the seconds before the sound cuts out, but it's clear that it comes at a key moment and that timing makes it very fishy.

Mike's soundman never could clear the exhaust fan noise. His calls for help from the FBI, Department of Justice, Illinois U.S. senator Dick Durbin, and the Vidocq Society also went nowhere, primarily because each of them wanted another law enforcement agency—usually a local one—to get involved and ask for help.

"It's not all bad," Mike told me after the U.S. Attorney declined to get involved until the FBI requested it. "I'm not at all that beaten up about it, to tell you the truth. I just got in it to keep the rope taut."

Instead, he had reason for hope. It stemmed from a meeting two weeks earlier, when he'd spoken with two sheriff's deputies and a representative from the coroner's office. Mike told them Warren was getting ready to sue, and they apparently suggested that the Illinois State Police was largely responsible for Warren's grievances. Mike, in a conciliatory mood, expressed sympathy for their position. In his words, the three men "bonded."

He'd reached out again to another FBI investigator, who, after reviewing Mike's website on the case, said in an email that it "seems like quite an interesting case." Mike's intention was to tap the agency's sophisticated forensic techniques and technologies to try to reconstruct a face from the skull and get DNA tests done on the skull—among other analyses—to determine for sure if it was a match with Mary Jane's body. Once his relationship was established with the bureau, who knew what revelations it might produce? Mike called himself "a liaison with the FBI," which I thought was an eloquent, extravagant turn of phrase. And, in fact, emails Mike shared with me show the FBI investigator setting up a meeting, telling Mike what to bring, giving directions to the Quantico facility, and discussing procedures.

I was amped to hear the results, I told Mike. But it never got to that.

After gassing up his truck on a Friday then packing his bags, Mike was planning to hit the road Monday morning for a Wednesday arrival in Quantico. Then he got an email from the investigator calling off the testing.

"Given concerns over loss of chain of custody," the investigator wrote, "we will not be able to do the facial reproduction."

It turns out that on Friday, the FBI guy had been in contact with an Ogle County deputy sheriff who apparently conveyed that county investigators no longer had possession of the key evidence—Mike did—and that meant the official evidence chain had been broken. County law enforcement couldn't verify that whatever Mike was taking to Quantico was the material pulled from Mary Jane's body. Mike was screwed again and fairly pissed.

"I don't think they [the sheriff's office] thought I was really going to go," he told me, "and then they were like, 'Holy shit, this guy's actually going. What the hell are we going to do now?'"

A few months later, he got smacked down again, this time in court after again trying to persuade a judge in a neighboring county to consider his suit claiming misconduct on the part of Ogle County officials.

That smackdown was notable for one other reason: it was the only time I heard from Vince Varco's son, William, the sole surviving immediate family member I'd been able to find.

Before filing stories on the case, I'd placed a call to William. He hadn't responded until now, when I had called to ask if he had anything to say about Mike's latest court rejection. William left a voicemail message at night on my cubicle phone.

"Hello, Ted," he said in a surprisingly cheery tone when I picked up the message the next morning. He cleared his throat. "William Varco. You left me a message. I'm returning your call. If this is a story about uh, I know that brother Arians and uh"—another throat clearing—"and the girl's brother, they've had an attempt going on here for quite a few years to hang my dad thirty years after he died. So if your part in this is to help them guys out, then you and I have nothing to talk about. All right? Thank you."

The phone went dead. I called back, got no answer, and left another voicemail message.

It was looking like Mike's last hope was exhuming Stanley's body, and that seemed like a very uncertain prospect. Mike told me he'd been in touch with what remained of Stanley's family—the two nephews and the frail and senile sister. They all had mixed feelings about digging up Stanley's body. Mike sounded agitated, but mostly fatigued and disillusioned, near defeat.

I couldn't help feeling for the guy, even if I doubted or outright disagreed with elements of his theories. I could relate to the case's capacity to bring on fatigue but also its capacity to hang on one's conscience, to make it impossible to shake free.

I started thinking about ways I could get back out to Oregon, maybe find another story in that neck of the woods that would allow me to stop in Oregon and poke around a little, talk to some people. I began story poaching—browsing online through small-town papers' websites, hoping to take a journalism whisk to an underreported story and create a *Tribune* soufflé.

I couldn't find anything around Oregon, but something elsewhere caught my attention, in Bureau County, about sixty miles directly south of Oregon and 100 miles southwest of Chicago.

Sleepy and pastoral by most standards, Bureau County has a rich, largely unknown history. A central figure in that history is renowned, fiery abolitionist and U.S. congressman Owen Lovejoy, an instrumental force in forming the Republican Party and Abraham Lincoln's best friend in Congress.

A Congregationalist Church minister, Owen used his house, now a historic national landmark, as one of the busiest stops on the Underground Railroad, and he was defiant when that was an extremely perilous stance. Reverend Lovejoy knew that danger firsthand. In 1837, a pro-slavery mob in Alton, Illinois, shot to death his brother Elijah, another firm abolitionist who also happened to be a journalist. Elijah's death bestowed upon him martyr status, drew waves of people to the anti-slavery cause, and made Reverend Lovejoy that much more committed to freeing slaves.

So committed, in fact, that the reverend, apart from the ripple effect he had as a lawmaker, personally helped hundreds of slaves find freedom. He even advertised his home as part of the Underground Railroad in an anti-slavery newspaper, *Western Citizen*, and gave a now-famous speech to Congress in 1859. He made his position very clear, in case any doubt existed.

"Let it echo through all the arches of heaven, and reverberate and bellow along all the deep gorges of hell, where slave catchers will be very likely to hear it," the reverent congressman proclaimed. "Owen Lovejoy lives at Princeton, Illinois three quarters of a mile east of the village, and he aids every fugitive that comes to his door and asks it. I bid you defiance in the name of my God."[1]

Stirring stuff, especially when I learned, about 155 years later, what was happening with a meandering, narrow creek a few miles from the Lovejoy homestead. It drifts for eleven miles through Bureau County's farms and small towns, and it carries an uncomfortable legacy, its name: Negro Creek.

Somebody in Bureau County thought that name needed to change, and that's what made the story poacher in me grin.

That somebody was Phillip Mol, a Navy veteran born and raised in California who had moved with his wife to a spot near the stream about two years earlier. After reading in the *Peoria Journal-Star* and *Bureau County Republican* about his effort—it's not news until the *Chicago Tribune* says it's news, dammit!—I gave him a call.

Phillip, an aerial surveyor who called himself a liberal Christian, told me the creek's dubious name was an awkward enough discovery for him and his wife when they arrived in the area. But what really got him agitated was hearing a few people utter the slang epithet for the stream: Nigger Creek. After praying about it for six months, Phillip decided to mount a campaign to change the name. It didn't go exactly as he'd planned.

He created a Facebook page, "Let's rename Negro Creek," that drew at one point around 150 members. Six weeks later, somebody else created "Leave Negro Creek Alone" on Facebook. A total of 358 members joined. As is the case with many social media "discussions," people began posting personal attacks on Facebook. Each side held gatherings to stoke their efforts. Tensions were running high, and emotions were fairly raw. Phillip even told me he'd started to think authorities were watching him.

Ding went the story bell in my head. I had me a field trip, distracting me temporarily—again—from the saga of Mike, Warren, Mary Jane, and Stanley. My editor gave me clearance to make a quick one-day drive down to and back from Bureau County, where I expected to find a story that pointed out how gnarled and agitated the community had become, how a public debate on race once again had brought out the worst in people.

But the news business continues to surprise me, and not always in disappointing ways that fuel despair for humankind. The surprise in Bureau County was that all the early agitation morphed into something different, something reassuring. This little overlooked county was giving the rest of the world a lesson on civility.

Instead of fist-shaking, invective-spitting demonstrators squaring off in a toxic exercise in community destruction—or worse—people participated in a healthy, calm discussion on race. They gained a renewed appreciation for Bureau County's important and not-so-important history. Both sides even reached something of an agreement.

I don't want to imply that people debating the issue were ready to hug it out. Their opposing positions were firm and passionate, and the social media debate at times got snippy. It had the potential to drive a wedge of hatred through the heart of the area that would last for years. That didn't happen. The overall restraint was fairly remarkable.

From where Phillip sat, the issue was simple.

"This is just about us being nice," he told me in our phone conversation. *Negro* is at best an outdated word, but more accurately, an offensive one, Phillip said, adding that the time for change was long overdue. "It's the decent thing to do."

His alternative name was Love Creek, the last name of a sizable black family who came to Bureau County as slaves in the 1830s and settled on forty acres near the creek. Phillip also liked the symbolism of changing the divisive name into perhaps the most unifying name in the English language.

His save-Negro-Creek-counterpart was Chad Errio, a trustee and volunteer firefighter in the tiny town of Seatonville, and a part-time stand-up comic. Chad characterized the renaming effort as "political correctness run amok."

While we sat in his living room a few steps from the creek one afternoon, he told me that very few people invoke the uglier slur for the creek and that local blacks he spoke with didn't object to the *Negro* part of *Negro Creek*. Besides, he noted, organizations such as the Negro League Baseball Players Association, United Negro College Fund, and the National Council of Negro Women are accepted by everyone, including African Americans.

And, by the way, Chad said, removing *Negro* from the creek's name wipes away about 200 years of history.

"It doesn't change the good things or the bad things that have happened," he said. "It's part of our history. You want to give credit and educate people. Telling our kids about the past makes a lot more sense than trying to change the name."

Which is why as an alternative to Phillip's plan, Chad proposed the idea of erecting a historical marker at the creek explaining the name and history.

As civilized as the debate had become, it hadn't unfolded organically. Phillip and Chad monitored Facebook traffic on their respective pages. When they saw postings that started the discussion down a repugnant path, they pulled them. Both men also attended the other's group meetings.

But it may have been local historian Sarah Cooper who turned Negro Creek into a stream of conscience, who saw the debate as an opportunity for history to bring both sides together. In a letter to the editor of the *Bureau County Republican*, Sarah noted that black history in the county dates as far back as white history and that "ultimately, it's about honoring everyone's history."

While we sat in the dining room of her spacious home, Satch, her friendly mutt-hound with a mysteriously curly tail, kept trying to hop in my lap. Sarah finally brought him under control and told me about the origin of the creek's name.

It appears to trace back to an African American man, identified only as "Adams" in historical records, who settled near the creek in 1829. Earliest references to the name started appearing in the 1840s, and at least one historical document I found on Seatonville suggests that people commonly referred to the brook as Nigger Creek in the 1870s.

She also told me more about Bureau County's African American history: twenty-four blacks had come there during the Civil War and enlisted in the Union army, and the county's African Methodist Episcopal Church was supported in part by proceeds from gigs played by the Colored Cornet Band.

We spoke of Bureau County's ugliest moment, a bloody race riot in 1895 in Spring Valley, four miles east of the creek. European immigrant coal miners who'd gone on strike attacked African American strikebreakers and their families. Sounded familiar. But, unlike the attacks on miners in "Bloody Williamson" County three decades later, the Bureau County assault yielded convictions of seven or eight immigrants (accounts differ). All were sent to prison.

After the uprising, blacks remained in Spring Valley, and in a development that might sound shocking, they bonded with more than two dozen different ethnic groups that also worked in the mines. To me, that tolerance suggested something about how, when placed in similar circumstances, we're really not all that different from each other, despite the color of our skin or the nations of our ancestors. It also gave me insight into why Bureau County was dealing admirably with the tempest over the creek name.

Sarah might have worded it best in her letter to the editor.

"What we can document, then," she wrote, "is that African-Americans who once called Bureau County home were pioneers, farmers, miners, soldiers, church-goers and musicians. They worked hard, served their country (in the Civil War, World War I, and World War II), raised families, built a church and gave concerts to support their community. Some lived here for generations. Descendants of Bureau County's black Civil War soldiers were still living in Princeton into the 1970s. And many are buried here in Princeton's Oakland Cemetery."[2]

She wasn't convinced that Phillip's effort to change the creek's name would prevent people from using the N-word when referring to it. She was more optimistic that a discussion about history—one that helped all sides understand the others' stories and their shared story—might be more successful in making the word disappear altogether from the lips of the good people of Bureau County.

"One can only hope," Sarah said, "that at the very least, because of the dialogue about Negro Creek, instead of letting a racist comment whiz by us in casual conversation—at the gas station or coffee shop or tavern—we will not remain silent."

Apart from the discussion the name-change controversy created, it also brought greater awareness of Bureau County's overall history. Chad told me that in recent weeks residents had given him vintage photos of a fire truck and squad cars dating back to the 1920s. He received a Seatonville State Bank check from the early 1900s and a 1936 article clipped from a local newspaper.

"People are dropping off stuff like that all the time," he said while we sat in his living room. So much stuff, in fact, that he was planning to decorate Seatonville's village hall with the memorabilia that people had handed him since the Negro Creek debate began.

"I think it's really brought the community closer," Chad told me.

"Darn right," Phillip said when I asked him about it later. "It's kind of working itself out in people's psyches. It's kind of cool to watch."

The truth is that the biggest reason for the relative calm might have been simple demographics. Fewer than 250 residents of Bureau County's 35,000 were black.

When I got back to my cubicle, I had just enough time to make a few phone calls to fill out the story. The first call was to an African American family in Bureau County.

The Klinefelters lived a little west of the creek in DePue. Geneva Kline-felter, the matriarch, said the name needed changing. *Negro* is a word that slaps an unfair characterization on an entire race, she said. The Negro-Creek-as-history argument held no water, as it were, with her.

"To me," Geneva told me, "that's not saying anything about my history."

Next I spoke with her son Cortland, who was nineteen years old and agreed with his mother. His perception of the word *Negro* was that it "comes from so much hate," and a time that represented obsolete notions on race.

"We should be able to show that we've come past all that," Cortland told me.

I thought the story needed more context and reached out to academia, a standard ploy of general assignment reporters who want to look like they know what they're talking about. I got lucky and spoke with Sundiata Cha-Jua, associate professor of African American studies at University of Illinois at Urbana-Champaign.

"*Negro* signified a kind of weakness and subordination," Professor Cha-Jua told me. He explained that blacks began rejecting the word back in the mid-1800s. Even then, African Americans believed the word *Negro* had been imposed on them, he said. "Self-definition, self-determination . . . naming oneself" are reflected in the words *African American*, or *black*, the professor said.

It turns out that Bureau County's Negro Creek was one of many geographical features with *Negro* in its name that still existed in Illinois. I poked around and found fifteen sites. There was Big Negro Creek in Warren County in western Illinois and Little Negro Lick in Macoupin County farther south and west. Negro Hollow was near Saint Louis, and Negro Lake was in Mason County in central Illinois. Two Negro Cemeteries —one in central Illinois and another in southern Illinois—existed. Even something called Negro Spring Salt Well was in southeast Illinois near the Ohio River.

I didn't find efforts to change those names, but in Bureau County, Phillip's next step was to lobby for a state law banning the words *Negro* and *squaw*, a highly offensive word among Native Americans, from official place-names in Illinois. First, he had to find a lawmaker to take up the charge and sponsor a bill. I didn't hold out much hope for finding that sturdy a backbone among Illinois legislators.

Chad, meanwhile, was working to create a nonprofit to obtain funding for a historical marker. Phillip told me it was a great idea that he would support "a thousand percent."

I got to work writing, pounding out the story and finding myself wondering about the delicate business of revising and updating history, an effort many might characterize as political correctness that somehow softens facts and obscures truth. At the same time, what is our duty to right wrongs or to change history now for the greater good of a peaceful, reconciled future? Does renaming Negro Creek to Love Creek deny history or acknowledge it in a way that says we have overcome a barrier that stood between us? We can't exactly compromise by calling it Love Negro Creek.

So what's the answer? That's what Bureau County was struggling with, what many places and well-meaning people struggle with. Phillip and Chad seemed ready to take it one step at a time and look for common ground. One of the reassuring things was that they saw the value in remembering the ghosts of Negro Creek.

"If all we'd see was a monument go up," Phillip told me as we wrapped up our chat, "and you combine that with all the conversation that has occurred, I would consider that a victory for everybody."

• • •

WHILE I WAS AWAY, reconciliation of sorts was occurring for Mike, and a certain critical mass seemed to coalesce around the case.

After months of delicate negotiations, he'd somehow gained the approval of one of Stanley's nephews to exhume the body. Then, Mike marched to the courthouse in Winnebago County and filed paperwork for a judge's approval. The judge set a hearing.

About this time, Mike was having a few drinks in the wee hours at the Roadhouse when he caught an episode of a reality-based cold case show on the Travel Channel. *The Dead Files* features a former New York Police

Department homicide detective, Steve DiSchiavi, and a medium, Amy Allan, investigating "paranormal histories and mysteries." At one point, the show solicits viewers who think they may have a case worthy of investigation to contact *The Dead Files*. Mike fired off an email from his phone that moment. Immediately after, the device shut down. Mike shrugged, figuring the email had disappeared into the internet ether.

It hadn't. But his more immediate, practical concern was the exhumation court hearing. In paperwork stating his case, Mike noted his establishment of the Stanley V. Skridla Chapter of the Mary Jane Reed Foundation, "the purpose of which is to seek out volunteers, donated funds, and contributions from individuals and organizations who are willing to provide services to help solve the murder mystery . . . on the behalf of the victims' surviving families in the name of justice and to bring those families closure." As noble sounding as those words were, the foundation seemed to exist only on paper. I found no records of it in the Illinois Attorney General's database of charitable organizations or in the Illinois Secretary of State's database of corporations and limited liability corporations. GuideStar, the database of information on nonprofits, had no record of it either.

Elsewhere in the court documents, Mike called Stanley a World War II hero and noted that since Mary Jane's exhumation, "an individual affiliated with the local coroner's office at the time of said exhuming" met with Mike and stated, "If you would have exhumed him [Skridla], all of your questions would have been answered."

Stanley's nephew, Steve Skridla, has "a question as to whether the remains interred . . . are the actual and complete and (only) the remains" of Stanley, Mike went on to say. His intention was to use advances in forensic technology and science to make that determination conclusively. A thorough examination of the remains would also yield information that "may solve or contribute to solving" the killings, and might reveal if Mary Jane's skull was in fact buried with Stanley, Mike wrote. Although he didn't state it in the paperwork, Mike also was hoping the exhumation would retrieve bullets that could be tested. He'd told me in somewhat cryptic asides that he had a few leads on the potential murder weapon from people who'd made contact with him.

The day before the court hearing, I spoke to Mike on the phone and he was encouraged, primarily because of Steve Skridla's approval to exhume Stanley's body. Often, a family member's consent is all a judge wants. It looked like Mike was going to have to come up with his own money to fund the exhumation, analysis of the remains, new casket, and reinterment, all of which would run about $10,000. It was an investment he was willing to make. And, Mike felt that the judge's order would give him obvious credibility to secure commitments from anybody who might be interested in funding his venture and forensic experts.

Near midnight the next day, I got a text from Mike: "All went great in court beyond my belief," he typed. "Judge even commended me for my patience and years of dedication to seek out justice . . . I'm on cloud nine."

I called him a day later, and Mike said the entire hearing ran for about a half hour, during which Winnebago County judge Eugene Doherty went over the paperwork, asked questions of Mike and Steve Skridla, then, according to Mike, complimented him "for pursuing every avenue to find justice." Then Judge Doherty signed the exhumation approval.

"He might as well have put a gold star on my forehead," Mike said. "I'm not used to being treated that way in court. I had to look away. I was starting to get misty a little bit."

Now he was off—to see if he could find anyone besides him to fund the exhumation, to get law enforcement and forensic experts formally involved, and then, finally, to divine answers from the grave. For my *Tribune* story on the exhumation approval, I asked Mike what he'd do if the autopsy failed to show anything definitively.

"Case closed," he said. "We've done everything we can."

About this time, another indication that momentum was gathering around the case arose one summer afternoon while Mike was relaxing in the woods of Wisconsin. His cell phone rang. He punched the answer button. A staffer at *The Dead Files* greeted him.

They were on the phone for an hour, Mike told me.

Three months later, a crew from the Travel Channel, including Steve and Amy, arrived and spent several days in and around Oregon filming an episode.

The producer reached out to me and wondered if I'd be interviewed on camera for the episode, an adventure I was anxious about but willing to try. He sent a release for me to sign, and I passed it along to my editors, who agreed, provided I had free rein to write whatever I wanted about the filming for the *Tribune*. The production company was uncomfortable with that stipulation, and my dreams of dramatic reality-TV stardom were dashed quicker than I could say Kardashian.

For Mike, the experience was exhausting, he told me. Crews had stayed at the Roadhouse, which he was forced to close for filming, for more than twelve hours one day and until three or four o'clock in the morning another time. They shot take after take after take. All that lost time might have cost him thousands of dollars in business. He said he wasn't sure he'd do it again if he'd known what he was getting into.

"The Obsession—Oregon, IL" premiered in the late spring after the crew's visit. To make a long story short, Amy tours the Roadhouse and doesn't like the "solid darkness" she feels there, especially in the basement, where she suggests one or more people might have been beaten or stabbed.

"This place just destroys," she says at one point. "Feels like my mind is being erased." She feels dead people wanting to talk.

Her best guess about what happened to Mary Jane and Stanley is that Vince committed or directed the crime, that his spirit is in the Roadhouse, keeping the other spirits captive to prevent the truth about his role from emerging.

Steve, who interviews a few people in classic New York homicide detective style, gets whatever official records he can on the case. He believes the two DeShazo brothers killed Stanley when he fought their attempts to rob him, and that Mary Jane was killed to dispose of the witness.

Amy advises Mike to take two steps: first, he must demand that the spirits of Mary Jane and Stanley leave the Roadhouse. "Tell them you're releasing them," she says, adding that it's hard for Mary Jane to depart because Mike is her hero. Then, Amy says, Mike should bring a holy man to the Roadhouse to clear Vince's spirit.

Mike followed her suggestions, but, he said, nothing much changed. In fact, another one of those peculiar incidents, one that gave me great pause, occurred about this time.

I called Mike to get an update on his latest exhumation venture, and he told me that a few days earlier an older gentleman came to the Roadhouse and interrupted Mike at about the exact moment he slid $20 into a video gaming machine. The man started explaining to Mike that he'd purchased an electrical warehouse and supply company in nearby Dixon and was clearing out the old building. Mike stared at him, a little annoyed at the distraction. The man handed him an empty envelope.

The mailing address, written in cursive with a pencil, read "Miss Mary Jane Reed Oregon, Ill. Ogle County Illinois." That caught Mike's eye, but not as much as the return address in the upper left-hand corner: "M. Ariens." Both addresses were written in the same unsteady, perhaps elderly, style, Mike said.

"I looked at him, and I was thinking, *You're screwing with me*," Mike told me. "And he just kept a very stoic face. I asked and asked him questions, and he kept answering them."

After a few minutes, the man didn't want to talk anymore, Mike said. "It scared the crap out of him. He just wanted to get rid of it and give it to me."

I was intrigued enough to ask to see it the next time I visited Mike, and he was happy to share it. I'd come out to Oregon for a story on the restoration of *The Eternal Indian* statue on the bluffs overlooking the Rock River and stopped by the Roadhouse. I walked in to a place that had changed in the last few months. Still living in the building, Mike had built a stage in part of the restaurant area, acquired and mounted old velour movie-theater seats, and staged seven performances of the play *Luv*, which he'd produced years earlier at his Oak Dell Farm Theatre. He also was bringing in the occasional belly dancer. You had to hand it to Mike: he was an innovative restaurateur.

He fetched the envelope and handed it to me. It was authentic, right down to the faded, stiff consistency of the paper, smudged cursive written in pencil, and two one-cent stamps on the upper right-hand corner. I could see printed cancellation strips across the top but no postmarked date. Holding it, I felt my palms tingle. I looked up at Mike.

"Pretty much anymore," he told me, "you just kind of throw your hands up and say, 'Thanks.' It bewilders you for a couple days, and then you make sure you document them so when you tell people about it they don't think you're crazy."

He told me of more "activity" in the place—little things that together amounted to a moderate level of creepiness: items moving and falling unexpectedly, tapping on a door that, when opened, revealed no one standing there. Once Mike pulled on a light chain and it kept bouncing and skipping for much longer than it should have. He had mostly gotten used to all of it.

We chatted more before I had to hustle back to the office. Mike told me that funding sources for the exhumation were more difficult to come by than he'd anticipated. Now he was planning on paying the $10,000 or so to cover the exhumation and related costs, placing his total investment in the case at somewhere north of $120,000. He also had a few more delicate negotiations with the Skridlas. One side of the family was grumbling about whether this exhumation would make a mockery of Uncle Stanley. Mike had to do a fair amount of reassuring, helped in large part by his ability to persuade a Catholic priest to preside over the reinterment and a local VFW honor guard to fire a salute there.

He pulled it together. On a Thursday morning late in May, I woke early and drove to Calvary Catholic Cemetery in Winnebago, about twenty-five miles north of Oregon. It was what I like to call Chamber of Commerce weather—sunny, clear, a light breeze, and seventy degrees. Red-winged blackbirds and yellow warblers flitted by as I drove in the main entrance, bordered by six American flags. Unsuspecting bugs had smeared my windshield in yellow streaks. Fluff from cottonwood trees floated in the air.

As for Stanley's exhumation, about twenty-five people had gathered around. But no one had set up a screen this time, which allowed me to walk within a few feet of the hole that had been dug the day before. Mike, who'd bought a new video camera for the occasion, set it on a tripod and trained it on the hole. Rita, Mike's close friend who, like me, Jack Fredrickson, and assorted others, had the Mary Jane Reed unsolved murder disease, was assisting.

With the hole already dug, the burial vault was loaded on a truck that departed the cemetery by 9:30 a.m. and drove to the back parking lot of a burial vault company about twenty miles away, in Belvidere. I followed. There, workers popped off the lid, found the wooden casket soaking in about a foot of brown water, then cracked a corner of the vault, allowing the liquid to drain. A filmy brown-gray puddle spread over the gravel and weedy grass in the bright sun.

Winnebago County coroner Sue Fiduccia and a technician donned blue gloves and started fishing through the sludge, finding skeletal remains and shreds of the body bag. A team of students from Loyola University and their professor, Anne Grauer, a specialist in excavation and analysis of human skeletal remains, lifted bones and placed them in plastic bags and a green plastic tub. I saw two of Stanley's nephews engage in an animated discussion—mostly one jabbing his finger in the face of the other before they separated. A Belvidere police officer pulled up and used a metal detector to scan the remains in the casket. He found traces of lead, iron, and tin in various places. A few minutes later, a young intern was directed to shovel the remaining sludge into a body bag. About 12:30 p.m., she dropped the last shovel of slop in the bag and the entire collection of materials was taken to a hospital in Rockford for X-rays.

From there, Stanley's remains were transported a few blocks to the Winnebago County coroner's basement lab. I got lost driving there, then hung up in a traffic jam in downtown Rockford in what looked like thousands assembling for a high school graduation. I used the forty-five minutes in traffic to expand my profanity repertoire.

I finally found a parking space on the sketchy outskirts of downtown, jogged to the coroner's office, and told the friendly receptionist I was there for the autopsy. I was expecting to hang out in the office for a couple of hours, standing and sitting, looking at pamphlets on death and home journal magazines until I heard the autopsy had ended and could try to collect the important players for comments.

About ten minutes later, the receptionist woke me from my stupor and asked me to follow her. We descended into the bowels of the county building and entered a bright, white, odorless cinder block room—the lab where forensic experts were assembling Stanley's remains. I was stunned for a few seconds that no one said as much as a peep when I stepped into the room. Then I started taking notes, thinking that I'd be kicked out any minute. I looked up at the clock. It was 2:20 p.m. I counted eighteen people in the room.

Brown waterlogged bones had been laid out neatly, forming most of a detached skeleton on a blue tarp on the examination table. Beneath that was the outline of a yellow box painted on the floor. In another section of the room, the coroner had set up screens atop two sawhorses and another blue tarp on the floor under the screens. She and a forensic specialist scooped material from a pile that had the consistency of peat moss, broke it up with their hands, and dropped it into a stainless steel bowl. Then they dumped the contents on the screens and rubbed the material through, plucking out the larger pieces that remained. All bones were placed in their suitable spots in the assembled skeleton on the table, and a couple of students were measuring and taking an inventory of the bones. Fabric, buttons, and related material deemed irrelevant were tossed in a red plastic biohazards box. A few feet away, a sheriff's deputy munched on a bag of pretzels and sipped an orange Crush soda. Someone had found a Christian cross in the remains, and one of the nephews directed that it be reinterred with what was left of Stanley.

"We got a lot here," Sue told me after looking through the sodden remains. "I don't know what we're going to find, but we got a lot here."

Shortly after 3 p.m., when another body was wheeled through the lab and placed in a viewing room, an intern and a Loyola student each found a bullet and placed them in separate sealable plastic bags. Professor Grauer told Mike that the group had collected nearly all the bones, except for many of the toes, which is to be expected in exhumations after the body has been decomposing for as long as Stanley's had. The remains were consistent with a male aged twenty-five to thirty-five who'd received a lot of dental work, Professor Grauer told Mike. She'd noted carbon residue on the skull, which might suggest it was burned, although that was unlikely, and there were no signs of acid. Those two findings were germane. Over the years, Mike and the Skridlas had suggested Stanley's head had been abused—set on fire or splashed with acid—during or after the shooting.

Most important were two damaged areas of the skeleton: a right rib, fourth or fifth from the bottom, was missing a tiny semicircular chunk, which defined a wound, Professor Grauer said. Two more semicircular chips in the pelvis also indicated bullet wounds, she said.

Professor Grauer planned to conduct a more thorough review in the upcoming weeks. The state police lab was going to examine the bullet slugs and scrapings from Stanley's skull to check for accelerants and acid.

By 3:45 p.m., the remains were placed in a white body bag, which Mike helped load into a coffin that funeral home staff then draped in an American flag and rolled on a gurney out of the room. About a half hour later, relatives and friends gathered under a gravesite canopy at the cemetery to listen to a Catholic priest conduct a memorial service over the coffin. Mike's friend Rita stood nearby, holding a bouquet of roses. Across a cemetery road, the twelve-man VFW honor guard had assembled. The priest talked about how those who believe shall not die and asked God to accept prayers for Stanley and grant him eternal rest.

The honor guard riflemen fired a salute, followed by one member playing a perfect version of taps through a silver bugle. A couple members handed a tri-folded flag to Steve Skridla. A few minutes later, the other nephew, David, gathered four or five shells the rifles had spit out, and the two men had a few moments of conversation.

That rendition of taps, I thought, was too perfect. I approached the bugler.

Turns out it was recorded. He explained that buglers for veterans' funerals are in very short supply. Then he showed me the bell of the device, which was a speaker. He grinned. "But you gotta make it look good for the family."

I talked to Mike, who looked exhausted. He said the exhumation had achieved progress on three fronts: First, Stanley's family was reassured that the bones in the coffin were his, unlike the situation with Mary Jane's remains. Second, the exhumation showed that Mary Jane's skull was not in Stanley's casket. And third, the forensic team had found two bullets that could be tested against a pair of handguns that may have been the murder weapons—that pair of mystery guns that Mike had referred to earlier.

I checked the time. It was 5 p.m. Only the gravediggers were left. I decided to leave them to their work.

The next day I drove out to the Roadhouse for a press conference Mike had called to sort through the previous day's action and pull everything together. Dressed in a pressed yellow short-sleeved shirt and dark tie, he moved a little slower and spoke softer. Steve Skridla sat next to Mike at a table. Crews from three TV stations and reporters for three newspapers showed up. I asked Mike where he was with his investigation now.

"Where I'm at right now is, I'm done," he said. "I've done all that I can do."

He went on to say he hoped that his efforts over the past two decades hadn't been in vain, that "enough of the dots that I've created can be connected that law enforcement can color in the picture. That would be a perfect world for me."

Steve said he was glad Mike had pressed for the exhumation, that the reinterment presided over by a Catholic priest and an honor guard pleased him.

"It was a long day for everyone," Steve said.

In the rear of the dining room sat a surprise attendee, Ogle County sheriff Brian VanVickle, elected a few months earlier. He kept silent the entire time, then walked out with a deputy. I caught up to him on the boardwalk a few steps outside the door. The exhumation failed to reveal anything substantially different from what investigators already knew, Sheriff VanVickle told me, and he disputed Mike's contentions about what caliber and type of gun were used in the murders. He also was skeptical about Mike's suggestion that perhaps two people who participated in the crime—one of whom would have been sixteen years old in 1948—may be alive today.

"I think it's a stretch, in that day and age, to expect a sixteen-year-old to be out committing a double homicide," Sheriff VanVickle said. "I don't believe that's credible."

And that was it. I drove to the Oregon Public Library, wrote and sent my story, then hit the two-lane for my drive home.

Weeks passed, and my contacts with Mike dropped off. I wrote stories about the U.S. Supreme Court's legalization of gay marriage and a gentleman who rescues abandoned urban chickens. I took a plane to Florida to interview the parents of a Medal of Honor recipient killed in Afghanistan, and I returned to North Dakota, this time to write about the oil fracking boom. Throughout all that, I held out faint hope that the analyses of the bullets or skull scrapings from Stanley's exhumation would yield a breakthrough.

By this time, it was obvious that the print version of the *Chicago Tribune* had become a cumbersome, expensive, obsolete content delivery system. Lovable and rich in history as it was, the newspaper gobbled resources like a gas-guzzling, smoke-belching jalopy. The guys who ran the dealership were rolling it to the back lot.

In staff meetings with top editors, they'd say the newspaper was an "afterthought" and a "byproduct of digital." They used the phrase *reverse publishing* and encouraged "digital first" as our mantra.

Revenue from the print version of the *Tribune* still was very robust, far outpacing digital, but it was declining rapidly, with no reversal in sight.

Layoffs and buyouts continued as ways of cutting costs and—in management's preferred phraseology—refining our mission. This new "digital first" organization viewed our website like a twenty-four-hour news channel. Rather than wait for a newspaper to be published every morning, we covered breaking news online as it happened and posted stories there as soon as they were ready—sometimes even before they were ready. Then editors decided which of those would fit in the next day's newspaper.

We tried to find the elusive formula for success in other experimental ways. Editors required reporters to get trained in and make well-produced video. Then they spiked the idea when they determined the videos weren't generating much website traffic or online subscriptions. Then they revived it. We experimented with a pay wall/registration system for premium content and then decided to go with a metered approach that gave readers free access to a limited number of *Tribune* pieces each month before said readers were locked out of the website. We were told to push our stories on every social media platform that would have us.

The shift to some kind of online-first strategy, painful as it was, made all the sense in the world. The digital freedom train is rolling down the tracks, sisters and brothers, regardless of whether "legacy media" like the *Chicago Tribune* choose to hop aboard, be passed by, or get run over.

However, to some who view the business with an emotional investment bordering on religious zeal, the structural changes can feel too datacentric, antiseptic, and artificial. It's almost as if this new version is a carnival barker calling, "Free clickbait for everyone!" That feels disingenuous.

Something else is bothersome. Although it's great that everyone has a platform, this new media landscape, with all its noise and traffic, is also a highly manipulative place. Newsmakers with power and money—whether they're politicians, athletes, musicians, actors, CEOs, you name it—can go directly to "the people" on social media or a blog or website. That way, they avoid the purported or real bias of the mainstream media. But they also avoid answering tough questions from influential, independent, steely-eyed mainstream media outlets, which are becoming increasingly weaker since the digital revolution because none of those outlets have found the formula to sustain themselves over the long term. And no solution looks to be emerging. That scenario leads to the powerful, moneyed interests controlling the message, and that can get sinister.

So, for brief spurts, those of us in a certain demographic could get a little bitter, a little fearful, a little weepy, and a little sentimental about this structural change. Not me, of course. Other people.

• • •

IT HAD BEEN something like sixteen years since Mike had embarked on this physically and emotionally draining odyssey. Besides spending that $120,000 and investing hundreds of hours of his time, he'd lost business at the Roadhouse and lost a house to foreclosure. He'd run for reelection as mayor and lost, at least in part because of what he'd done on the case, then run two more times for that office and lost those campaigns, too. Then, on a March morning, he lost his mother, who died after a lengthy illness. Several hours later on that same day, Warren's ailing wife Vickie also passed.

Seven months after Stanley's exhumation, Sheriff VanVickle released a brief statement on the state police crime lab's examination of the two .32 caliber bullets retrieved from Stanley's remains and a .32 caliber handgun "obtained during the investigation." Mike had provided the sheriff's office with a couple of leads on possible murder weapons.

"An analysis of the bullets revealed only one bullet was suitable for comparison," the release said, "and that bullet was not fired from the submitted .32 caliber handgun."

The statement went on to mention the sheriff's relatively recent investigation of the deaths of Mary Jane and Stanley.

"We believe," the release concluded, "all the people involved in their murders are deceased."

The Winnebago County coroner followed that release about a week later with the announcement that an analysis of scrapings taken from Stanley's skull failed to reveal the presence of accelerants or acids.

Then came a loss more devastating to Mike than anything that had happened since he'd taken on his investigation: June, his dear friend, roommate, and ex-wife, collapsed in the shower at their Roadhouse apartment and died immediately from an apparent stroke. It was shocking to everyone who knew June, a lively, engaged retired schoolteacher who was seventy-one years old.

It happened on a Saturday afternoon a couple of hours after Mike had left to head up to Rockford to see a band perform. When he called June's cell phone to tell her he'd arrived, she didn't answer. Mike called the Roadhouse, and Marge, the hostess, said June was in the shower. Mike asked her to check. When June didn't answer, a bartender forced open the door. They found June—her clothes laid out, ready for work—on the shower floor.

"I was just in shock," Mike told me three days later, between sobs. "I couldn't even compose myself."

He said she was his biggest supporter. No matter what idea Mike would concoct, June would always tell him to go for it. He recalled how they would sit in the bar after closing, or in their apartment, have a couple of drinks, and watch TV together until two or three o'clock in the morning. He spoke of her attending church, praying regularly, and reading from the Bible on her nightstand.

"I told her I loved her constantly," Mike said. Then he broke down again. "It's just like twenty-five years and *poof*, she disappears, but all her stuff's here. So, it's hard."

Apart from the emotional component of their relationship, June took on a heavy workload at the Roadhouse. Although the two were co-owners and both their names were on the loan papers, June handled the books, Mike said. She also was president of the company.

"I used to tell people nothing gets done unless it's cleared through CEO June Bug," he said.

Now Mike was left to untangle a snarl of ownership and management agreements on the Roadhouse, which he closed after June died. He'd have to try to run the place mostly on his own, but he had no specific plans to reopen. Also, he couldn't bring himself to stay in the apartment there. For the time being, Mike was sleeping on the couch in his hostess Marge's apartment.

The Illinois State Police exacerbated his heartache by investigating June's death to determine if foul play was involved—news that I'm sure overheated the rumor machine in town. Dr. Mark Peters, the same forensic pathologist who participated in the examinations of Mary Jane and Stanley, performed June's autopsy and confirmed that she died from a stroke.

Mike scheduled a visitation, including a brief memorial service, for the following Sunday at a local funeral home. I drove to Oregon that afternoon, and when I stepped from my car, I bumped into Jack Fredrickson as he was leaving. He told me Mike didn't look well. I got inside, where about seventy people mingled and spoke in hushed tones. Photos of June—including a baby picture, a photo of Mike and her on their wedding day, and one of her from the back side, bending over in pink pants—had been placed on tables. There was a photo of June with a cat and, among others, the famous photo of Nixon meeting Elvis Presley at the White House—an image that always made June laugh. Two white spandex jackets from the Roadhouse hung near a red-and-white striped apron June wore while working.

I found Mike. Jack was right. Wearing a black suit and tie, Mike looked ashen, exhausted, disheveled. He introduced me to a few people, then, when we had a moment alone, told me the state police investigators wanted him to call them back, even though the cause of June's death had been confirmed. Mike was pulled away, and I stepped to the casket, where June was wearing a powder blue T-shirt with "official roadie" in a sheriff's star on the left breast. A Bible had been placed at her left side.

A few minutes later, Marian Boesen, one of the psychics Mike had consulted who also worked as a pastor, gave a seven-minute eulogy. She talked about how "June Bug" would not want us to be sad, she merely was in another room, and that she loved her cat and loved to go to Mike's retreat in Wisconsin. I met a niece and nephew from June's small hometown in southern Illinois. They said she was their cool aunt who, after graduating from Southern Illinois University, headed to Chicago and never looked back. She'd traveled the globe before settling down with Mike.

The visitation ended and I bumped into Warren, who looked frail and unsteady. We stepped outside to the front landing of the funeral home, where he introduced me to his new girlfriend, Marti. She'd welcomed Warren into her home a few weeks earlier. Although he was as convinced as ever that the case of his sister's death was rife with corruption, Warren sounded like he had no realistic options.

June was cremated. Half the ashes were given to the niece and nephew. Mike kept the remaining half. His plan, he told me, was to spread some near the couple's Wisconsin getaway and to have some buried next to his right hand.

All of it—the deaths of Mike's mother, Vickie, and June, the sheriff's and coroner's conclusions—made this feel like the end. I wasn't sure where

Mike or anyone else would go from here, or if anyone—especially Mike —had the energy for it.

I met Jack Fredrickson for coffee again to commiserate, and he said it was an impossible case to resolve. He reminded me of something I kept trying to ignore: everyone involved was probably dead, and those who were alive and knew something were laying low, disinclined to step forward and create more havoc. There was nowhere for anyone to go on this, he said.

And, like me, Jack had started to doubt some of Mike's more recent logic. It seemed as if Mike was becoming more desperate as his scenarios and options shrank. Exhibit A was Mike's current contention that Jerry Brooks, the former sheriff, might have been the gunman.

• • •

HISTORIES —call them stories if you like—never really end. It's more like they continue to unfold, but we've left them; they've ceased to resonate.

At this point, thirteen years from the first piece I'd written on Mary Jane's and Stanley's deaths, I was ready to leave this story, especially after all the paths that had led to dead ends, the absence of any concrete leads, and the lack of interest in, even downright antagonism toward, finding answers.

And I did leave it, but only for a few weeks. Then I had two dreams on the same night.

In the first, I was walking in a cluttered, messy, run-down apartment in search of something related to the Mary Jane Reed case. I saw an easy chair, but without arms. A large towel was strewn across it. I wandered to the bathroom, which had a handheld showerhead attached to a hose. I picked it up, and even though I was fully clothed—it wasn't *that* kind of a dream—I was going to use it. But I stopped and turned. I saw a woman, who may have been Warren's wife Vickie. I walked to another room and saw Mike, a small boy maybe ten years old, and a dog sitting around a table. They greeted me and we talked. The boy became anxious and upset, and he started crying. Somebody—a young woman who appeared out of nowhere—comforted him and took him away. The dog walked over, wanting to be petted, and I scratched him under his chin and on his chest. He was very pleased. That was it.

The next dream followed immediately. I came to the shore of what I think was Lake Michigan. I walked along the water's edge then followed a rocky path that jutted far into the lake and ended under an archway of stone. The lake narrowed into a small waterway. I waded in and came to a large, tall fireplace mantel made of stone, which I scaled, and ended up again at the cluttered, messy, run-down apartment. Then I had to go, but a woman—the same I'd seen in my previous dream—told me another newspaper reporter was there today. I became nervous and asked what he was up to.

"Oh, he's got a story on sightings," she said.

"Sightings of what?" I asked, but I knew. They were sightings of Mary Jane's ghost. I got nervous that I'd miss it, but I still had this powerful notion that I must leave, and I did.

After that, the case started cropping up again, as it had before, at the most unexpected times—in conversation, while working on other stories, while folding laundry, reading, walking, driving, taking a shower.

I knew the case was unsolvable, as sure as I knew the newspapers of today would continue devolving into a cute, niche retro item like vinyl LP records.

But I had questions, maybe not fully formed questions, but curiosities. I saw a few places to mine a little deeper, a few people who might know something. In my role as distracted savant parachuting into Oregon over the years, I'd spoken with many people involved, but not all, and I'd looked at most, but not all, of the documents. Those documents I had reviewed had received only the most perfunctory skimming while I chased a deadline. I hadn't really had the time to look at them in depth, or together all at once, or to probe some people and places I thought might yield important information. Maybe I could do that now, as sort of an extracurricular endeavor, on my own time.

When I started thinking more about it, I realized some of those people had retired and had nothing to lose by speaking with me. What if I reached out to them just to chat? What if I poked around for documents and simply made a more comprehensive commitment to the case?

If nothing else, I'd feel as if I'd exhausted all options, and maybe that would make the case disappear from my conscious and unconscious self.

I told myself that at the very least, I'd gain a clearer understanding of what happened. At best? Well, that was impossible.

I came up with a defined game plan: what documents I would review and who I would speak with. Not all that much was out there—five or six people, maybe a handful of documents. I told myself to keep an open mind.

I could do that.

Shortly after compiling that list and making my commitment, something serendipitous happened. His name was George Seibel.

George, Doug, Jerry, Greg, and Mark

• • •

GEORGE CAME TO ME by chance, through another story—this one placed in my lap by the gracious Pulitzer prize–winning *Tribune* reporter Patricia Callahan. She'd been contacted by a woman who was looking into the unsolved death of a twenty-four-year-old neighbor, Jenna Crandall. Her body had been found the previous fall in a forest preserve.

Trish was fully consumed by the final stages of what would be an illuminating series on herbicides and wondered if I was interested in Jenna's case. I started making phone calls. I learned that Jenna had led a troubled life that mostly revolved around drug use, and the autopsy showed she'd had drugs in her system when she died. But the amounts did not appear to be enough to cause a fatal overdose. Besides that, Jenna's body was partially clothed—she was naked from the waist up and her yoga pants had been pulled down near the middle of her thighs. The neighbor who'd reached out to Trish, Sally Messenger, and Jenna's mother, Donna Gerhartz, were trying to figure out exactly what had happened to Jenna. I wrote a story about it, and a few days later, George contacted Donna and offered to help.

He was in a rare position to do so. A retired Chicago Police Department violent crimes detective, George ran a cold case program from a community college in a gritty working-class Chicago suburb. He and his students would scan unsolved cases, then dig into those that looked intriguing. In the decade since he'd created the Institute for Cold Case Solution at

Morton College, George said he and his students had contributed to the solutions of at least a dozen cases. I'd heard of at least three they'd worked on. He'd also written a handful of books on policing.

His involvement in the Jenna Crandall case seemed like a story to me. My editor agreed. I called him, and we met in a Morton College parking lot at dusk on a cold February weekday. Wearing a black leather jacket and blue jeans, George walked with a slight limp while he led me through a darkened stairwell to his cluttered, windowless office next to a loading dock.

On bulletin boards were photos of suspects and victims, official-looking documents, and scraps of typed notes. Lean, tanned, and weathered, George wore glasses behind which was a perpetually furrowed, studious brow. His gray hair was styled in that fashionable, mussed look.

George sat at a desk overflowing with papers and told me he was motivated to get involved with Jenna Crandall's case because he "felt like Jenna needed a break, in terms of the truth being found." He wanted to give Jenna's soul and her family some peace, he explained, and he mentioned that he had a soft spot for addicts, but didn't go into much detail about that.

About three minutes into our conversation, a little bell sounded in my head—more like a gong, really—but I didn't mention Mary Jane Reed, Stanley Skridla, Mike Arians, Oregon, lovers' lane, exhumations, or anything about the case. I asked him his age. Seventy-two, he said. He looked better than many sixty-year-olds I knew.

By the time of our chat, George already had stirred the pot on Jenna's death, talking with at least one mutt who clearly had some involvement with her in the final days of her life and pissing off at least two investigators. We wrapped up our talk, and I asked him to keep me posted. I also told him I'd check in from time to time.

We talked a couple more times over the phone in the next few weeks. George hadn't solved the mystery of Jenna's death in that short time, but he'd moved the case a few steps forward and come up with a plausible scenario—that one or two guys had been doing drugs with Jenna and she'd passed out. The drug zombies panicked, brought her to the preserve, dumped her body, and made it look like a rape.

A few days after that phone conversation, George told me that he'd gone about as far as he could on the case for the time being. He was going to let forces play themselves out, then circle back to see what surfaced. Seemed like an opportune moment to bring up a certain other case that had been on my mind from time to time.

I asked if he'd be interested in taking a look at this case I'd been covering for the last thirteen or so years. Then, even though I'd rehearsed my next lines in what I'd describe as very laissez-faire fashion, I came at him now with all the subtlety of a fire hose, rushing through the basics of the case and dropping in random details. I said I had some material and asked if he'd take a look at it and let me know what he thought, that I'd really appreciate it.

George was quiet for a few seconds. Then he said he was flattered, but that a case this old was problematic for the obvious reason that Jack Fredrickson had been trying to communicate to me—everyone involved most likely was dead. Still, George said he was willing to take a look at whatever I could get him and that he'd get back to me in a few weeks.

It just so happened that I'd already copied every official document I had, including the unedited report from the sheriff's reinvestigation, which I'd obtained a while back but hadn't read closely. I also had reports on Mary Jane's exhumation, state police supplemental reports on that endeavor, Linda Klepinger's analysis of Mary Jane's remains, and all fourteen stories I'd written on the case. I drove to George's house that afternoon and shoved the folder full of materials into the mailbox at the sidewalk. On the narrow lawn near the front door was what looked like a very tall weed or a very small tree that had died and been painted green, perhaps for Christmas. Among the assorted items on the porch were a red suitcase, cooking pot, and stacks of books. At the curb was a restored forest-green 1950 Ford with a polished chrome spotlight on the driver's door, one of about nine vintage cars, I was to learn later, that George owned.

He texted me with his first question less than an hour after I'd stuffed the material into his mailbox. George wanted to know who created the Mary Jane Reed website. Mike Arians, I told him. The next day he posed more questions based on what he was reading on the website, which was a blend of facts, interpretations, and theories. I cautioned him against placing too much credibility in the website. I was unsure about some of the sources of information posted there. Over the next ten days, George asked more questions, did some digging on his own, and came up with a couple of theories, then scrapped them. He wondered where Bill Spencer, the elderly former sheriff of Ogle County who seemed to know more than he was sharing, might be found. He died about three years ago, I told him. George wondered about a name mentioned in the more recent sheriff's report—Amos Blanchard, son of a former sheriff—whom investigators wanted to speak with in relation to a pair of suspects. George was suspicious that the report seemed to dismiss Vince Varco as a suspect quickly and without much discussion about why. He was intrigued by Mary Jane's family using a psychic. He reached out to the Oregon Public Library and Ogle County Historical Society to get more information.

Twelve days after he'd received the materials, George met me at a diner next to a body shop. He'd finished a workout at the local YMCA and was wearing a neon yellow hoodie with OREGON, as in the university, stitched in green across the chest. I mentioned the irony.

"I just like the colors," he said.

Over the next two hours, George ate a vegetarian skillet, drank two diet Cokes, shared a bit about himself, and offered his theory on the case.

Born and raised in Chicago's Rogers Park neighborhood, George played baseball at Sullivan High School, where, it turns out, two of my cousins played as well. He continued in college, then realized that his dream of roaming center field for the Chicago Cubs was never going to happen. Married and the father of a baby girl, he looked around and found what he saw as the next most fun job: police officer. He started in a rough neighborhood on the south side and made detective after three years, then was sent to equally rough and dangerous neighborhoods on the city's west side. He worked for a decade, was haunted by too many murders, drank too much Russian vodka, and burned through two marriages.

He started teaching at Morton and, at the urging of a dean, established the cold case institute. When we met, he'd been sober for twenty-five years and received extremely high ratings from students.

"It keeps my juices flowing," George said of his work. "It's kind of what makes me tick. The coolest thing is they place a lot of trust in me."

His theory on the murders of Mary Jane and Stanley, I was somewhat shocked to discover, was very similar to Mike's: Vince Varco and one or two henchmen were the killers.

I was still reluctant to believe that Vince was responsible and was concerned that George had relied too heavily on information from Mike's website. But he brought up some points that made me stop and think.

First of all, George said, a successful robbery is all about maintaining control. The robber doesn't want to kill anybody; he wants valuables and then he wants to split, as clean and as quick as possible. In the case of Mary Jane and Stanley, the assailant or assailants shot Stanley five times—mostly in his groin—then took Mary Jane.

"Why wouldn't they have just killed her right on the spot and be done with it?" George said. That question had bothered me since the early days. "They're driving around the countryside with a girl who could talk? They wouldn't have done that if this was a robbery. That's too far-fetched. They wanted her for some reason."

He answered my next question—Why?—before I could ask it.

"Because the whole thing was about her."

Which led to the even more disturbing heart of George's theory: Vince not only was having sex with Mary Jane, he was making her available to others in town, some of whom were powerful people. Mary Jane had had enough and started threatening to go to a higher law enforcement authority. That notion rattled Vince and others who were engaging in sex with Mary Jane, George said. Maybe she was confiding in Stanley, a mature, perhaps fearless Navy vet from out of town, and that made those powerful people extremely nervous. They disposed of Stanley and then tried to coerce Mary Jane into staying in line or, even more horrifying, decided to punish her by raping her before killing her, George said.

Now I was the one thinking about far-fetched notions.

"Come on," I said. "That seems pretty wild."

George welcomed my doubt and conceded that it was only a theory; he doesn't ask people to agree with him and doesn't care if they do. He approaches every case the same way—by collecting everything he can on it, coming up with a theory, then testing it.

"I can't do it here with this," he said of the Reed-Skridla case, "because everybody's freakin' dead."

There it was again.

A few other things fueled his conspiracy theory. He seized on an overriding theme throughout the material he'd read, particularly Bill Spencer's comments in my first story on the case suggesting that people throughout the community knew a fair amount about the murders but few spoke to authorities. That reluctance indicated widespread fear, George said. Spencer said as much to me when I'd interviewed him for the *Tribune* story years earlier.

George also pointed out that no formal autopsy was performed on Mary Jane back in 1948.

"You tell me why, when you have an apparently innocent victim shot execution style, even in 1948, you don't have an autopsy?" George said. "Hello? Hello?"

An autopsy, even in 1948, would have revealed a number of important factors about Mary Jane's death, perhaps even if she was raped.

And then there was Fred Horner, Ogle County coroner at the time of the murders. His signature is missing from Mary Jane's death certificate. I had to agree that if one death certificate was important for the coroner to have signed—perhaps the most important of his career—it would have been this one. Instead, his name is typed on the line designated for his signature.

Four lines below that is another curious, startling detail. The name of the person filing the death certificate, also known as the registrar and quite possibly the person who typed the form, is Martha Varco, Vince's wife.

"This whole thing is such a dark case," George told me. "It's not as simple as two people being killed. It's too big. My gut keeps telling me . . . nothing short of something very dark could explain the fear that has gone on for two-thirds of a century."

Fear certainly was a factor, I think. But decades after the murders, indifference may have been just as prevalent.

He offered to do more, but I hesitated. I wanted to talk with at least three people who'd investigated the case. Previous experience had suggested to me that one investigator dropping in and questioning another investigator's work is about as productive as a wrestling match between two angry bears.

I told George I appreciated his offer and that I'd keep him posted. Now I had an expert off whom I could bounce various findings.

I made a couple more phone calls to Vince's son, William, but got no response, then wrote him twice and received the same silent treatment.

My next move was to call Doug Oleson, the reporter who had written the series on the fiftieth anniversary of the killings and had worked briefly with Mike on a book project about the case. In going through my reams of notes, I'd seen a barely legible reference from our first conversation years earlier about Mary Jane being involved in prostitution. It shocked me, and I called Doug to talk about it.

What he told me was that he'd gotten a look at police reports from Rockford, where Stanley had lived, and one of the reports outlined an interview with a landlady who rented an apartment to two young women. Those two young women, according to the landlady, had numerous male friends visiting at all hours of the night.

"The phrase they used was that the girls had plenty of boyfriends," Doug told me. "They didn't always have a job, but they always had money to pay the rent."

And, he said, the landlady recognized Mary Jane as a frequent guest of the two young ladies. That was all he could glean from the report, Doug said, but he strongly encouraged me to get my hands on the Rockford Police investigative file from the case. I couldn't believe I hadn't thought of it earlier. I reached out to a detective and waited to hear a response. He called and suggested another detective. I reached out to him again and again and never got a response.

But I got Jerry Steinmetz on the first try.

I'd been looking to talk with people who'd been alive back in 1948 and were old enough then and lucid enough now to provide context. I reached out to the pair of senior residential facilities in Oregon and a third nearby. I talked with a few elderly people in the region. I also contacted a senior services center in the area. None could help.

Then, one of the people involved in Mary Jane's exhumation suggested Jerry and gave me his number. He'd worked at his family's grocery store one door down from the Reed house. He was twelve years old at the time Mary Jane and Stanley were killed. Now he was eighty. I called and he picked up after about twelve rings. He was at home recuperating from a truck-driving accident on Interstate 88 in which he broke his neck, ribs, and an arm. I apologized for bothering him, but he was perky and happy to chat.

"Mary Jane was quite a girl," Jerry said. He recalled her and the entire Reed family visiting the store, often to use the store's phone, the only one in the neighborhood. He enjoyed watching her come in.

"I was pretty young back then, but I do know she had one helluva body on her," Jerry told me. "I was old enough to recognize that."

She had "a lot of boyfriends," Jerry recalled, and a lot of guys pursuing her. Some of them wore badges. One in particular had an ongoing relationship with her, but Jerry declined to name him.

He remembered someone coming in the store to announce that a body had been found on County Farm Lane, and he recalled hearing four days later that Mary Jane's body had been found and that it was severely decomposed. He didn't remember much else about that time, except hearing Mary Jane's mother say that the person responsible would confess before he or she died.

"But she was wrong," Jerry said. "After that, we didn't hear much about it."

I asked him who he thought committed the crime.

"I'm not going to say," he told me. "I'm pretty dumb, but I'm smart enough to avoid that shit. A lot of people like me, they figure it's all been a cover-up deal since day one. But how we prove it is beyond us."

I asked if he could explain why no one was arrested. He said several influential people, notably law enforcement officers, "were all getting a little nibble there, and it was, you know, you keep your mouth shut. I'll keep my mouth shut."

We talked about Mike, whom Jerry said he wouldn't recognize if Mike knocked on the front door. We talked about Jerry's crash, which occurred about six months earlier when another driver cut in front of his semi, forcing him into the median.

After a half hour of talk, visitors came to Jerry's front door and he had to go. I thanked him and returned to my list of names.

I decided to reach out to Dr. Mark Peters, the forensic pathologist who performed Mary Jane's autopsy a few years earlier, participated in the examination of Stanley's remains, and determined June's cause of death. I also contacted former Ogle County sheriff Greg Beitel.

Years earlier when I'd interviewed him, Sheriff Beitel struck me as a particularly candid and open-minded law enforcement officer. He played a key role in the reinvestigation that Mike had sparked a few years earlier and now was retired. I thought he may have had less to fear in the way of repercussions. Maybe he'd be even more candid and open minded.

Both men agreed to sit down with me.

I met Dr. Peters on a Saturday afternoon in the parking lot of the Winnebago County coroner's office, where he was listening to an audiobook, *The Last Coyote*, a Michael Connelly crime novel about protagonist Harry Bosch reopening a thirty-year-old unsolved murder.

Dr. Peters led me into the bowels of the office, just a few feet from the examining room where he'd sifted through Stanley's remains nine months earlier. About ten feet away, behind glass, was the body of an elderly woman set up for viewing by whoever might be interested. Otherwise, the place was vacant, eerie.

A stout man dressed in jeans, black T-shirt, and dark baseball cap, Dr. Peters sported glasses and an ambitious goatee, which faded to gray an inch or so from the bottom of his chin. He was a busy man, covering about a dozen counties in northwest Illinois and performing something like 500 autopsies a year, he told me. His total body count over a thirteen-year career was about 6,300.

Dr. Peters plowed through books at the same pace. For the past decade, he told me, he had been into mysteries and thrillers, although he would venture into vampire and zombie tales, coming-of-age novels, and memoir.

We sat on black plastic chairs at a rectangular table in a cinder block room painted light blue. A phone and box of lavender tissues were on the table. On a short corner table were a microwave and a small bottle of Motrin. I opened my laptop, slid in the DVD of Mary Jane's exhumation, autopsy, and reinterment, and we started watching, fast-forwarding until we got to the autopsy. He explained what he was doing at different points—pulling fingernails, finding a ring, clipping samples of undergarments, conducting vaginal swabs; there was no way to detect if she'd been raped, he said, adding that many of the internal organs had decomposed completely.

"The skin kind of mushed away," he told me. "I don't know why, but this reminds me of meatloaf," he said at one point, and that brought him to the idea for his own project, *The Pathology Cookbook*, merging his three primary interests: books, cooking, and forensic pathology. One chapter would delve into his professional work, he explained, followed by another chapter that would connect thematically to a related recipe. I was unsure exactly what he was getting at or if he was joking. In the interest of getting the full story, though, I asked for details.

"Did you ever notice how maggots look like rice?" he offered. Then he gave a quick description of how he'd follow a chapter on the workings of maggots with a chapter on rice recipes. He told me to run it by people in the publishing business. I laughed nervously and felt my stomach do a slow turn then rise toward my throat.

When the DVD got to the audio break, I asked if he recalled anything noteworthy at that moment or right after. He said he hadn't; he was focused on his examination of Mary Jane's skull on a corner table of the room, looking for the bullet marks on the skull.

"Maybe it's Mary Jane's ghost," Dr. Peters said of the reason for the sudden audio silence. "I wonder what her ghost would feel, watching her body being dug up. I wonder if she followed us."

We talked about Mike's theories on the case, that I had my doubts about some of them. Dr. Peters agreed—to a point.

"Some of the stuff he's said seemed off the wall, but not all of it."

A few things about the autopsy and the case in general did look peculiar to Dr. Peters. First, the vibe in the room was tense. The judge had ordered the investigation, and Dr. Peters sensed that the coroner and law enforcement wanted no part of it. The two factions—law enforcement and the coroner and Mike, Warren's family, and their attorney—stood in different areas of the room.

"And never did the two mix," Dr. Peters recalled. "That's probably why nobody bothered introducing me, because they didn't want any of those people there anyways."

He was a little peeved that no one introduced him around, and he figured he could have helped explain what he was doing and what he was finding.

Also, he was perplexed by the path of the cut that separated the top of the skull from its main section. The skull in the casket was cut in a straight line from the top of the forehead around the circumference of the skull, in the way a bicycle helmet sits on a head. He'd never seen a cut like that before. Common practice is to start the cut above the forehead then work back to a point near the ear and ascend up and across the top to the other side, then take a path forward to the front, Dr. Peters said. The cut on Mary Jane's skull was strange, but he didn't know what to make of it.

Like George Seibel, Dr. Peters agreed that a full autopsy should have been done, "no matter what year it was. I don't know the environment down there at the time; obviously none of us do. But it's just hard to believe that you wouldn't do a full autopsy on one of the victims, you know?"

Most troubling, downright shocking, was that the skull had been removed from the body, Dr. Peters said. He thought it might have been done to find the bullet, but he still found it deeply troubling.

"That severing of the head, that's weird no matter what," Dr. Peters told me. "I don't care what anybody says. I've never seen it before. I've never even heard of it before. I've had to dig around in plenty of necks and never done anything like that. There's no reason to take the whole head off."

Before ending our visit, we talked briefly of Stanley's exhumation, which he was less involved in. He recounted his time in the examining room, sifting the denser material with his hands. He remembered that two anthropology students found bullets while sifting looser material through the screens.

The most interesting thing to him about Stanley's exhumation was that he got to drive a Jaguar. His assistant, Mabel Jean Mann, drove her boyfriend's Jag to the cemetery, and Dr. Peters drove it to the vault company. "That was the first time I'd ever been in a Jaguar, so that was a thrill," he said with a little cackling laugh.

After a little more than ninety minutes, I told him I was set; he could get back to his Saturday afternoon of waiting for the next grim service call. I thanked him for his time and closed my notebook. That's when he offered this assessment, unsolicited:

"It probably is a cover-up, you know. That's the only thing that makes sense."

I stayed silent, looked back at him while reopening my notebook.

"I mean, no one is that dumb not to do a big investigation on a high-profile case like that unless they're trying to cover something up."

"When you say investigation, you mean an autopsy?" I asked.

"An autopsy would be part of it, yes."

At that point, one word Jack Fredrickson pointed out to me resurfaced in my mind: *desultory*, an adjective meaning half-hearted, unfocused. In reading newspaper clips from 1948 on the case, Jack found one story by legendary *Tribune* reporter Frank Winge particularly intriguing. Frank, who'd lost an eye in combat in World War I, personally solved two murders during a raucous, colorful career that ended with his fatal collapse in the *Tribune* newsroom on New Year's Day in 1958. While covering the Reed-Skridla case, he'd used *desultory* to describe the investigation. It struck Jack as a small but very important signal that the intrepid reporter sensed investigators' objectives were not altogether honorable or decisive.

"That's why I think the rumors are that the sheriff was covering for his deputies, or whatever," Dr. Peters told me. "That's the only thing I can think of as to why it would be such a shitty job done, with no autopsy on one of the victims, just a bullet recovery."

"Can't it be gross incompetence?" I asked.

Dr. Peters chuckled.

"Can anyone be that dumb?" he said, and he answered his question by conjuring characters from *The Andy Griffith Show*, a classic 1960s sitcom depicting a small-town sheriff in Mayberry, North Carolina. Sheriff Andy Taylor was surrounded by lovable goofballs. Deputy Barney Fife carried an empty service revolver and a bullet in his breast pocket as a safeguard against a twitchy trigger finger; cousins Goober and Gomer Pyle were dim, naïve hayseeds. Wild-eyed ruffian Ernest T. Bass was a rock-throwing backwoods nut who wreaked havoc virtually everywhere he went.

"You think about Barney Fife in Mayberry and shit, yeah, if he and Goober were running it, or Gomer, yeah, definitely," Dr. Peters said. "Maybe they had Ernest T. Bass. Maybe he was the coroner. You never know."

We both laughed, and he led me out of the room, past the lonely, waiting corpse and an artificial skeleton draped in a sheer plastic apron, wearing blue latex gloves and matching blue slippers. In its eye sockets were two eyes drawn on tiny slips of paper. Getting into our cars, Dr. Peters reminded me again of his book idea. I nodded and smiled, grateful that my stomach behaved.

My meeting a week or so later with former sheriff Beitel was in a more stylish place. The Prairie Street Brewing Company is a newly restored brew house built in 1857. Today it's a cavernous but warm, handsome brewpub in Rockford, with a deck on the banks of the Rock River. That day's menu offered dozens of handcrafted beers and an array of food that stretched from burgers and pulled pork sandwiches to lamb shawarma wraps, farro salad, seared salmon, and coconut custard. Not a corpse or mock skeleton to be seen anywhere.

I barely recognized Greg, who'd left law enforcement after losing his reelection bid six years earlier. Four years before that unceremonious departure, he was chief deputy sheriff, one of four people involved in the reinvestigation of the Reed-Skridla murders.

Since he left law enforcement, Greg had worked as a jail consultant, served as chairman of the buildings and grounds committee at his church, regularly visited Disney World with his family, and spent time with his grandchildren. He also worked out aggressively, which is why I barely recognized him. Greg had dropped fifty pounds and looked buff, relaxed, and younger than when he was in office. When we met, he was training for a half-marathon, and he wore bright red, stylish running shoes. We ordered a couple beers.

"From what little information and reports we had," Greg told me of the investigation's early days, "it really did kind of look like Vince was the guy who did it, but we were going to follow the leads wherever they went. If evidence pointed to Vince, so be it."

Vince had a reputation as a nasty cop and womanizer, Greg said. It's also clear he'd had a relationship with Mary Jane. The one crazy thing that stood out to Greg was reading an old police report that said Vince had arrived at work without his service revolver the day after Stanley's body was found. When Vince was asked about it, the report stated that Vince said he'd sold it to some guy in a bar, Greg recalled.

Then there was the shocking condition of the sheriff's case file, the same thing I'd noticed. Greg said at one point, years before the reinvestigation, he'd found a dusty leather satchel on a shelf in a closet. Inside were papers, at least one bullet, and one casing. It was part of the Reed-Skridla file, he was told. When the team started the new investigation, the leather satchel was missing, as were the bullets.

But former sheriff Jerry Brooks showed up for an investigative team meeting and carried with him a box of material, Greg recalled. He was shocked at how complete Jerry's file was and how decimated the sheriff's file was. After the meeting, Jerry took the box with him, Greg recalled.

"Didn't that make you feel, uh, uncomfortable?" I asked.

"It pissed me off," Greg said. It's one thing to make copies of documents in the file and bring them home, he said, but quite another to have a personal file that's much more comprehensive and organized than the one law enforcement has.

No formal action was taken against Jerry, Greg said, and the investigation got under way. Greg said he never heard of or found evidence of a deliberate cover-up.

"If I had any inkling that we were covering anything up," he said, "I would have made a stink about it. I would have walked away from the agency."

But something fishy had happened during the original investigation in 1948, Greg said. Some people in power back then knew more than they were sharing.

"There were people who knew and didn't do anything or did not do the right thing," he said, "and that's what really disappoints me."

Captain Rich Wilkinson did an exhaustive job tracking down information and speaking with people, Greg said. Even George Seibel, who'd theorized that Vince was responsible, said the same thing about Captain Wilkinson's evidence gathering. We talked about his nineteen-page report that stated that "almost nothing in the investigation" supported the notion that Vince Varco was involved.

I was troubled by the report's lack of detail on why Vince was cleared, considering all the talk and circumstantial evidence suggesting his involvement. Greg said Captain Wilkinson's conclusion that two brothers killed Mary Jane and Stanley in a botched robbery was plausible. But he stopped short of fully endorsing that conclusion.

"Well," I finally said, "what do you think happened?"

He laughed, put his head in his hands.

"God . . . " He sighed, staring straight ahead. After a few moments, he said, "Somebody got the jump on them."

That seemed evident, I thought, and asked him who it was. Could Vince have been that guy?

"Yeah, theoretically," Greg said. The report about Vince showing up for duty the next day without his service revolver was "mind blowing," Greg said. And, yeah, he agreed that Stanley's wounds suggested somebody who was jealous, and Vince could have been one of those jealous people.

"But from the sounds of things, it could have been others," Greg said, noting Mary Jane's reputation for promiscuity. In the end, investigators were unable to find information that led them to believe Vince was involved. Greg was sticking with what that limited information provided.

I pointed out elements that suggested the crime was something more than a robbery gone awry—that Mary Jane had been taken, her head had been severed, no autopsy had been performed on either body, neither death certificate had the coroner's signature, Vince had asked Jerry Brooks to investigate and clear him, experts believed something bigger had happened. I reminded him that even Captain Wilkinson wrote of corruption, negligence, and "suggestions . . . that pointed to political, as well as social connections appearing to have some influences on this [earlier] investigation."

Greg acknowledged that investigators conducting the recent probe could have been "sandbagged," or lied to. Fifty-seven years had passed by the time they undertook that reinvestigation, he said, and some people still refused to talk. But he declined to go much further down the path of speculation. The retired sheriff was playing it safe.

What about the mismatched skull? I asked.

Greg's short answer was that the Illinois State Police boiled the skull and bones to clean them—a move that agitated Greg and other sheriff's investigators who'd hoped to preserve material on the bones for testing. Boiling the bones might have disfigured them, he added.

"When Rich and the rest of us found out about that, we were not happy," Greg said.

Mike disputed that contention, noting that some of the vertebrae did fit; others did not. I asked Greg if he thought Mike would be devious enough to find a different skull and pass it along as Mary Jane's.

"I have no idea."

I asked what he thought about Mike, and Greg broke out laughing. He called Mike an "entrepreneur." Greg doubted the existence of ghosts swirling around the case and said Mike "obviously" was out to make money. Why else would he bring in a screenwriter? Greg asked.

I pointed out that maybe Mike had been out to make money *and* get to the bottom of the case; the two aren't mutually exclusive. After all, Mike had sunk more than $120,000 into his effort with no payoff. Greg grudgingly conceded my point.

We ordered food. The place looked a little empty for a late Friday afternoon. I asked about the audio gap in Mary Jane's autopsy video.

Greg looked a little perplexed and said he was surprised. I described what the scene looked like at that point in the video, what snippets of audio I could pull from replaying that segment several times. I told him it sounded like the audio cut out just as a discussion was heating up. He thought for a few moments, then grinned and nodded.

State police and sheriff's investigators were discussing what to do with the skull and bones pulled from the gooey remains, Greg said. Some wanted to bury everything, arguing that the primary reason they'd dug up the body was to check Mike's premise that Mary Jane's skull may have been missing. Others, including Greg, wanted to keep the bones for further analysis. He agreed that the conversation may have gotten a little heated.

The food came. Greg ordered another beer. It was getting hard to hear him. I looked up and saw that the Friday after-work crowd and families were streaming in the place. Every seat seemed taken. I told him I'd like to talk with the mysterious Captain Wilkinson, who, like Greg, was retired. Maybe, I said, Captain Wilkinson would be interested in getting a few things off his chest. Greg said he doubted that.

I asked Greg what he thought the prospects were for finding the truth. He paused, said he was unsure. I didn't say anything for a moment; neither did he.

"I think that there are not many people in the county who care," Greg finally said, "who really want to know. The dominant thought is that this happened long ago, who cares. Let it go.

"But if it was one of your family members or loved ones?" he said. "How could you let it go?"

We walked to the parking lot. I thanked him and wished him luck in the half-marathon. He got in his SUV and drove off. I pulled out an old notebook and found three phone numbers for Captain Wilkinson that I had tracked down months earlier. I stared at them for a few seconds and took out my phone. Then I tossed it on the seat and pulled out of my parking space.

. . .

CAPTAIN RICH WILKINSON had been the one guy who may have had the most information and yet he was the one person I was most reluctant to approach. I'd heard things about him: that he had a fierce, unpredictable temper; that he was a loose cannon; that he would intimidate people. Once, while interviewing an official two counties from Ogle on a completely un-related topic, my interviewee happened to tell me that he'd worked in law enforcement and bumped into Wilkinson a time or two. "The guy's a little off," he told me.

In my most cowardly moments, I had visions of reaching out to him and setting him off, leading him to track me down and shoot me or discour-age me in very clear and present terms from going any further with this. Over time, the vision kept growing more menacing. I saw him bearded and wild-eyed, living in a dilapidated shack deep in the woods, outfitted with an arsenal, a pit bull–German Shepherd mix that had flunked police training, and a grudge to settle against the world, starting with me.

But I called the numbers anyway, telling myself the tired bromide about confronting my fears, as I did when I attended the séance. I expected not to find him, and admitted to myself that part of me hoped he simply would not respond. One of the numbers was disconnected, another rang into eternity, and a third had one of those robot-woman voicemail greetings. I left a message on the last one and waited but didn't get a response. I could've tracked down his address, driven to his house, and knocked on his door, but that scenario shot a bolt of fear through me. Plus, what if he happened to be out or the address I'd gotten was incorrect?

I decided that would be my last-ditch Hail Mary effort. Before taking it, I had one more idea. I wrote Captain Wilkinson a letter and sent it by certified mail.

He called the next day.

The Perilous Line between
Truth and Loyalty

• • •

I ANSWERED THE CALL, and in something like 1.6 seconds, my cheek went sweaty against the cell phone.

The first thing Captain Wilkinson said was that he had a lot of information to share. He had in fact called Mike and one of Stanley's nephews about eighteen months earlier to share material that he hadn't included in the official report. But they had blown him off. He'd even offered to sit down with Stanley's sister a decade earlier when he investigated the case, but she didn't want to stir up the anguish that had been buried somewhere deep.

We talked for a half hour. He was humble, friendly, direct, respectful of what I was doing, willing to help. He preferred that I call him Rich. I said I'd like to sit down and talk, Rich. He said we should do it quick. I said how about we meet on the upcoming Sunday afternoon.

"Honey?" I heard him ask in a sweet tone that sounded nothing like a backwoods ogre living in a hut. "Do we have anything going this Sunday afternoon?"

They didn't have anything going. I offered to buy him lunch so that I wouldn't have to intrude on his home. Police can be particularly guarded about their homes.

"Nah," he said, "come on out to the house and we'll fix some coffee or something for you."

He gave me specific directions to his home, and for the next three nights before I went out there, I had trouble sleeping.

When I pulled up to his white ranch on that bright afternoon, I saw birds flitting around the two feeders dangling from a tree in the front yard. Rich was in the backyard. Gray haired and lean, a red splash of sunburn on his forehead, he'd been retired for a decade. He smiled, shook my hand, and led me into the bright, immaculate home he shared with his wife, Deb. They had two dogs, dachshunds named Misty and Max who wanted their bellies scratched. Deb offered me a cold drink, then Rich and I descended the stairs to their equally immaculate, carpeted family room, painted in lavender. On the coffee table was a dachshund statuette, and on a wall was a taxidermy fish trophy. I could see a treadmill around the corner.

We talked for three and a half hours.

Some of the information Rich shared with me during our conversation was in the report he had prepared and submitted more than a decade earlier.

The difference now was that I had the original, unedited report, and I had read it three or four or five times. This unscarred version included names, and its author sat in front of me, anxious to share more information.

"I didn't want any part of this case," Rich told me. "I had other cases I was trying to finish up, and I was getting ready to retire. And my personal opinion was that the case never had gone anywhere." He'd even investigated it back in the mid-1980s, when an informant had reported that her ex-husband had bragged about committing the murders, a report that turned out to be false. "I didn't think it was even possible to come up with anything else," he said.

But, twenty years after that investigation, Sheriff Mel Messer asked Rich to reopen the case, and Rich had enormous respect for Sheriff Messer.

He started by going through the old files again, and, yeah, former sheriff Jerry Brooks had some, and yeah, the prevailing opinion among law enforcement was that Vince was the killer. Rich decided the best place to start after that review was to sit down with Mike and find out the sources behind his theory. The two met at the Roadhouse, and the conversation soon turned acrimonious.

"He basically wouldn't give me any information, and I guess I made him mad because I told him I didn't care about . . . the spirits," Rich said. "I might have mentioned something to him, something about the movies— 'cause I was getting upset and I'm well-known for having a temper." ("The movies" was a reference to Mike's effort to get a film made on the case.) "And, I think he got upset with me, which I don't blame him. So," Rich laughed, "we called it off at that point."

What he discovered was that the more he looked at the theory that Mary Jane was the reason for the murders, the more dead ends he encountered.

"You'd hear something, and then you'd go talk to the person and they'd say, 'Well, no, I didn't know that. I heard it from this person, I heard it from that person,'" Rich said, "and so it was not going anywhere."

While examining all the materials and talking with people, Rich didn't see much follow-through on evidence that focused on Stanley, and he wasn't exactly sure why. So Rich figured he would head down that path. Very quickly, pieces started falling into place.

It began with a former Ogle County animal control officer, Gary Miller, who knew many people from Oregon around the time of the murders and who had worked with the guy who was county animal control officer in 1948, "Doc" Stevens. Doc had told Gary that the murder weapon was at the bottom of the well on the property of Delos "Hap" Blanchard, who was sheriff years before the murders. Rich had the well dredged, and although some metal pieces were found, they were not parts of the gun.

During that time, Rich established a rapport with Hap's son, Amos, who offered a different version of events he said his father had told him.

While he was Ogle County sheriff, Hap developed a reputation for solving challenging crimes, Rich told me, and was brought on as an investigator to help with the Reed-Skridla case shortly after Stanley and Mary Jane were killed. A person Amos declined to name but who purportedly was involved in the murders came to Hap and told this story: Two men related to each other knew Stanley had $70 on him and were planning to take it from him. They trailed him to lovers' lane and confronted him. Stanley got out of the car and was uncooperative. In fact, he strode toward his would-be robbers and might have scuffled with the older one, who pulled back, drew a gun, and shot Stanley. Stanley kept coming, necessitating several more shots. Mary Jane had to be killed because she'd witnessed the shooting. Right after the killings, one of the two attackers hotfooted it to Iowa, where he'd been living at the time.

Hap got the gun, went to State's Attorney S. Donald Crowell, and tried to negotiate a deal but failed, Amos Blanchard related. Hap then purportedly hung on to his information and the gun, hatching a plan to run for sheriff, win the campaign, then present the solution to a relieved and grateful citizenry. Only one problem: Hap lost the election.

After talking with Amos Blanchard, Rich expanded the investigation. His officers kept hearing about two tall men in a beat-up old black car tailing Stanley and Mary Jane that evening. One source said Hap had given him the name of one of the men who confronted Stanley and Mary Jane: a local fellow named Lloyd DeShazo. Lloyd DeShazo lived next to Hap Blanchard. Rich returned to Amos Blanchard, who confirmed that Lloyd was the man who'd come to Hap Blanchard, but he was not the shooter. Rich found Lloyd's stepdaughter, Elizabeth Merrimen, who told him that her mother, Lloyd's wife, had told Elizabeth that Hap Blanchard knew all about the murders and possibly was involved.

Rich then told Elizabeth the scenario he'd heard, and she fell silent. Finally, she told him the older man, the shooter, probably was Lloyd's older brother, Perry DeShazo, who'd lived in or near Waterloo, Iowa, under the name Robert Schay and worked at John Deere Tractor Works there. By the way, Elizabeth said, Lloyd's car was a beat-up black Reo that would have been at least twelve years old at the time.

Rich searched for the DeShazo brothers and found that both had died: Lloyd in 1968 in Oregon, Perry in 1958 in Waterloo. After our conversation, I searched for Elizabeth and found that she'd died at age ninety-one in 2011. Hap Blanchard and Doc Stevens also were dead. Amos Blanchard passed in 2014.

Rich shared other intriguing information with me, specifically that the report was a source of aggravation for him. He was annoyed at being ordered to black out huge chunks of it and upset that a judge sealed the edited report, blocking it from public view.

Then Rich told me three very compelling things that he'd never revealed. After he submitted the report, people kept calling him, credible people with intriguing information. Elizabeth Merrimen was one. She wanted to sit down with Rich again, he said, and when they met, she said her mother had told Elizabeth that Lloyd did in fact go to Hap Blanchard to tell the former sheriff about the killings. Elizabeth declined to share that nugget during the formal investigation because she was afraid that she'd then be called to testify about it, she told Rich.

A second contact came from a source in Rockford, Stanley's hometown, who reached out to Rich through a mutual acquaintance. The source, an elderly gentleman whom Rich declined to name but who "knew Stanley very, very well," told Rich that a group of telephone company employees regularly gambled in the basement of a church a couple of blocks from Stanley's home. Stanley appeared to have organized the gambling. In a session there that occurred on the late afternoon or early evening of June 24, 1948, Stanley caught Lloyd and Perry DeShazo cheating. He grabbed the money they'd had on the table—$70, the source said—and ordered them to leave. The source also told Rich that everyone in the game that night knew Stanley was heading to Oregon for a date with Mary Jane.

"There was no reason for him to come up with this," Rich told me. "He didn't say anything about a murder. He just told me what was going on down there." So there it was: Stanley caught Lloyd and Perry DeShazo cheating in the church basement on the early evening of Stanley's murder. Stanley took their money and kicked them out, and then headed to Oregon for a date with Mary Jane.

But the third post-report contact was even more revelatory.

A trusted source from the Reeds' neighborhood told Rich that the slightly salacious photo of Mary Jane was taken at a judge's home, and this judge had a cabin on an island in the Rock River a little north of the bridge, a place where, this source said, men would congregate and Mary Jane would visit regularly "to entertain the men," as Rich put it. Those men included the county animal control officer, Doc Stevens, Vince, and the judge. It's unclear how many others congregated there.

That's where talk of conspiracy begins to coalesce into something very believable. Let's imagine the reactions among those men—a judge, deputy sheriff, and county officer whom Mary Jane had entertained—when they heard that her date had been murdered and she kidnapped. The Illinois State Police and a swarm of reporters descend on Oregon, search teams are scouring the countryside for her. Then, four days later, she turns up dead in a ditch, possibly raped. That same swarm of authorities and reporters shift their full attention to an intense, comprehensive hunt for evidence and suspects.

My guess is that those local gentlemen of status would have been somewhat reluctant to cooperate and might even have taken steps to slow down, divert, or close the investigation, given what it may have done to sully their reputations and—if things got carried away—lead to their arrests for murder, rape, and kidnapping.

Add to that mix Hap Blanchard, the former sheriff who was holding onto the killers' identities and likely the murder weapon to further his personal ambitions. He wanted to win an election—or burnish his reputation as the lawman who achieved justice for the most shocking crime in Oregon history, a crime that received coast-to-coast headlines.

I was about to ask Rich why he didn't report any of those later findings to authorities, but he was ahead of me.

"The problem," he said, "was that I was under the impression that the case was sealed, boom, okay? So why add to it? I figured that since the suspects were dead, it was over."

I also think he might have figured, based on how higher-ups and the judge handled his report, that they weren't interested in whatever findings he had uncovered.

I asked about his more recent contact with Mike and the Skridlas.

When *The Dead Files* producers reached out to Rich, he explained, he initially agreed to participate, then the notion of validating ghosts and the producers' reluctance to share their sources on the case prompted Rich to reconsider and decline. That's when, days before the episode was to begin shooting, he said he contacted Mike and Steve Skridla to share information that wasn't in the report. But both blew him off. Mike had told me a different version: he interpreted Rich's call as an attempt to intimidate him from participating in the program.

Wherever the truth is about those conversations, the scenario Rich laid out for me on that Sunday afternoon in the basement, while Deb watched TV upstairs and the dachshunds patrolled the backyard, has its soft spots.

For starters, Rich gave me the same explanation that Greg Beitel did when I asked about the skull and vertebrae mismatch: the Illinois State Police boiled the bones, which could have disfigured them. But I called Illinois State Police captain Matt Davis, who attended Mary Jane's exhumation and autopsy and later analyzed the bones. He told me that disfigurement was impossible.

Analysts did place the bones in water that was near boiling, which is standard procedure when trying to remove tissue to examine trauma to bones, Davis told me. But they don't become disfigured in that process.

"It's not like putting a sweater in a washing machine and dryer," he said. The process is designed specifically to remove tissue without damaging bones.

That point may be peripheral to Rich's scenario, but I also was suspicious about why he declined to give me the names of a couple of key sources unidentified in his report, especially those who had died and the two sources who contacted him after the report. That reluctance is something an excitable conspiracy theorist could whip into a plausible argument that Rich was protecting the Fraternity of the Thin Blue Line.

Except not really, not when you take everything he's provided and think for a couple moments. When you do that, you see strong suggestions that some informal conspiracy was in effect.

I recalled a snippet he said during the first minutes of our phone conversation a few days earlier.

"I have nothing to win, lose, or gain on this thing," he told me. "Period."

Also, three comments in Rich's unedited report are particularly telling. Two of those comments—about political and social connections influencing the investigation and his conclusion about a corrupt and mishandled investigation—I saw when I skimmed the report way back when. The third—more nuanced but in some ways more damning—I picked out after I read the report leading up to my meeting with Rich. It's toward the end, overshadowed by the fiery conclusion.

"The leads that I pursued seem to have been there from the start of the investigation," Rich wrote. "Some of the leads were revisited . . . Some of the leads leave questions opened as to why the lead ended where it did."

Sitting together at his basement table, Rich flipped through his notes and a copy of the infamous report. Then he repeated the suspicions about unfollowed leads he noted in the report.

"Why it wasn't done in 1948, I don't know," he lamented. "But that's why I put down in that report that something was politically wrong, as well as hidden information."

Those are not the observations of a man trying to conceal a conspiracy or cover up police misconduct. Those strike me as the comments of an honest man dealing with an incomplete history, trying to walk the perilous line between truth and loyalty.

Still, I had questions for Rich.

Why was Mary Jane taken from the scene if this was a botched robbery? Why not simply kill her there?

First of all, Rich didn't view it as a robbery. He felt that the two brothers merely wanted to get back the money Stanley had taken in the church basement and be done with it. He said Lloyd, who was driving the car and probably was shocked when his older brother pulled a gun and shot Stanley, started arguing with his older brother immediately. That bought Mary Jane time. But at some point, the older brother persuaded the younger one that they had no choice, Rich said.

Why was her head severed and why did investigators fail to order a thorough autopsy?

She'd been in a roadside ditch through four summer days and nights. Her neck was so severely decomposed, perhaps from blood that had collected near the wound, that Mary Jane's head had almost become detached, a funeral home director from the time told Rich. As for the lack of an autopsy, he said 1948 was a primitive time in Oregon. The coroner saw that she'd been shot once in the head and that she was dead. That's about all he needed.

I have my doubts about his theory on the lack of an autopsy. Just a gut feeling, but given the tension circling around her murder and the influential people who had some involvement with Mary Jane, I'm thinking the quicker they could get her buried, the simpler it was to move past any difficult questions.

Then we got to the audio at Mary Jane's autopsy, the audio that fell silent the moment it appeared an argument was building. Rich said he was unaware that the sound had cut out, but he readily acknowledged that a heated argument ensued, primarily between him and the state police. Rich wanted to return the bones to the casket and bury them with the rest of Mary Jane's remains, he said, blocking Mike and Warren from conducting more analysis. He saw no rational reason for more examination of the bones, only potential mischief. State police investigators and Greg Beitel held the exact opposite opinion, and they prevailed.

"The fact of the matter is that she was dead; she was murdered, okay?" Rich told me. "There had been a doctor that had examined her at the time of the death. With everything that's going on with movies and films"— another reference to Mike's early effort to make a film on the case—"I'm saying basically, okay, you got the grave dug up, there's her body. What are they trying to find? What are we trying to do here?

"I was upset because the Reed family were all saying Varco, Varco, Varco did it, and I'm simply saying give me the damn evidence where you think Varco did it. Tell me where you're getting it from." He stopped and took a breath. "Sorry. I was getting very, very frustrated on this thing, and so that's where the argument's from."

It came time for me to leave. Rich led me up the stairs, where one of the dachshunds demanded her belly be scratched. He escorted me to my car. He thanked me for coming out, shook my hand, reiterated that his primary goal was to get to the truth on the case. If I needed anything more, he said, call him. We stood at my car, the driver's door open. I had one foot inside. I could tell he wanted to say more but maybe wasn't sure what else to add. After a few seconds, I got in and pulled away.

The next day at my cubicle, my phone rang. It was Rich, saying he really enjoyed our talk and he hoped he was helpful. He repeated a few of the things we'd spoken of the day before and added a nuance or two: he was "shocked" the judge ordered him to black out large portions of the report and then sealed it; everybody in town knew Vince Varco back in 1948, and if he'd have been following Stanley and Mary Jane around, many people would have reported it. I wasn't so sure about that.

Finally, he shared with me his most enduring regret.

"The only thing I ever wanted to do," he said, "was sit down with the families."

The Messy, Noble Pursuit

· · ·

SO MIKE WAS WRONG, at least I think he was. But he was right, too.

I don't think Vince pulled the trigger, and his direct involvement simply feels unlikely—I don't know how else to say it. I do think, at the very least, he had some powerful hunches about what happened or where to find answers. He might have gotten those answers and turned a blind eye. He might have known better than to ask questions in the first place.

And Mike? For all the criticism fired his way, he played a most honorable role as the man who pressed the issue. Remember: Mike's agitating led to the reinvestigation, among other things, and that showed what I think was persuasive evidence of a cover-up. Mike at times might have looked like an amateur boxer wildly throwing punches, but he landed a few blows in key places. He might be an eccentric fellow who perhaps fell in love with a young lady's ghost, but he drew attention to a murdered woman whose town largely had grown indifferent to her. In the process, he tried to ease the long heartache and unanswered questions of two families. Even Rich Wilkinson commended him for that.

My friend Jack Fredrickson said it clearly and simply, I thought, during a chat over Diet Coke and tea at a library café. He told me that he was having breakfast a couple of weeks earlier and found himself wanting to wrap his head around the entire case again. All these years, and "the disease" had stayed with him. He told me the best he could hope for would be remission, that it would never go away, and that what Mike attempted in examining a seventeen-year-old girl's murder was noble, even if the crime occurred seven decades ago.

"I sound much more pious than I am," Jack said, "but it just seems to me like we should always give a damn about stuff like that, especially if it's been covered up, especially if people are conspiring to cover it up, okay? I think that matters."

I still don't know what motivated Mike. Maybe it was something in his personal history. Maybe he saw heroic righteousness in his role as Mary Jane's redeemer or found purpose in an otherwise mundane life. He might have started out trying to make money then became immersed in something much more complicated that was too difficult to extricate from—commitments to Warren and the Skridla family or to an auburn-haired young woman he never met. It's probably some mix of all that, and I'm reasonably sure Mike himself doesn't understand fully what pushed him on his odyssey.

• • •

ELEVEN DAYS AFTER talking with Rich Wilkinson, I drove out to the Roadhouse to see Mike. It was cold and drizzling. He walked me to the empty, dark dining room where he had stacked a few three-ring notebooks on a table so we could revisit some of his research. He'd reopened on Fridays, Saturdays, and Sundays, but his lucrative video gambling machines were still dark while he tried to untangle June's contract on them. He wasn't sure how long he'd be able to stay open. Five months after June's death, Mike still wasn't spending nights at the Roadhouse apartment. He said it was taking more vodka to get to sleep at night and more black coffee to wake up the next morning.

He'd come up with a new twist on his theory about the crime. This one started with the notion that many people in town back in June 1948 were anticipating a showdown between Vince and Stanley, and that it occurred on the lovers' lane. A cluster of people gathered on the road and saw Stanley knock down Vince, infuriating him and prompting him to shoot Stanley. Once Stanley was down and nearly or fully dead, someone poured gasoline on his face and lit it, Mike said. He showed me a black-and-white photo, purportedly of Stanley's body at the morgue. Skin on his head looked like black plastic from a garbage bag stretched tight against the skull. His teeth were exposed. But I couldn't see valid proof of whose body it was. I'd gone back and forth with investigators on the question of Stanley's head being set on fire and was unable to reach a definitive conclusion. I didn't ask Mike for more details. I'd grown weary of thirteen years of tempting twists like this that I was unable to nail down.

He rejected much of what Rich had told me. The trail leading toward Vince as the killer went cold, Mike said, because everyone was afraid to cooperate with authorities who were in on the conspiracy, which I think makes sense. He was suspicious when I told him that Rich held back naming a few sources.

Mike remained convinced that the skull in Mary Jane's casket was not hers, that hers was taken as a trophy—a powerful indication that this was a crime of passion, he said. He also noted that authorities never charged him with evidence tampering, a step they would have taken had they believed he substituted a skull for Mary Jane's. As long as we were on the subject of the authorities, Mike was suspicious about whether they'd really run any gun through ballistics testing after Stanley's exhumation, and he was upset that the sheriff's office was not returning his phone calls.

He was pressing onward, although he wouldn't tell me his next step. He said he didn't want to tip off the opposition. We walked through the kitchen and to the back door. I thanked him again for all his cooperation over the years. He said to stay in touch. We stood silent for a few moments.

"As soon as I get back on my feet," Mike told me, "I'm going after their asses."

It was getting late. I wasn't sure when or if I'd return to Oregon, and I had one more thing I'd wanted to do for years. I drove three blocks east of the Roadhouse and caught the aroma of Italian food. Alfano's was open, and, as I saw when I entered, busy. Seated beneath a portrait of the pope and next to a depiction of the Last Supper, I looked at the menu and settled on the obvious choice: the Sicilian, a pizza featuring fresh garlic, fresh tomatoes, onion, oregano, and a thick layer of cheese. It was, as the Sicilians say, *delizioso*.

• • •

HAVING MOVED three times in the six years since we occupied the building on a manicured lawn near a swank shopping plaza, today I report to a
former Zenith television distribution center. The company went bankrupt
in the late 1990s and disappeared.

It's a two-story brown brick building that had ceiling leaks in the
kitchen and a trash-strewn parking lot pocked with potholes the size of
folding card tables. It stands on a weedy frontage road next to the interstate. Around it are giant illuminated billboards for no-snip vasectomies,
Actors, Models, and Talent for Christ, and $10 Tuesdays at a gentlemen's
club called Polekatz. Down the road is a truck stop.

In November, I was dispatched to the coast of Peru to write about the
Chicago Zoological Society's conservation efforts there. About the same
time, three dozen people on the news staff took buyouts. A few weeks later,
they split. I gave it serious thought, but it turns out I really enjoy what I do.
I'm willing to ride the turbulent surf until it tosses me.

In February, we got a new chairman of Tribune Publishing, a man who
made a few hundred million as a technology entrepreneur. He says he
wants to save journalism. I'm cool with that. Less than three months later,
he was fielding a slightly hostile offer to sell for $815 million, news that
generated more anxiety among the troops. I simply was glad somebody
viewed the newspaper—digital or print—with such overt desire.

In June, the new management team changed Tribune Publishing's name
to tronc, short for "Tribune online content." *Philadelphia Daily News* and
Inquirer columnist Ellen Gray responded by tweeting, "If I had a pet dino-
saur, I'd probably name it #tronc, too."

Painful, but funny.

That change was followed later in the summer by news that a Los Angeles developer was buying Tribune Tower for as much as $240 million. So
it goes. History never ends.

My niece-in-law and nephew delivered a great-grandson to my mother
in spring, which thrilled her beyond words. She keeps asking his name and
verifying which of her grandchildren are married. But she loves looking at
pictures of him, and when she holds the little peanut, she sings to him in
Greek and the light of the world emanates from the two of them.

Near as I can tell, she's the most popular resident in the senior home where she's lived for four years. Sometimes she thinks she's been gone for an extended period from her tidy, comfortable apartment on the seventh floor, even though she hasn't. Sometimes she calls in the middle of the night, worried that one of her children is ill or one of her grandchildren is missing. As often as she asks the same four or five questions and circles the same four or five topics, the message she repeats the most is that gratitude has gotten her through life's cruelest setbacks. If we take one lesson from her life, she says, that's the most important one. She also keeps asking to give her children and grandchildren their inheritances before she dies.

• • •

TO THIS DAY, I can't say with certainty who killed Mary Jane and Stanley or why. I still can't explain the mysterious skull or why Mary Jane was kidnapped after Stanley was shot. But I tend to believe that events on June 24th and 25th of 1948 more closely resembled the scenario that Rich presented than the one that Mike did.

I don't dream about the case anymore, and it doesn't surface in my conscious mind very much these days. I guess I've taken it as far as I can and accept that getting the full truth is next to impossible, which is the way it is with all stories. General assignment reporters learn that. We work a story as hard as we can. Then we move on to the next.

I read someplace that stories connect our histories and memories to our future, that they help us remember how we got where we are. I like that. I also like that stories, even those filled with romance, mourning, mistrust, and cruelty, bring us together, help us grow. When real journalism recedes, that capacity to grow, reform, and build our communities fades right along with it, almost imperceptibly, and that's an unsettling thing.

Those stories—our histories—rarely are tidy and always compound. Sometimes they are repackaged, like a heinous Abraham Lincoln statue transformed into a worthy project for folks with disabilities. Or they evolve in the form of a corpulent flying fish remaking a rich river ecosystem. They can grow like towns confronting shameful episodes from their pasts and becoming better places for it. They can shift and illuminate, like disregarded teens and lost old people changing who they are, who they will be, and how they are perceived simply by sitting together. Or they can resurrect and give life to the dead, like when a man gets caught up in an unsolved double murder.

That's what makes history and memory risky when we embark on expeditions to look for more. Our pasts can become messier, murkier, unflattering. But the adventure of pursuing the story might be the best we can do to honor our pasts. It might not be about the ending or finding the solution at all, but about trying to keep the stories alive, telling them, rescuing the ghosts, and then maybe helping them find a place of repose. The search for the truth, the courage to face and accept it as our own, the value in trying to gain deeper understanding—that's the noble journey.

NOTES

CHAPTER 2

1. Chicago Police Department, 2011 Murder Analysis Report, http://4abpn
833conr1zvwp7447f2b.wpengine.netdna-cdn.com/wp-content/uploads/2014/12
/2011-Murder-Report.pdf; "Crime in Chicagoland," *Chicago Tribune*. http://
crime.chicagotribune.com/chicago/homicides; Drum, Kevin. "Raw Data:
Here's What Violent Crime Really Looks Like Over the Past Decade," *Mother
Jones* magazine, February 12, 2017. http://www.motherjones.com/kevin-drum
/2017/02/raw-data-heres-what-violent-crime-really-looks-over-past-decade.

2. Associated Press, "How Average Is Your State? http://hosted.ap.org
/specials/interactives/wdc/average_state/index.html?SITE=JRC.

3. Wilson, Chris. "Time Labs: Find Out If Your State Is America's Past or
Future." *Time* magazine, July 13, 2015. http://labs.time.com/story/census
-demographic-projections-interactive/.

CHAPTER 7

1. Hild, Theodore W. "The Rock River Colossus." *Historic Illinois* 32, no. 5
(February 2010).

CHAPTER 13

1. "Speech on the Fanaticism of the Democratic Party," February 21, 1859.
In *His Brother's Blood: Speeches and Writings, 1838–64, Owen Lovejoy,* edited
by William F. Moore and Jane Ann Moore (Champaign: University of Illinois
Press, 2004).

2. "More Than Just a Name . . ." *Bureau County Republican* (Princeton, IL).
September 9, 2011; updated January 23, 2012. http://www.bcrnews.com/2012
/01/23/more-than-just-a-name/aeukvo4/.